Stoner Meditation

By Withered Tree

In Collaboration with Lao Two

ISBN-13: 9781492889274
ISBN-10: 149288927X

Front and back cover Art by Translucent Studios, Digital Creative Services.
josh@translucentstudios.com, 415 250 3515
Back cover – Manjushri Statue from Nepal, owned by Lao Two.

Ozymandias
I met a traveler from an antique land
Who said: Two vast and trunkless legs of stone
Stand in the desert... Near them, on the sand,
Half sunk, a shattered visage lies, whose frown,
And wrinkled lip, and sneer of cold command,
Tell that its sculptor well those passions read
Which yet survive, stamped on those lifeless things,
The hand that mocked them, and the heart that fed:
And on the pedestal these words appear:
"My name is Ozymandias, king of kings:
Look on my works, ye Mighty, and despair!"
Nothing beside remains. Round the decay
Of that colossal wreck, boundless and bare
The lone and level sands stretch far away.

Percy Bysshe Shelley (1792 – 1822)

Contents

Read This Introduction

This book is about Stoners partnering with meditation, and about how to achieve a low-level enlightenment—a sudden awareness of nondual reality (nirvana).

Stoner Meditation excludes all drugs except for psychedelics, which includes marijuana. If you use any other drugs, this guide probably won't be as helpful for you, because it focuses on direct entheogen experience. This is not a book on religion; it's a book for wizards. We will teach a specific type of meditation called calm abiding, but we didn't invent it. We expect that our book will make a lot of strict religious fundamentalists rage that psychedelics have nothing to do with meditation, or enlightenment—we disagree. We don't expect religious fundamentalists, or governments for that matter, to understand the Stoner quest, because psychedelics and the freedom they bring scares them.

Psychedelics have a unique effect, and when used as a spiritual tool can help you reach predictably high levels of attainment—it's as simple as that.

This book is aimed at Stoners, teaching advanced esoteric techniques. If you are a novice, please pay attention to the warnings throughout the book. If you are under 18 we recommend you wait until your body has grown before you jump into daily smoking and taking psychedelics.

If possible, please use only naturally grown psychedelics. We love LSD, but unfortunately, purity or strength guarantees can't be given for any street-bought powders or pills. As with ALL drugs, become

informed, and use at your own risk. No drug is inherently good or evil—
for example, taking 100 aspirin will kill most adults.

Educate yourself and use drugs responsibly. No matter what is written in this book that might influence you one way or the other, YOU are
ultimately responsible for obeying or disobeying laws. Do not consume
psychedelics just because everyone else does or because you think it
sounds cool. Only do psychedelics for spiritual attainment, direct experience, and realization.

Lao Two says: "Respect the power in psychedelics for spiritual
growth."

Our universe is currently estimated to contain anywhere from 100
billion all the way up to 300 trillion galaxies—but that's really just a
best guess. Astronomers are more confident in their range for the number of stars in our Milky Way galaxy—that's 200 to 400 billion "suns"
like ours. And more recently, astronomers have estimated that there are
at least 100 billion planets circling many of these local stars. It makes
sense that some of these planets harbor life of one kind or another. It
then follows that some planets will have intelligent life like our Earth.
Think on this—right now, there is a swarming multitude of life of all
kinds, shapes, and forms throughout our galaxy. And a few of those
alien beings are more intelligent then humans on Earth.

Neanderthals roamed our planet for 300,000 years before we
evolved into *Homo sapiens*, around 40,000 years (400 centuries) ago.
It took us a long time to make the leap from the Stone Age, maybe
20,000 years, but something happened when metals were accidentally
discovered—we suddenly changed the way we lived. Unfortunately, our
ancestors' brains were stuck in the past, and instead of making the world
better, they kept killing each other. It's embarrassing to look back on the
history of the human race—we've had great advances in technology, but
not a day has gone by without humans killing each other. Some primal

fear caused us to work against each other, instead of finding ways to live together. Strange, isn't it?

Basically, we've been "scientifically intelligent" for only 150 years (since the Industrial Revolution). Our real problem in the twenty-first century is that humans are still not competent.

Well, we've got another chance coming to get it right: computers and robots will be taking over most of our jobs, so work will be almost obsolete. War could also become obsolete because of robots and computers (drones). Overpopulation will have to be reduced, and we must find ways to live in cooperation with planet Earth. Then more people will be able to explore inwardly, realizing higher mind, using psychedelics and meditation. This coming change will be more dramatic for humanity than adding tin to copper to make bronze.

They say our universe started from the Big Bang 13.75 billion years ago. That makes the 150 years of "intelligent" *sapiens* less than a blink of the eye. We like to believe that any intelligent alien species that are smarter than Earth humans are flying around the Milky Way right now. But unlike us, they are sane, and don't have murderous wars or greed and inequality. I like to imagine them hovering above planet Earth and studying us for about fifteen minutes. They would certainly come to the conclusion that visiting Earth must be avoided, and although we can't see it, we're betting there is a flashing neon sign out past Saturn that says to bypass the third planet. No wonder we haven't met any other species.

On the most mundane level, we evolve generation after generation, but we can't seem to break through and organize Earth—we're still bogged down fixing the holes in our boat, the holes that we humans have caused. Imagine the benefits real peace would bring, if we stopped pouring our resources down the drain in wars. Our goal as Stoners is to get our own act together; then as mature, sane adults, we can start to repair our world—together.

We are inexplicably born on this planet called Earth, and that is part of our karma (the effect of the cause of birth). Since there are so many planets spread throughout the universe, why were we born right here, right now in history? It's really not enough to imagine what it would have been like to be born in some other country. We have to expand our minds out from Earth to the solar system, galaxy, near star group, universe, and possibly multiverses, or dimensions. It's incredible in such a vast cosmos that here we are, born and living on Earth right now.

The musings I just presented are familiar to anyone who smokes marijuana and takes psychedelics. This kind of far-out thinking typifies many psychedelic Stoners, a group of somewhat extraordinary seekers, eccentrics, and psychonauts. We are eager and willing to explore our inner universe, because we've overcome our fears. Unlike the casual marijuana smoker, we Stoners crave visionary experience.

About us: Lao Two is both my longtime childhood and Stoner friend and, more recently, my Stoner Meditation teacher. You will find his high-level wisdom quotes, and his stories, throughout this book.

We've spent a lot of time together, and I've been writing down Lao Two's insights and stoned reflections over the years. By the time I retired from my job, I had collected a box full of notes and a scribbled notebook.

At the time of this writing, Lao Two and I are 68 years old. But this book is really not about me, it's about the higher-mind that is Lao Two. His whole life has been spent on the outside looking in—He's one of those people who just never fit in, so being a countercultural hippie was perfect. Now that he's older, looking back, he's proud to have rejected a conventional lifestyle. Since his mid-twenties he's smoked marijuana nearly nonstop, probably a zillion reefers, and for eight years (more or less) in the 1960s he took somewhere between 300 and 500 trips on various psychedelics, mostly LSD (also known as acid). Three or four of those years were spent selling the legendary LSD made by Owsley, with street names like purple haze, blue cheer, white lightning, etc. Then Owsley quit producing and other LSD suppliers came in. Lao Two sold lots of

Mexican marijuana back then, and occasionally got his hands on some magic mushrooms or peyote cactus. He's taken amanita mushrooms; drank ayahuasca; smoked DMT; experienced STP, PCP, methadrine, heart poppers, cocaine, regular and opium hashish; and was dosed on heroin several times by a "friend." He's never been much of an alcohol drinker; he would rather slip outside to take a couple of hits on a reefer.

He was living in San Francisco, studying philosophy at San Francisco State University, during the 1960s, generally not going to classes very often, taking LSD in Golden Gate Park or on the beach instead. One morning Lao Two woke up and realized there was nothing he could do with a philosophy degree except teach, and his perfect dream job didn't exist—"Philosopher wanted: Sit on beach and contemplate the meaning of life. Good pay and benefits." So he dropped out and became homeless on the road. He spent a lot of time backpacking up and down the California coast and into the Sierra Mountains, dealing LSD and marijuana to support himself. He had a great life living part-time with a girlfriend in Los Angeles and with a different girlfriend in San Francisco, and often had casual sex with women he met when hitchhiking. He likes to imagine that he was really good looking back then, but in reality it was just the '60s, and birth control had just been introduced—women were liberated, experiencing their own freedom, and everybody was having casual sex.

After somewhere around 300 or 400 trips, Lao Two realized that LSD is a fine tool for realization and understanding—opening the doors of the mind and heart—but the results are fleeting, ephemeral, and it's hard to hold on to what's been learned after the come down (the next several days after tripping). Then inexplicably, the strangest thing happened: after taking LSD so many times, he quit coming down—he discovered he was psychedelic all the time. He would take LSD and nothing would happen, even though the people he sold it to told him it was excellent. It was obviously time to give up swallowing psychedelics, since he wasn't getting high on them.

Over the years the quality of marijuana improved greatly, but LSD disappeared for him. Lao Two sold marijuana brands that were labeled by their country, like Columbian Gold, Panama Red, Thai sticks, Maui Wowie, Kona Gold; and the stuff from around Mendocino in Northern California, known as the Emerald Triangle, which we just called "home-grown," "California," or "local" weed. He knew dealers of marijuana, connoisseurs like he, who were always on the lookout for something special. He never made much money but enjoyed the clientele, and it was nice to have extra income along with what he earned from his straight jobs.

After a while, the scene around him changed, and people started doing cocaine. He didn't like it very much; it seemed like a stupid waste of money for something that brought no hallucinations. One of his oldest friends knew some pilots who had just returned from the Vietnam War. They were already excellent pilots, so they gladly flew half-crazy low-altitude flights from Mexico or Colombia to small airfields hidden in the southwestern deserts. These pilots were smuggling pure, non-Mafia cocaine, untouched. He bought a microscope and compared the coke his friends were getting on the street with what the pilots were bringing in, and there was a huge difference in purity. So because he had a trusted source, he started dealing cocaine, with the mind-set that he was helping his friends get a pure product instead of the horrid street cocaine. To this day Lao Two still thinks that dealing cocaine was his biggest mistake along the way, and he regrets it—especially since he didn't even enjoy using the stuff. In his defense, he was recently divorced, and dealing coke was an easy way to meet women for sex. The glitz all ended when he got busted for a pound of coke and about a hundred kilos of Thai sticks. All the money he'd made went for lawyers.

These are Lao Two's credentials. Neither of us is an expert in anything; almost everything in this book is from personal experience. In addition, it must be understood that we're not the only people who could have written this book—we are simply two of many who have had higher-consciousness experiences. There are people who continue to take psychedelics, still pushing the boundaries of the inner path. To all the psychedelic wizards of the past, present, and future, this book is dedicated.

Lao Two says: "Be willing to sound crazy, act and be crazy. Let the crazy come fearlessly. Tomorrow after the experience wears off the world will be changed. I never met a magician whose feet could touch the ground."

There will be lots of far-out ideas presented here, as we've decided to not hold back on anything. Instead of painting a rosy picture, we'll also discuss the downside. Lots of this stuff has been secret for centuries, but we're swinging the door wide open. As a warning—since information can be powerful and dangerous—we have to assume the reader will not go further than their comfort level or common sense.

It's important to emphasize that this is NOT a book on religion: Stoner Meditation demands that you create your own spiritual path. There is a mountain to climb with many paths, so it's entirely up to you which way you'll go. Stoner Meditation will join you along the path now and then, pointing out easier trails. As we walk that path, let's smoke some marijuana together and discuss some truths. At the end of our conversation we will have entered another realm. And our realizations will resonate to open our minds and hearts, apprehending mind-to-mind, unspoken awareness.

Lao Two says: "ALL fundamentalists fear free speech, new ideas, and satire."

Both Lao Two and I hope you enjoy this book, and profit from it. Our goal is simple—to get you to meditate daily.

Lao Two says: "Do not take meditation lightly; in the long run, it's more powerful than the strongest hits of LSD."

Holy smokes!

We created an email account for you to contact. As you read through this book keep in mind that we are open to your suggestions, additions, and corrections. However, changes can only be made to the eBook, but maybe that will change. Let us know if you would like the quote credit, or remain anonymous. Please, no questions concerning specific personal problems. Apparently we can edit this book online, so contact us: Stonermeditation@gmail.com

Spirit

Old adage: "Head in the sky, feet on the ground."

At some point, everybody stands on the cliff of epiphany. It's the life-changing angst-filled moment we all share: realizing that life is quickly ticking by, and then facing the relentless human question: "What's it all about?" If we're not careful, we might miss the significance of this questioning moment. Do we take our brief life seriously, or do we shove it under the door into the locked room of denial—living half a life?

The fact that this book is in your hands says that you are already thinking about meditation, and probably you've also been wandering a while on the noble path toward higher awareness, smoking marijuana, and maybe taking psychedelics. Welcome.

Marijuana has been smoked for centuries, possibly even in our prehistory by those Neanderthals—but now it is being cultivated for stronger and higher-quality buds. Traditionally it was wild-growing hemp, used as animal food, until someone realized the sticky stuff on the plant could be collected, dried, and smoked as hashish. As we understand it, there are a series of chemicals like THC (tetrahydrocannabinol), THCA, and CBD that are the main ingredients that affect humans. There are two main varieties originating in different parts of the planet, *sativa* and *indica*, each having specific effects. But those revered old strains are currently being mixed, resulting in thousands of new subvarieties.

Did you know that the United States has thrown an entire industry away? The stalk and fibers of the marijuana plant are used for hemp, a product with an astounding number of industrial uses such as paper, rope, clothing, canvas, building materials, food, and water purification; it could effectively replace oil in making plastics. At present, the United States imports all of its hemp products from abroad because it's illegal for our farmers to grow it.

Scientists are discovering that medical marijuana brings relief for an amazing number of physical problems, including body aches and pains, uptight body tensions, mental anxiety, and mild depression. It's efficacious for glaucoma and cancer radiation-therapy patients; increases appetite for those suffering from AIDS; is immensely helpful for insomnia; shows promise in slowing breast cancer, brain cancer, and Alzheimer's; and could possibly help epileptics. Medical marijuana has become more and more established and accepted. It's important to remember that no one has ever died from smoking marijuana.

Marijuana is much different now from when we first started smoking it some fifty years ago. Growing it is now an advanced science and an art. Compared to the wild-growing Mexican brick weed we used to get in the mid-sixties, it's like night and day. We used to smoke reefer after reefer, usually in a communal circle, passing to the next person. It was a lot of effort to clean out the seeds and stems, constantly rolling joints in a lot of smoke-filled rooms. Among our group we quickly realized that Mom Nature has created a symbiotic relationship between the marijuana plant and humans. Unlike the apple that nourishes our bodies, marijuana nourishes our mind, and natural psychedelics nurture our soul.

Smoking marijuana makes us ask a million important questions: What is our life purpose? Why are we here? Is money all there is? How can we find peace of mind? What's the best way to live? Will I get laid soon? These questions and so many more are a natural and inherent characteristic of the experience. From our introduction to smoking marijuana or eating some magic mushroom, we discover another world, a *nonordinary* world.

For our discussions, we'll use two levels of h

First, we can get "high," having a fun night fi
lot of lying around, some trippy visions, a stomach fi
ies, and great sex. Then we wake up the next morning b
bushy-tailed.

Second is getting "stoned," where after years of tripping, w
the same amount but it affects us differently. Or beginners smoke
more than they are used to, eat too much brownie, or smoke a rea
strong brand and get super high.

The best-case scenario is that Stoners become creative, open-minded, and willing to change. We engage the world on our own terms, leaving behind the judgmental and erroneous beliefs we were taught—becoming loving, mellow, understanding, and aware. This opens us up to a well-worn path of insights and visions, and gives us a few answers to long-standing questions. Our natural curiosity becomes so strong we educate ourselves, trying to unlock the mysteries we encounter. Best of all, we learn how to be happy amid the craziness of life.

But in the worst-case scenario, we Stoners get stuck in an undirected high where thoughts are repetitious and control us. We become emotionally disoriented, with temperamental ups and downs, and feel confusion and lack of direction. Anger is suppressed and often internalized. Instead of becoming more creative, the mind goes blank and we end up lying around all the time, which can lead to minor anxiety attacks and potential paranoia. This lazy-dopey Stoner state is the hackneyed persona portrayed in most media (the Dude, Cheech and Chong) and comics.

Either way, for Stoners it's usually a psychedelic experience that pulls the rug from under our feet, changing everything forever. Stoners enter the nonordinary world and for some of us, there is no turning back. Both the best-case and worst-case scenarios have their place and time, and neither is really right or wrong—but we are assuming you

er Meditation, we can begin to
ove in our endeavors and even
ıt?" And Stoners still wake up
tailed.

ın to calm emotional anxiety
ong marijuana and most psy-
ght, but they come too fast to
nces are fleeting, and we long
while stoned would remain
on is another meditation tool

...experience, with practice. We postulate that we Stoners do enlightenment ass-backwards, oppositely: instead of putting in years of daily sitting meditation, learning concentration, and moving toward enlightenment, we have our enlightenment first, then learn how to get grounded, centered, and balanced through meditation.

Let's take a break—and do Exercise 1. This is a good opportunity to get stoned together.

The first exercise is inspired by a story Lao Two heard at least forty years ago. The story revolves around a woman who goes by the name of Dusty Street, who in the late 1960s was a famous San Francisco nighttime radio disc jockey. Historically, this was the time when AM radio was pretty damn square. FM radio had just been introduced; right at the time that LSD was catching on, and was considered the place to find alternative music (rock and roll). We hippies wanted to listen to psychedelic music, so we tuned in to FM and found stations playing the Beatles, Dylan, Stones, Grateful Dead, etc. There was a certain risk for disk jockeys being in the spotlight, as it often led to getting busted for narcotics (marijuana), which meant not only jail time but also, in those days, completely ruined careers and lives.

Also, women disc jockeys were few and far between. Dusty broke down the wall, and we suspect she was a Stoner—at the least, we can say that she had a huge Stoner audience. We contacted her a few years ago via email to ask about the veracity of this story. She said she used to do a lot of different warm-up techniques to get ready for her popular radio show, so it's entirely possible this exercise did come from her. She's still a disk jockey, and you can find "Fly Low," her current radio show, on the national airwaves.

Lao Two originally heard this warm-up technique from another disc jockey, XYZ, whose radio show was in Marin, a wealthy bedroom community just north of the Golden Gate Bridge. Lao Two would go into XYZ's studio during broadcasts and they would get stoned together while he was on the air. Of course Dusty Street wanted to perform with an energetic voice. The Marin disc jockey XYZ described this stunning warm-up of hers that he'd witnessed before one of her radio shows.

Exercise 1: First smoke some righteous marijuana, and let it come on for about fifteen minutes. We recommend you find a place where you can speak as loudly as you want and jump up and down if you want to.

Dusty Street would close her eyes. Then she would first say to herself slowly, quietly, "I am alive," feeling the vocal vibrations in her throat. She would open her eyes and say louder, "I," pause, "am," pause, "alive," pause, and feel the effect of her words. She would add expansive body gestures, moving her arms and body simultaneously with the phrase. She would say it until she was bursting with joy at being "alive." Please keep saying, "I—AM—ALIVE!" until you feel separated from the gravity that holds you to Earth. Notice how the vibrations connect to the air you are breathing and the ecstatic body you reside in—feel the vibes. Tap your toes, jump around, dance, flap your arms, and turn on that smile!

You should feel pleasantly aware and euphoric when you are finished, and in the mood for the concepts and definitions that will follow.

End of Exercise 1.

Lao Two says: "Life is a river, we are bubbles in the water."

Enlightenment: There are several ambiguous levels, or states, of enlightenment. We'll consider three classifications:

1. The first is analytical enlightenment, where we understand emptiness, much like an intellectual, scholarly appreciation.
2. Then we have the personal experience of emptiness enlightenment, usually on a psychedelic trip or sitting in meditation. The word *satori* describes this experience, also know as an intuitive realizing of awareness, or sudden enlightenment.
3. Lastly, there is a type of enlightenment where we have passed through the door and view life from the shamanic "other side." We accept the paradox that we exist and are also emptiness, existing in an indescribable tactile, mindfully aware void. This emptiness is not nihilism, nothing, or depression—it is alive, loving and active. Living in conscious bliss, we move through the everyday world as an awakened being.

Lao Two says: "If you are trying to control the world around you, trying to figure it out with analysis, you will discover it's counterintuitive. Analysis won't develop realization or happiness. Instead, letting go lets us be aware and accept the mystery, living gracefully with unanswered questions. Accept that you haven't figured it all out yet. This is called living with a sense of wonder."

Albert Einstein said: "He who can no longer pause to wonder and stand rapt in awe is as good as dead."

Three Assertions

1. Marijuana's greatest benefit is as a tool for mental and spiritual exploration. Every marijuana bud has the potential for imparting insight, education, and transcendence. When marijuana is combined with meditation, our view changes to clear high awareness, our heart opens to compassion, and dualism is resolved.

2. Although marijuana (and psychedelics) opens the door, it is meditation that enables us to walk through to the other side. On the other side of that door is Stoner Meditation.

3. Stoners should advocate the use of marijuana and psychedelics. Most of this book is written as if psychedelics were already legalized, easily available for adults, taxed, and labeled with warnings, advice, and other pertinent safety information as necessary.

Let's face it: even when marijuana and psychedelics do become legal, not everyone will try them—psychoactive experience is not for everybody. But those people who become Stoners, who consider their psychedelic tripping as the path of wizards, will be rewarded for their spiritual motivation. The ones who add meditation will realize their true nature. If only one person reading this awakens to highest enlightenment, then writing this book has been worthwhile. If a thousand people learn how to trip better, then our efforts are justified. And if ten thousand, million, gazillion people try marijuana for the first time, then wowza!

Lao Two says: "Every human who takes a natural psychedelic like magic mushrooms will understand that entheogens teach peace on Earth is possible."

Dreams

Marijuana demands a great deal from us. After smoking marijuana awhile, we realize that we're going to have to change a few things. Personally, we'll be glad when cars drive themselves automatically so we can relax instead of drive. And, we can't smoke everywhere. Sometimes we even have to quit smoking marijuana for a while, for example, when traveling to countries where it's inadvisable to smoke, or during and after pregnancy, while performing brain surgery or flying in a jet, or flying a jet. We have to be careful how we speak, act, and live. We Stoners wouldn't do all this if we didn't think it was worth it.

Stoners have to learn to adroitly balance many worlds. We have our regular material ordinary-reality world. And we have our Stoner transcendent, hallucinatory nonordinary-reality world. Of course the responsibilities of kids to raise; a wife, husband, or partner; and a job all take different types of concentration, and are worlds in themselves. We intuitively suspect that beyond all these material worlds is a wizard world, an extraordinary reality where insights, wisdom, and teachings arise magically, as if from nowhere. The wizard world is the yet unknown, interconnected higher world. But with practice, we discover an ever-creating reality around and within us, using the meditative state of calm awareness as we integrate the wizard world.

We juggle work, social life, education, and our families for our "hobby"—our joyful preoccupation with smoking marijuana. We smoke because it's the most reliable and predictable way to experience visionary thinking, loving body feelings, and magical, unexpected synchronicity. It even makes mundane, repetitious work fun. Because marijuana is illegal, we have to weigh our wanting to get high with the difficulty of secretly finding some smokes through underground sources. Unless it's medical marijuana, we are always aware of the possibility of getting busted, and getting busted sucks. We put a lot of effort into our lives, trying to bring everything into harmony just to be high. Sometimes life goes along successfully; other times we're stumbling, or faking it.

There are many ways to live; we've already decided to get stoned. Marijuana and psychedelics are absolutely NOT necessary to reach the higher states of mind and consciousness we'll be discussing. But getting stoned is nothing new; humans probably discovered higher mind while living in caves and mud huts—after all, psychedelics grow naturally on almost every corner of the Earth. It seems meditation is also a natural predisposition for us, as staring up at the stars was probably considered entertainment back then. We don't know how far marijuana, magic mushrooms, peyote, etc., go back in history, but it's possible the Neanderthals before us got stoned. We like to think that if those plants did have psychotropic ingredients back then, Neanderthals ate or smoked them and had those same magical experiences we have.

Many religions have meditation as part of their teachings, and whole schools of thought have been developed to achieve higher mind. So here we are, stoned in the twenty-first century, adrift in an ocean of psychedelic nonordinary reality, trying to fit in with the straight world around us, and we've heard that meditation is helpful for sorting everything out and can give us peace and wisdom. With Stoner Meditation, we don't have to use meditation alone to discover higher mind—times have changed. We can combine marijuana, psychedelics, and meditation to achieve awareness.

Marijuana and psychedelics give us visions and teach us insights that can come too fast, growth is ephemeral, and we are left with partial wisdom, and often confusion. This is like flying a jet.

Meditation brings stability, relaxation, and a more solid grounding of wisdom. However, results can take too long, and using meditation alone is difficult. Meditation will eventually break us through to the other side. This is like trekking up a mountain on foot.

Combine marijuana and psychedelics and meditation, and we get Stoner Meditation. Awareness has lots of labels: satori, *kensho*, calm abiding, natural mind, Buddha nature, nirvana, and enlightenment—and now, with Stoner Meditation, we have a new key to open the door of realization.

From the misinformation of the media, many people have mixed or negative feelings about marijuana, including assorted preconceived notions about the people who smoke it. Nonsmokers wonder if marijuana is a scourge because they don't know fact from fiction. Marijuana became illegal about the same time as alcohol, in the 1920s and '30s. It remained illegal mainly for racist reasons in those days. There have been so many lies fed the public for the last fifty-plus years. ... But lately there is hope; with each passing year, people are seeing that marijuana criminalization isn't working.

The truth is that marijuana is not addictive or lethal, and will not destroy the fabric of society. The DEA's (Drug Enforcement Agency) biggest fear has been realized, there is no longer any need to smuggle marijuana between countries. Almost anyone can grow a few marijuana plants inside with growing lights. Soon it will be clear that their misguided efforts for the past five decades were all based on lies. When it's legalized, people will smoke peacefully, giggle at movies, order take-out pizza; taxpayers will see the cost of the "drug war" disappear; and the marijuana taxes will actually bring in a little new revenue.

Lao Two says: "Marijuana and psychedelics are a health issue, not a criminal issue."

As a rule, Stoners are harmless, intelligent, loving, and concerned about the destruction of Earth's environment—not evil, stupid addicts like the drug war or Stoner movies portray. Our position is that marijuana and psychedelics are medicinal and ultimately spiritual—not in a religious sense, but in a moral and ethical sense.

Lao Two says: "We don't need any new religions. Once it's figured out how magic works, it's no longer called magic—it's called science."

Here are some far-out (speculative) opinions of ours: Buddha, Muhammad, and Christ probably smoked hashish, and possibly took psychedelics—although not in a group get-together. Jesus lived in a time when *cannabis* was central to survival, and was used as hemp in products like anointing or lighting oil, clothing, shoes, and rope. Also, we consider his lost years wandering in the desert a road trip to visit India. Muhammad proclaimed alcohol is prohibited, but hashish is not. Buddha renounced being a prince and left his family to become a wandering ascetic some 500 years before Christianity, and before Hinduism. Historically, hashish was smoked in pre-Vedic times, at least 1,500 years before Christ. During Buddha's time there were a great many enlightened holy men wandering around, many who had stumbled on awareness one way or another—perhaps getting their insights from hashish. Lastly, there was soma—a legendary psychedelic brew known as the drink of the gods, possibly the fly agaric mushroom, also known as amanita muscaria.

Today, there are hashish-smoking sadhus (followers of Shiva) in India and Nepal who can trace back their hashish use for thousands of years. Shiva is one of the three most powerful gods in India. He has many attributes, one being his love for hashish. ... As far as I can research, it seems hashish has been smoked in India and the surrounding Mediterranean and Baltic regions since forever.

Each time Lao Two visited Nepal he interacted with many of the playful, joyous *sadhu*s who wander the streets of Kathmandu and the high mountains, living on donations. They are considered holy men, renunciants, mendicants. Although he never smoked with them, he often gives them marijuana and hashish as offerings. Marijuana grows wild in the mountains of Nepal, and Nepalese hashish is world renowned for its potency. It's ridiculously easy to score hash in Kathmandu. It could be said that we in the West have rediscovered this same ancient path, except we call ourselves Stoners or psychonauts these days.

Marijuana users can achieve the very highest extraordinary states of consciousness by being guided naturally toward awareness. Serious Marijuana smokers will inevitably find the path. Only the most rare of humans are like Buddha, Muhammad, or Christ in their attainment. But every time we strike a match, burn some marijuana flowers, and inhale the smoke, we are essentially trying to break through to the other side, and even if we're not paying attention, it's happening. But, the other side of what? Do we really need to be a saint to experience some of the legendary breakthroughs?

During nighttime sleep we have different kinds of dreams, and after death is supposed to be dreamlike. Using lucid dreaming, it's possible to be an aware participant in our nighttime dream experience. Once we start participating in our dreams, they take on a different flavor.

We also have waking dreams, known as daydreams, and have a whole world outside our bodies that is said to be nothing but a dream. We have the dreams that arise out of psychedelic experience as hallucinations. It seems our consciousness is very adaptable.

In the wizard world it's possible to merge our inner and outer worlds as a paradoxical experience—where the dream and the real become one. The concentration we learn through meditation is what will make those waking dreams and nighttime dreams useful. Our life obviously has many levels of being—from the solid material world to consciousness, emotional and sensory states—yet we generally take them all for granted. Most people go through life with no concern for these distinctions; we unambiguously live here in this body, and our brain thinks. Simple enough. ...

However, those notions of an unexamined life don't feel so substantial for Stoners. We spend time being straight people, and then we become Stoners. Then we walk through the real world making the distinctions blur together, and life takes on a more contrasting, dreamlike quality. Everything reveals its ephemeral and transitory nature. Our daily life has become dreamlike, because life is a dream. But we wonder then, what's real? What can be known for certain?

As long as we are alive we can experience being human; when we die, our human existence changes to something else. Unfortunately and historically, humans on Earth are not too bright; even with our amazing material possessions and industrial accomplishments, planet Earth right now is steeped in the Great Second Dark Ages. Politically, economically, and as a species, we are hell bent on self-destruction.

We have to be more than just human if we are going to live a life with purpose—we have to become enlightened beings, or wizards. Letting life slip by without questioning the various worlds around us just won't cut it anymore.

A few of us have already opened up the mostly uncharted map of our mind's potential and have sailed bravely into the unknown. They search everywhere for ways to navigate and stay clear of storms, reefs, and sea monsters. But the psychedelic map isn't much help because it uses no compass. Up, down, east, and west have no relevance on the map of the mind. First we need to find an island to use as a safe harbor. From there we can explore the farthest psychedelic destinations, knowing that whatever comes can be navigated.

"Stoner" and "straight: are not value judgments—they are descriptions of being high or not high. Straight people don't have any concern with "extraordinary reality" and generally accept their beliefs on habitual "faith." Stoners question reality, beliefs, and habitual memories—or at least they should.

Beginning smokers tend to get high and float away, enjoying their experiences of bliss. Stoner Meditation is learning how to guide the high so we can relax and float downstream unimpeded. It turns out that our habitual thoughts, and the things we take on faith, are why people have "bad" trips. The extraordinary reality of Stoner Meditation requires training in control, concentration, then letting go, and eventually paying very close attention. The payoff is awareness, and the ability to view life as magical existence.

Do you remember that awkward lunchtime at work, when you sneaked the smallest puff of marijuana? You figured you had an easy afternoon, and one little hit wouldn't make any difference, but that smallest puff got you higher than you expected. On returning to your job, you were informed that the boss just announced an unscheduled conference in five minutes. Whoops, now you felt even more stoned, and would to have to really try to maintain your composure. There you were in nonordinary reality, and everybody else in ordinary reality. That meeting was exhausting, requiring intense concentration, and full of awkward emotional body sensations. Maybe you were anxious about being discovered and had difficulty keeping from smiling or falling asleep. This happened because you haven't learned to use meditation to keep your center, balance, and concentration.

A Stoner Meditation wizard in that same situation would be able to actively participate in the meeting, no matter how stoned, with focus, concentration, creativity, and the ability to ignore self-doubts and enjoy the ride. Stoner mindfulness is seeing everything that's going on from the viewpoint of higher mind. We notice our physical and emotional reaction to whatever is happening around us, then make wise choices using wisdom and awareness.

Lao Two says: "We are not our material things, we are not our body or thinking mind. When we discover that we are only awareness, we are liberated. This is the true nature of reality."

The inherent eternal nature and underlying vibration of the universe is *aware love*. It could be said that everything that exists at this moment is vibrating, and the highest, purest vibration is love. It's had lots of names and labels, and it's been rediscovered over and over throughout human history. From the very beginning of our first smoke to the highest levels of Stoner Meditation, we can connect with this universal love. Aware love can be felt in the body as joy and bliss. It can be called God, Buddha-nature, highest mind, super stoned, breaking through, or whatever, but when we access it directly, we recognize aware love. This fundamental quality, power, energy doesn't care what we call it, or even if we notice it or not. It exists beyond human comprehension and senses, creating every complicated component of existence. Love is nothing but pure, yet somehow intelligent vibration. We can connect to it through synchronization, much as the same musical note played on two separate instruments synchronizes. When we become synchronic, we uncover the transcendental wisdom that is available if we then know how to receive it.

In other words, love is the ever-creating, never-ending intelligent force of the universe. The farther we get from it, the more discordant and out of harmony we find ourselves. If we are not feeling love, we are probably feeling angry, emotional, or depressed. Enlightened people are often called blissed out, because they directly feel vibrational love within them. They are able to see the people farther removed from the vibration of love as suffering. And although they understand that other people feel suffering as real, for an enlightened person suffering is now an abstraction, viewed as delusion.

The Stoner Meditation journey can be described as figuratively leaving a comfortable, laid-back valley homeland and going on a life-long climb through the forest of trees, up a mountain, trekking higher and higher in elevation. We begin by leaving our mindless, distracted culture and setting out on our own quest, maybe because we've heard there is another way to live. Maybe we are sick of our beliefs that don't make sense, or of our inner turmoil and our suffering, so we are searching for the answers, peace of mind, and wisdom that come from direct experience.

In answer to the question posed above—the other side of what? The symbolic mountain is inside of each of us, and our journey is traveled alone. When we can accept that we are being transformed by it, we can start to give up our identity, just enough to become one with the world around us. This identity, or ego, is not evil or a chain around our neck—it is who we are, right now in time and space. But there is another aspect to ego, and that is our erroneous assumptions about the reality around us. The world is not what we think it is. ... If we're able to let go of our ego beliefs and do everything with intense concentration, then we actively create our future, by participating in the present. It's easier said then done, and that's why we need to start right away to balance our life. We found the psychedelic map and we started on our journey, but we have no idea where we are. We're somewhere on the map, but quite lost for the moment.

Lao Two says: "We create our future by our choices in the now."

In real life (not metaphorically), have you ever backpacked up a mountain? Hiking up most mountains requires walking uphill through trees and brush. But there is an area beyond which trees will no longer grow, known as the tree line—a gradual or sudden ending leading to a panoramic view. So switching back to our metaphor, tree line is where we have opened up our minds to a much larger awareness. In the trees we can't see very far, but at tree line we can clearly see the unobstructed vistas, or awareness.

Tripping on marijuana and psychedelics, and practicing medita-tion, is hiking in the trees. When we break through tree line to where the clear heights are visible, this is our first enlightenment.

But this is not enough. Even though we can see much more around us, we can also look toward the mountain peak rising above and under-stand that we still have to go higher. Once we've broken through tree line, we see other people who are just milling around. They've set up (religious) communities, but they mistakenly think they are at the top of the mountain when they're only halfway up. They are being helpful by yelling down to the people still stuck in the trees to help them find their way, but their voices are confusing—it's difficult to know exactly which direction they are yelling from. Tree line gives us our first realization of where we are on the psychedelic map.

Since there are "levels of enlightenment," tree line can be considered the first breakthrough. We learn very important lessons in the forest, but it's nothing like the view from here. It's not that we have one enlightenment and then boom, we're finished and life is perfect. During the Stoner Meditation journey, we can have higher and higher enlightenments until we enter nirvana at the mountaintop.

Since the trip from the valley through the forest to tree line must be taken without knowing where you are on the psychedelic map, we are here to guide you. We hope to show you how to get there—not an easy destination in itself, but very achievable.

Don't let the terms we use throw you. We're just talking about ways to get high, and then higher, and live a righteous life. To guide you, we first have to explain a few more terms and make sure we are all talking about the same concepts and ideas. We need this information to be able to understand how our thinking directly affects our ability to trip.

Lao Two says: "Never take anything on belief or faith. Test my recommendations in the fire of your own experiential truth."

Mind

Lao Two says: "Fundamentally, we are a focus of eternal awareness experiencing constant transformation on the physical and conscious levels, while living in a finite body/mind. We all have our identifying ego story that describes and labels us, yet on a higher level we are nothing more than a conglomeration of aware energy in the here and now."

Natural Mind: Please note that we are using the capital N and M, to mean highest mind awareness, reality, or enlightened view of nirvana. This mind includes everything with no separation. Physical body, conscious thinking, the world around us, and the entire universe is Natural Mind—it functions on the microcosmic and the macrocosmic levels. Included in Natural Mind is our karmic propensity, as the driving force on our path, and the historical period we are born into—in other words, whatever brought us to exactly here and now.

Natural Mind awareness has transcended our deluded, misinformed ego consciousness. Judgmental thinking is gone, along with our negative or positive attachments, like grasping and clinging. Arising thoughts are neutral, coming and going unimpeded. An apple is new each bite—there is no worrying about a future apple, or stressing over an apple incident that happened three years ago. Apparently, Natural Mind awareness as the highest level of pure perception doesn't change, no matter what dimension we are in (life or death) and exists in the here-now—awareness remains as awareness.

We describe **thinking mind** as our lower, instinctual, judgmental mind. This is where our emotional feelings and body senses arise. Our inner voice, emotions, and unpredictable habits come from thinking mind. This is sometimes called the monkey mind because it jumps wildly from subject to subject. It is standard consciousness, our habitual deluded mind, and the book-learning mind of facts. It's important to remember that mental consciousness on this level is just a sense, in many ways not much different from smell or hearing. It has a limited way of interacting with the world because it relies on ego (survival instinct)—for example, it keeps us from getting burned on a hot stove. Thinking mind's method is using the past and the future to keep us from being ambushed. This is the controlling mind of endless chatter, the mind we want to move away from enough to see it clearly. When positive, it is the deliberate analytical mind where we use past experiences to judge future actions. Or conversely, if negative, it's the voice of doubt and fear that arises from confused emotions. Thinking mind operates in the dark, and our goal is to acquire a candle and an endless supply of matches. This is the mind that most of us are stuck in without even knowing we're stuck. It could also be called brain consciousness— acting as a sensory organ.

Doing mind is the mind that looks at thinking mind, moderating the inner voice, and then transcends intention and goes into action. This is the mind that we want to move toward—the mind that gets things done. It consciously acts without the big argument or analysis we get from thinking mind. This doing mind sees directly, all things, thoughts, and experiences exactly as they are, before thinking mind labels them. This is the mind where creative and intuitive intelligence arises, beyond good/bad, right/wrong. When we get stoned, we enter doing mind; this is where our best insights and inspiration come from, or conversely, where we act out on our bummers, or get completely zoned out and do absolutely nothing. Doing mind also has a voice, but it rarely speaks – it is the wise ethical voice.

Please understand there is ultimately only ONE mind (Natural Mind), and these categories are designed for describing certain ways of perceiving. Mind is like an orchestra, many instruments playing together to form a group sound.

Enlightenment is not all that difficult to achieve, but thinking mind likes to complicate the situation, so it's knowing where and how to look that opens the door. We think our descriptions, exercises, and instructions will teach Stoners how to recognize a "low-level" enlightenment. Lao Two firmly believes that sudden enlightenment is possible for every single Stoner. We'll point out the path and give you the psychedelic map, but it takes your footsteps to walk to tree line. There's an old saying, "If you meet the Buddha on the road, kill him," because you can't be Gautama Buddha—you can only be you. Stoners have a unique advantage over nonStoners because we have already encountered non-ordinary reality. The jump to "extraordinary reality" (enlightenment) is just a matter of training, changing perspective, and being trusting enough to become "invisible" for a little while, to let insight dawn. Each and every exercise presented here is a direct path through the forest up to tree line and the expanded view of enlightenment. Some are extremely simple, others intense and intimidating. Sudden enlightenment is glimpsing or suddenly being aware of nirvana—waking up. Please investigate (Google) Vipassana Jhanas for more information on levels of enlightenment.

Nirvana, on the other hand, is an experience that can't be described using language. This is the awareness that can be glimpsed as sudden enlightenment—our goal in this book. Or, in the case of the Buddha, Muhammad, Jesus, and many others, nirvana is total immersion in a selfless state. The word "nirvana" means to "blow out," like the flame of a candle, or in our case, ceasing the chatter of thinking mind and letting go of ego.

Nirvana is advanced realization, usually after years of changing the way we think about existence using dedicated meditation. But we Stoners know that taking a series of psychedelics in an attempt to transcend the world completely washes clean the mental universe. As we said, psychedelic nirvana is difficult to sustain. Stoner Meditation bridges the gap between the ordinary world and nirvana.

The "opposite" of nirvana is our clinging to the material world. When we can temporarily renounce our attachment to it, we glimpse nirvana and are forever changed. We are released from wants, anger, fears, and ignorance—and discover desires have no hold on us. Nirvana is an active spiritual state of being, unaffected by but engaged with the comings and goings of the world, yet fully alive, passionate, and wise.

Nirvana is absorption in emptiness on the one hand, and keenly aware concentration on the other. These two together allow us to transcend ordinary existence and step into an amazing nonordinary view—direct experience.

Traditionally, enlightenment and nirvana have been interchange-able terms—but Stoner Meditation is giving them new and stronger definitions, because we need to describe at least two different levels of attainment. Enlightenment will be described as the first leap into nonordinary oneness, more like a completely transforming epiphany, a mind-bending exceptional "aha" moment, when we come upon pristine awareness for the first time—walking out of the dense forest and seeing the sweeping panoramic view above tree line.

Nirvana is sustained clear consciousness, connection with univer-sal love beyond space-time, and liberation from all suffering and attach-ments. We like to describe nirvana as sitting 100 feet above the summit of the mountain in the sky, experiencing extraordinary superconscious-ness, a vast view, and an astute, inherent wisdom that is beyond our dualistic way of understanding.

Lao Two says: "Change is all we have. We rent this body, using the sands of time as payment."

We said before that our life is not how it appears to us. This is because we've been taught to believe our dogma and accept the notion of what someone else has told us reality is. That's not only misinformed, it's sad.

But what happens if we stop and look honestly, fearlessly at life? We'll soon be teaching you how to sit in a meditation position and what to do while there. While we don't do anything except learn concentra-tion at the beginning, our sitting there is courageously questioning real-ity. Instead of being busy and distracted every moment, we are chang-ing the momentum and building a new dynamic.

We need you to also change the dynamic of getting stoned. Instead of getting high and watching TV, or grooving endlessly on music with headphones on your ears, you'll use the power of marijuana and psychedelics to take a close, accurate look at the astonishing world inside of and surrounding you.

By the time we hit our stride in our late teens, we've accepted a lot of assumptions about how to view our world. But what if almost everything we think is wrong? Let's play a short game and flip our world on its head: visualize that we are without any knowledge at all, that we never learned scientific facts or read a book; there is only what surrounds us at this very moment—we don't even know how we got where we are. Picture having no past or future, mother, father, children, or even a planet called Earth to stand on. Focus on this very moment in time and space and see it as distinct from all other past or future moments. Imagine having no emotions, feelings, or senses, so instead of scratching that itch, we discover that body signals don't have to be obeyed. We don't have to control our breathing; the body continues even when we sit unmoving in our meditation position. Without all these accepted things to hold on to, we have nothing, yet here we still are—awareness. We can't put our finger exactly where the awareness is located, but even with our eyes closed we have presence, existence. It turns out we are immersed in a river of ever-changing phenomena—we, and the water around us, are changing all the time.

Body and mind is just another illusion. If we turn our attention to the thinking mind inside our brain, we realize its just producing word-image after word-image, all of which quickly fade away. Our worries, analysis, and fears are temporary, with no importance.

We are not what we thought we are. Metaphorically, we are hiking in the trees, but we need to ask exactly who or what is doing the walking, when, and why. The smudged glasses of delusion can be taken off and cleaned, and then we start to see clearly no matter where we are. This is Stoner Meditation.

Before we were born, we were in the embrace of the nirvana of Natural Mind—the same nirvana that Gautama Buddha realized while he was alive. Imagine a superconsciousness that is nothing but aware-ness and transcends both time and space, yet appears to exist as a solid continuum. Awareness of superconsciousness arises for anyone who sets into motion the causes and conditions that are developed through meditative acuity—we actually experience what it's like to be unborn and eternal, and we "stand" in Natural Mind as cosmic consciousness.

Let's step back for a moment—we have to get used to no beginning and no ending. For example, before we are born, there is the potential of causes and conditions that have been in existence eternally. From that potential we are born. As long as that effect remains in motion, we are alive. When a new cause comes along, such as our body aging, we die and return to nirvana. We'll leave rebirth and reincarnation to the investigation and personal realization of you readers, and not impose our own beliefs here. We'll only say that death is not the end of every-thing we are.

It's no different with time and space; there is still cause and effect. To think that the Big Bang started into motion everything that exists in time and space is shortsighted. All the Big Bang did was create OUR time and space. Also, everything is in constant creation in every moment—everything.

Lastly, please remember that we're trying to write about an inef-fable, beyond ordinary experience, which we describe as breaking through the trees to the expansive view of tree line. Words can never do either the path or the experience justice.

As children, we must adapt quickly, and after a while the Natural Mind we are born with is suppressed. Eventually emotions like love, faith, trust, and innate wisdom become hardened, atrophied. By neces-sity we must become street smart, able to endure under adverse circum-stances and survive. Our development requires that we leave Natural Mind to develop thinking mind—otherwise we would not survive as a species. To be more accurate, Natural Mind does not actually go away;

our awareness of it fades into the background. Housecats developed an ability to be instantly ready for a potential ambush, and they're always super alert. Humans have developed an ability to adapt to, mold, and define the environment around us, so we have evolved into materialists.

As we grow as children, something is gained, but something incredible is lost. Fortunately, we can reclaim our Natural Mind awareness through Stoner Meditation. To do this we have to dissolve the judgmental impressions that have become our reality.

Being insecure is part of being a teenager, and our thinking mind spends an inordinate amount of time weighing the pros and cons of this and that—endlessly trying to figure out our experiences, putting labels and judgments on everything. To make matters worse, our emotions are heightened, and our body goes through a change. No matter how cool our parents are, we feel a strong urge to make our own way, stand on our own feet, and look toward the future.

By the time we mature we have become opinionated and have solidified our worldviews—we either have figured out how to survive, are still struggling, or in the worst case, have drifted into confusion. We all have an individual story that we constantly write to describe our life. From these stories we use our narrow viewpoints to create our self-identity, called ego. Ego is part of thinking mind, and our thoughts grasp at made-up beliefs to reify a solid reality: our "I" and the surrounding world as separate entities. Thinking mind helps us survive by assuming that our existence is indeed solid, permanent, and worth continuing. If not for this ego belief, we can easily die. Ego does this because if the body or brain dies, ego dies.

Of course, Stoner Meditation is here to tell you that thinking mind is paradoxically both right and wrong. Right when thinking mind guards our body and mind, even when we make stupid, reckless life-and-death choices. And wrong, by not listening to the wisdom of doing mind in the first place.

Maybe you've heard of the ego death experience. What usually happens is that we understand that our "I" is NOT solid, and separateness and duality is just an illusion. In ego death the boundaries we consider sacred are smashed, and all space and time becomes here and now. And since our illusions are demolished and deconstructed for that moment of ego death, we see ourselves as we really are, warts and all.

All our viewpoints come directly from what we think to be true—often despite the fact that our view of reality is wrong. We put up a wall, deny the suffering of others, are drawn to pleasure, and are never able to sit still for a moment. Try as we might, our own suffering keeps resurfacing and our emotions are dragged through our thinking process over and over. This scrutiny of thinking mind, dwelling on our problems, is part of the existential crisis I described at the beginning: "What's it all about?" Eventually dissatisfaction sneaks into everyone's story. Dissatisfaction with our life is not a bad thing—it forces us to wonder and investigate what is worth doing during our short time on Earth.

One of our very important goals is to see the world as it really is. Sometimes seeing things as they really are can be scary, upsetting, even disgusting. For example, did you ever want to be telepathic? Read people's minds? It's not like you think it might be—when you are telepathic you'll see just how crazy people are, full of good, bad, evil, guilt, confusion, etc. ... Telepathy is not like talking on a phone. Both people stand inside the same head.

When we realize that we are suffering inside, despite our chasing after pleasure, we want to know if there is any way to have lasting happiness. Watching TV, getting high, ignoring our suffering can only be a temporary soporific. "What is long-lasting happiness, what's it all about?" This can be the beginning of our breakthrough: looking toward this dissatisfaction, not avoiding, seeing it exactly for what it is. Dissatisfaction can be a great teacher.

The solution is to relax and let go of rigidity and solidity, let things start to flow. Remember when you first learned to ride a bike? The trick is to be moving faster than we would like; if we move too slowly, we can't steer effectively. Instead of erecting a dam in the river, we'll learn how to let the river flow; then Natural Mind will manifest automatically for us again. We don't need the constant intense, analytical effort of thinking mind to try to figure it out.

If you are smoking marijuana you are probably spending at least some time relaxing, and that's excellent. By adding meditation, we can bring awareness to that relaxation. Just getting high all the time can be numbing and hold us back, because thinking mind seeks pleasure. We need to transcend thinking mind for the higher view of doing mind. Over time, combining getting stoned and daily meditation, we start to notice insights that are different from the chatter of thinking mind. This new voice is the creativity entering from doing mind, and the dawning of stable awareness. Think of your daily meditation practice as a drop of water, each day filling a bucket. The bucket gets full and we have that breakthrough. Then we empty the bucket, but that's another story. ... We want to look closely at our thinking mind, exploring what it is, how it affects us, and what we can do about it.

The rules and regulations of Stoner Meditation are pretty simple: to smoke marijuana as often as you like, meditate daily for at least twenty minutes, and learn some new life techniques. Psychedelics are optional, but can be used for extra credit toward your final goal.

That twenty-minute meditation can have a big impact on your life if done every day. The effects are gradual, and although we might see it as a strange thing to do, it will have a payoff bigger than imagined. Meditation has been around for thousands of years; it would be frivolous to disregard what has already been discovered, so herein we include some information about the classical systems and their teachings.

If you are convinced that your life is just fine and perfect the way it is, and you don't need marijuana, meditation, or any improving, changing, or other crazy hippie Stoner Meditation philosophy crapola nonsense—but you've read this far anyway—then at least try meditation. If you could read every book ever written, meditation would teach and benefit you more. I don't care if you quit reading now, the important thing is for you to try meditation —please, at least a daily twenty-minute session for a few months—and see how it affects you. I predict that if you continue, you will find that meditation is life affirming, makes you feel well grounded, increases your ability to concentrate, and is conductive to good physical health by reducing stress. And best of all, you might discover who you really are.

Lao Two says: "Why don't we have young school kids meditate? Start meditation in preschool and make it fun, with absolutely no religious overtones. Continue into the first grade and beyond. Meditation is cost-free, and science is beginning to prove meditation's benefits."

When you start your meditation practice, take a good look at the thinking mind, best visualized as a flowing river, stream-of-consciousness, or monkey mind. Try to let your mind flow unhindered, without going for a ride on each thought that comes up. It's no secret that it's very difficult not to go for a thought ride. Before we start meditation, we don't even know it's happening; it's an invisible habit until we notice it. Watching concentration getting snagged by a thought IS the beginning practice, and seeing how little control we have over our own thinking mind can be a wake-up call.

We Stoners have to stand in front of our mental mirror naked, truthfully accepting whatever we think. Unembellished truth with our inner thinking should also show you that we humans have been fed a load of crap. Know bullshit when you think it: sometimes our thoughts are just plain wrong. For example, we are not here to dominate other species or to turn Earth into a junkyard. The truth is that we are here to be the loving custodians of Earth. After all, Mom Nature gives us everything we need, even our life. Humans are just another animal species, special in some ways, not so special in others.

When you become a wizard, you will understand your powers and how to control and use them. Of course, we'll never finish our training; it should continue throughout our life. But we can evolve beyond being just another mindless unaware human animal bumping and stumbling through life. We can learn how to be graceful, intelligent, and kind, dancing through life. Will you look in the mirror and honestly look at your thoughts?

Nikola Tesla said: "The day science begins to study non-physical phenomena, it will make more progress in one decade than in all the previous centuries of existence."

Stoner Meditation is not lazy meditation and demands some effort to make it work. If you have been getting stoned, living alone without a social life, watching TV and eating take-out food every night, you will have to get up off your ass. It's time to leave beginning marijuana and move on to the next step: intermediate marijuana. Intermediate means going out your door looking for adventure. Start walking in the mythical forest we've been describing, look around at the trees, look closely.

Probably the best place to get high is in a real forest (not a mythical one). Nature is an incredible teacher. However, if you are inexperienced in hiking, Google the "10 essentials" and take every item with you, even for day hikes. Stoner Meditation recommends every type of exercise, including work, play, dance or yoga creativity, and sex—instead of sloth.

Here's a tip: it's said that if you do something day after day for a certain number of days, it will become a life habit. For me, it seems a new activity takes about three to four months to become a life habit. Perseverance does pay off. ...For example, I taught myself tai chi by

DVD. Then while in Bangkok, Thailand, I was able to keep up with the "experts" I met in Lumphini Park, as the moves are standardized worldwide. Each morning before sunrise, Lumphini Park fills with people exercising—running, walking, tai chi, dancercise, weight lifting, etc. There is even a food area with awesome local Thai specialties. Then the national anthem plays and everyone stops in their tracks. Once the anthem has played, it's over, and everyone finishes up to go home or to work.

After some years of this stoned meditation, we'll have learned how to carefully observe the world inside and around us. There will be a point where we start to interact with the world in a different way, allowing doing mind to arise from balanced Natural Mind. We will discover that we naturally have more compassion for our friends', and our own, mistakes, and become forgiving, lighthearted, wise, enjoying whatever comes our way.

Lao Two says: "You can lose your money or your things, and all your stuff. But when you lose your time, you never get it back."

We can have magic and the miraculous in our lives, and Earth could be a paradise. Human potential is evolving toward a higher mind, and that mind will have a spirit body that can communicate with our vibrations beyond the physical body. We have myths of telepathy, magicians of all types, wondrous healing, flying through the sky, walking on water.... But as they say, "Miracles ended when the camera was developed." Now when someone claims they talked to God or saw a burning bush, we ask for photos or a video. Does that mean these miraculous powers are all invalid? We suspect some powers are real, but complicated to perform, with karmic implications. In other words, if we manipulate someone, or something, than we have to accept the effects of our action (cause).

If the physical bodies of humans can survive for another four thousand years, then our potential is unimaginable. When we look back to our Egyptian history, over 4,000 years ago, we can start to see what is possible. I see science confirming the energy centers (chakras) along our spine, the third eye on our forehead, and the energy center at the top of our head. I see all adults safely exploring nonordinary reality, and machines that travel anywhere we can visualize—who's to say what's possible or impossible? Mom Nature seems to have her own program for us, and we're basically along on her ride—we live only because she says so. But all we've done is squander Earth's bounty.

Hallucinate

Think of the times you've been your stonedest, when the hallucinations took over and your thinking mind was lost in the far background. You connected with something that allowed you to release a fountain of hallucinations. But sometimes, just when you are reaching for visions, something holds you back, won't let you break through so you can trip.

Lao Two says: "It pains me to say this, but smoking marijuana is a lower-level high than the practice of meditative awareness."

Hallucinations are serious business. When we experience them, we sit back and watch the show of pretty colors and imaginative cartoon images. But something else is happening too—there are deeply imparted meanings and lessons, and we want to retain those teachings. Unfortunately, the visions happen too fast, cascading endlessly one after another. Because of the rapidity, it's not completely a learning experience; it's more like a joyous, bewildering pinball roller-coaster ride. After the substance wears off, when we try to remember the visions and insights, they're at best vague—and more often already gone and forgotten. Great fun while it lasted, but something's missing: the stabilization and concentration from meditation.

There are two types of hallucinations. The first is completely *unique to the viewer*, based on the user's state of mind and the type of substance taken. Next there are *archetypal visions*, hallucination templates that everyone experiences: the paisley shape, seeing living images in rising smoke or clouds, the cascading faces reflected in mirrors, kaleidoscopic geometric visions, and cartoon characters. Even though these are archetypal hallucinations, they will be influenced by the user's own mental creativity. Physical body shakes, chills, vomiting, impulsive dancing, laughter or tears, intense bliss and peace, or expressions of anger, loneliness, and problems like abandonment issues are also common archetypal hallucination experiences.

Lao Two says: "If you are planning on tripping, at the outset courage is necessary."

Stoners want, and seek out, hallucinations and insights; it's part of the allure and magic of getting high. But if we continue to take psychotropics over an extended period of time, we can feel blocked, and the hallucinations just won't come, even if the dose is doubled or tripled. This is a big problem, and we can blame it on thinking mind. Remember, thinking mind is the controlling chatterbox; it grabs on to each arising thought, then labels and judges it. So let's say we just bought some excellent weed, grown organically with great care, full of sticky buds, with a reputation for celestial tripping. We expect to hallucinate, so we settle into a comfortable position, fill our bowl, and light it up. In just a few minutes we feel it in our body, and then our mind starts to let the environment settle around us. We might even close our eyes, waiting for whatever comes. But instead of visions, a romantic fantasy bubbles up. We think maybe a person from work could be a potential sexual partner... and we are distracted, off on a thought ride. Instead of hallucinating, we've been interrupted because thinking mind looks for ways to dominate our input. As the inner voice of analysis, it bubbles up thoughts that were relevant before we got high. And, unlike doing mind, thinking mind is never sure which is the best course to take, and seems to thrive on confusion. Thinking mind has no discrimination; a negatively critical voice is just as possible as a reasonable voice. We might hear that we're not good enough, pretty enough, rich enough, and self-assured enough to have that person from work as a sexual partner. Then emotions are triggered that are either enjoyable or painful ... until that particular fantasy is gone, replaced by a new epic inner-dialogue argument to keep thinking mind engaged. At this rate we will never get out of the forest, and never be able to trip unblocked.

Let's try: Smoke some excellent weed and lie down in a quiet room. Close your eyes and let your mind drift on the weed. Do not fall asleep. First try to completely relax your body, and then try to completely quiet your mind by not listening to your inner voice. Once you realize that you have been caught by your thoughts and have gone on a ride, stop yourself and return to silence. Try really hard not to think any thoughts at all. After struggling a while against the inner voice, you will notice that thinking mind does not want to be quiet and has lots to say about everything, and not only that, will put up a robust fight to retain control.

To find some peace of mind and be able to freely hallucinate, we have to learn how to relax thinking mind. The remedy is learning meditative concentration, and we recommend using breath meditation—a powerful authentic wizard technique that uses *doing mind*: instead of thinking about how to breathe, doing mind just breathes. There is no judging, commenting, and being emotional. Doing mind doesn't care if something is good or bad, enjoyable or painful—it's just breathing. We want to get to the point where we stop physically influencing our breath by taking control of it. When you can let breath be automatic, peace will arise. By changing our focus and our attention, we can bypass thinking mind's incessant interrupting thoughts and get righteously, peacefully stoned. Then, with training over time, we learn how to let hallucinations come unhindered.

Through breath meditation we come to understand a universal law: that all of existence is a rhythmic vibration. Thoughts are not evil, and thinking mind is not nefarious—wanting to mess us up. It's habitual, and thinking mind can be unraveled as the mysterious, malleable, ever-flowing illusion that it is. Then, once it's under our "control," we can delight in the thrill of our personal evolution. What a ride.

Spiritual awakening is what we seek; Stoners can change the world around them by their intentions and choices, using their creative energy, and developing an understanding of vibrations. Stoners don't need "religious awakening" or some outside imposed dogma. Stoner Meditation can be tested in the fire of life—it's right inside each of us. We're aiming to change the way we think. Taking over thinking mind is probably the most powerful mechanism we have for life change, and when we can do it, we fully understand the message of hallucinations. Imagine living in a conscious, aware mind without the interruptions of the judgmental thinking mind, without bummers bringing us down—seeing the world as sensitive to our experience.

Our eye-sense vision is only a small, flawed interpretation of the reality outside. Our eyes see an insignificant part of the total possible spectrum—but we're certainly grateful for what we do see. Recent quantum physics theories suggest we live in nine dimensions, with a possible tenth being a dimension of time. Other scientists are suggesting eleven dimensions, or even twenty-six dimensions. We definitely aren't the three-dimensional beings we thought we were. Anyone who has taken a psychedelic can attest to that. The scientists point at very large (stars, universes) and very small (electrons, neutrinos) locations where dimensions change according to the circumstances. They speak of multiple or mirror universes and suggest that time doesn't even exist. As humans, we are held back from new levels of superawareness by our thinking mind. Our consciousness is so wrapped up in ego that we have no idea what kind of creature a human being really is, and what it is capable of. We can either wait for evolution or get stoned. Everything is hallucination.

But perception goes much deeper than what our senses comprehend each day. When we reach death's door, we don't want to realize we didn't fulfill our life's potential. Why die in ignorant fear, or maybe full of chemicals that tranquilize us, and avoid the death experience entirely? Lao Two tells me there is an after-death world, much more complex, and with different laws then the world we live in now. He also suspects that people get buried or cremated too soon, not allowing our awareness energies from this world to manifest in the after-death world. We aren't born instantaneously, it takes plenty of time to arrive, so can't we give death a few days? We don't die suddenly, it's gradual. We're going to discuss death a little, without denial or fear, in this book. Think on the name of the rock-and-roll band Grateful Dead—the name gives us a clue how to live.

A Stoner's final breath should be confident—an amused sigh making the whole body smile as he or she falls into the tranquil superawareness after death. You can learn how to do this through Stoner Meditation. At death everyone leaves intellect, material things, and body behind. What then do we take with us? Higher awareness.

Lao Two says: "Death is the supreme instructor, but don't be confused; the true teaching is living life fully."

Meditation

If you have already been meditating, you can skim this section. Every meditation technique taught the world over is effective; don't limit your exploration to only Stoner Meditation. If you find a method that is more beneficial for you, then use it. The following is for beginning meditators; we will describe some advanced meditation techniques later.

When starting Stoner Meditation, we need to follow all the usual meditation practices—keep the spine straight, sit without moving, learn to intensely concentrate. Strangely, meditation is difficult at the beginning, and then one day suddenly becomes easy.

The Buddha said: "Breathing in, I am aware that I am breathing in; breathing out, I am aware that I am breathing out."

The truth is, no matter how clever or strong we are, there is an emotionally fragile part inside each of us. There is so much we will never know, and we will never get all the answers to our questions. We pretend to be just fine, but every now and then, when things don't go our way, we crash. Anger, desperation, tears, and possible emotional outbursts—even if we don't say anything, we're screaming inside. We're not alone in our suffering; everybody has his or her difficult days and dark nights. We discover over and over again that everything constantly changes, and we miss opportunities to get things right and then agonize about our mistakes. There are mean, despicable people out there, and world politics is crazy and unorganized; we are afraid, shocked and dismayed by what we hear on the "news." We truly have so little control over the world around us. ...

We might think the storyline we describe in our thoughts of "our life" is reality. But it's really a movie we wrote, and our actions are out of habit. The stories we all write are about a world that is secure and solid, but in actuality we are adrift on a small raft in an immense ocean. Although we are in pain and confusion, all that chaos is good. The deluded story we are telling ourselves is not good. All these collectively are a big reason we meditate.

Lao Two says: "Stoner Meditation is a method, one of many meditation methods. Like all techniques, Stoner Meditation will not suit everybody. The 'practice' is to examine the workings of consciousness."

How to Meditate

This is for those Stoners out there who have *never* tried to meditate. This is the beginner's introduction for a first sit-down meditation. Meditation is a come-as-you-are party, and everybody's invited. Meditation is demanding at first, and every one of you will hit the wall and want to quit. But if you don't give up, we guarantee it will get physically and mentally easier. If you meditate every day for a few years, it will pay off in surprising ways, and then—breakthrough. We don't care if you meditate stoned or not. We don't care if you are in jail, are a gangster, the president of the U.S., or a ballerina. It doesn't matter if it's the first thing in the morning or you just finished dinner, or it's 3 a.m. Let's meditate!

Beginner's Exercise: If you are going to meditate, you'll need a timepiece. (Stoner alert! Check the time before you start, and look at it when you finish.) Also a blanket, a bunch of pillows, and a place to sit in front of an empty wall. After you've been meditating for a while, treat yourself to a zafu and zabuton (traditional Zen sitting cushion and soft pad—they now come in cool colors and patterns).

Lay the blanket on the floor and fold it thick enough that your knees and ankles don't dig into the hard floor. Put the pillows on the blanket so you can elevate your torso comfortably—fold a pillow in half so it feels firm, your butt two to four inches above the floor. You might prefer to borrow the cushion off a chair or the couch for more firmness. If you can cross your legs like a buddha, that's cool; if not, try one leg over the other. You've seen the pictures of Buddha sitting in meditation, but, truly, most Westerners can't sit like that, especially at first. It's no big deal. Try sitting with your two legs underneath your butt, or your legs to the side of your butt. There are stools, specially shaped meditation cushions, and other new sitting options, and you should be able to find a satisfying, comfortable way to sit. We want your spine straight but not inflexible, so the muscles can develop to keep your back aligned and stable. But in the beginning, don't be afraid to experiment with more pillows or a folded blanket. Maybe a chair works best, but don't rest against the back. If you lie on a bed you might fall asleep, but if you have to—lie flat on your back on the floor with a blanket or carpet underneath.

You'll know when your back feels straight; pull the shoulders back a little. Put your tongue to the roof of your mouth. Align your neck so it's comfortable; let your head tilt forward just a touch, so your eyes are looking about 45 degrees down, and keep your eyes half closed, relaxed, not forced. Feel the top of your head pushing gently upward. Breathe through your nose. Put your hands in your lap, palms up, one hand on top of the other with thumbs touching. Optional: if you are right-handed, put your right hand under your left hand (and vice versa for lefties) as a reminder that during meditation it's time to relax. Or you can put each hand on a thigh, palm up, with first finger and thumb touching. Stoner Meditation didn't invent any of this stuff—it's all from various traditional methods developed centuries ago.

If you have any serious physical problems, adjust these instructions to suit your condition. The most important thing is to learn how to be still, with only your breathing moving your body. So there's no intentional physical movement—your body does enough just existing. Of course, all this will feel unnatural for a while, but in the end you'll understand the reason for a straight spine and sitting in this style.

Single-point breath meditation (calm abiding): Now that we have our bodies sitting, this is what we should be doing with our mind-consciousness. We'll put our attention at the nostrils where the breath comes in and out. Focus on the delicate feeling of air coming in and going out. Just let your breath come and go naturally, without being pulled away by thinking mind. For the moment, ignore breathing in different parts of the body and really zoom in on where the breath enters and exits your nose. Two senses are actively involved: the concentrated mind sense directed at the nostrils and the concentrated sense of touch, feeling the air passing in and out.

Thinking mind is a control freak. It will start sending signals and you'll find yourself controlling your breath, or feeling pain in your legs or back, or itching around your body. Thinking mind will do everything to pull your attention away from your focal point. At the beginning, don't stress about any of this—just notice what's happening. Feel free to adjust your body and scratch itches, but you'll probably find there is no comfort and no peace. The goal here is to just be an observer of everything, including your uncomfortable physical pain, your moving to try to adjust it, or your itch and scratching. Always return to observation of the breath. If it's unbearable, then sit for five minutes and try again tomorrow. It's very important to be kind to yourself, not cause injury or make meditation burdensome. After meditating for a few days, you'll see results. It's the everyday, regular part of meditation that matters, not how well a particular session went. Doing this for a brief part of each and every day will be the most important teacher—even if you only meditate for five minutes at the beginning.

It's like we have two amplified speakers—there are really loud lyrics coming out of one and extremely soft instrumental music coming out of the other. Thinking mind is the insistent, loud lyrics, and doing mind is the barely heard soft instrumental music of breath, and our body. We want to eventually be able to turn down the volume on individual thinking-mind lyrics, and turn up the volume on the instrumental breath of doing mind. During meditation, give up ALL your thoughts, be intense. For those twenty meditation minutes, thinking about the past and future is unnecessary. Regard every thought as an unnecessary illusion. Almost all afflictive thoughts arise out of habit, anxiety, and fear. But that doesn't mean we want to silence, repress, or stop thoughts; what we want to do is make peace with them. At first all we aim to do is equalize the vocals with the music. Then down the road we can turn up the instrumental music, completely turning off the vocals. Then we start to understand a little what silence (emptiness) is.

At the beginning, when we first notice how many insistent thoughts there actually are, we can go a little nuts trying to "control" them. It can feel overwhelming, trying to keep attention on the breath and never being able to get past two or three attentive breaths. We understand the process: thinking mind just has to ask, "Did I say the wrong thing to X at that meeting?" That thought catches the attention, and like a fish, you are hooked and going for a ride. "How did X react?" "I should have said," "Could I get fired for that?" and you've got yourself into a thinking-mind loop. Of course this is the exact practice—to catch that we got distracted. And if you can catch yourself somewhere along the thinking-mind loop and short-circuit it, give yourself some credit. This is your first success at mindfulness.

If something big is going on in your life, meditate anyway. Even if you can't concentrate on your breath, at least you will be able to stop and see what I call "the color of my thoughts." I'm not saying to dwell on bummers, but even dark thoughts can be teachers if we observe them and see what color they paint on our life. Also useful is the bargaining technique of taking a break from thinking. You can say to your mind: "This is my time to just sit here quietly. Just give me twenty minutes without too much interruption, and then I'll think about all this stuff later, when I'm done." This seems to take all the urgency and fear away from thinking mind and allows more relaxed concentration. But you should know that your breath concentration will fail over and over again, and you will wander constantly back to thinking mind, so don't freak out. Every gymnast falls a thousand times before mastering graceful balance.

Observe any comfort or discomfort, and your thoughts, feelings—you can even list them in your mind. Listen to the jackhammer sound from two blocks away, or the dog barking incessantly. Feel the movement of your body, how it rocks slightly with each breath. If you need to distract thinking mind, think about what each breath really means to you. This is called analytical meditation. Try holding your breath until you can't any longer—no breath, no life.

Lots of people use mantras (chanting)—words or phrases repeated over and over again to overcome thinking mind. We will describe this technique later.

At some point after meditating alone, you may want to give sustained meditation a try. Advanced meditators can sit for hours at a time, some all day long. Try to find someplace near your house that teaches meditation, or an online practice group, or travel to a retreat to learn more advanced methods.

But for now, at the beginning, really concentrate on the breath sensation right at the nostril entry/exit of your nose. Exert yourself. Try to sustain the concentration for as many breaths as possible. Get right into microscopic focus on each part of the breath cycle. For example, each breath has four components: in-breath, then a very short pause, out-breath, then a coasting toward the next breath. After you have been meditating for a few weeks, try Stoner Meditation stoned, or if you've been getting stoned, try it straight. Mix things up, challenge yourself!

When your timer goes off, before you get up, sit for just a few seconds longer so you can experience the impatience and resistance to sitting. Feel your body, then fully open your eyes and just relax for one more moment. Try to remain aware of the complex physical motion required as you stand up. So? How long did you sit this first time? Congratulations for giving it a try.

Another method: Some people do better counting to ten breaths over and over. Place the beginning number count at the in-breath, and when it starts, say "One." After the in-breath you will notice a very short pause. Right after this pause the exhale starts. You'll discover that thinking mind loves to interrupt during the coasting of the out-breath. If you lose count, restart from one again.

Another method: Try to feel the air around you. Become the air around you.

As noted, there are hundreds of different meditation techniques, all of them more or less effective. If one doesn't feel right for you, try a different one.

End of beginners exercise.

A summary:

Meditate daily; twenty to thirty minutes is a good amount.

Don't put yourself down if you can only meditate for five minutes.

Find a mostly quiet, relaxed place. Things like traffic noise are all right.

Wear loose clothing, no shoes.

Keep your eyes half-closed, unfocused; tongue at roof of closed mouth.

Sit on a cushion on the floor and look at a spot on the wall.

Concentrate on your breath at the nostrils.

Don't go on thinking-mind loops; try to catch yourself thinking.

The goal is to be aware of the present moment, not past or future.
Turn the volume down on thinking mind, and up on doing mind.
Your mind will wander; gently bring it back to the breath.
Do not ignore body sensations, emotions, or thoughts.
Pay attention.
Physical pain, mosquito bites, and emotions can be the best teachers.
Meditation is not shutting down, it is opening up to awareness.
Thoughts range from irrational fear to ecstatic bliss—but all thoughts are just temporarily passing through.
All thoughts are illusion—during meditation.
Be the watcher, watching.
Don't cling to, or get attached to, any type of thought, emotion, or experience.
Work toward letting things be as they really are.
Meditation takes practice, so at first, just learn how to focus concentration on your breath.

Extra Credit: An important mantra (chant) to learn is the AOM. Aaaaaahhh oooooooooohhh, emmmmmmmmmm. Put your front teeth together on the m, feel the vibrations all through your body. Imagine your vibrations go into the earth, and throughout the universe. Find a rhythm and length of each sound quality for the AOM that works for you personally. Lao Two does the AOM three times with eyes closed after each daily meditation.

Although some of these instructions might seem contradictory, they are not. The only way to really understand how to meditate is to sit down and try it. Then, sit down the next day and try again. There will be a point when you intuitively know that you are doing it right—there will be a balanced feeling between holding your body in the awkward, rigid skeletal position and then being able to relax the muscles within that skeleton. But no matter how long we meditate, the concentration at the nose will continue to be destroyed by thinking mind, even though the effect becomes different. After a while, the meditation will transcend concentration itself and become pure awareness.

Since our style of meditation feels the in-breath and out-breath at our nostrils, it's possible to use this technique during the day, off the cushion. Whether you're in motion or sitting still, you can have what we call multiple attention. When walking, put your attention on breath concentration, and when sitting, on breath concentration. Try it when you are speaking to someone: talk and put a small part of your attention on noticing the air coming in and going out of your nostrils. Whenever you can think of putting your attention at your nostrils, it will remind you to be centered, right where you are, engaged, attentive.

Lao Two says: "It's not being without thought. It's turning down the volume (attention, reaction, attachment, clinging) of thoughts. Let thoughts just pass through without grasping. Give thoughts the same value as the sound of your breath—thought arises, persists, and fades away ... exactly like each breath. If we are not grasping at anything, thoughts will naturally become quiet, without effort. Once silence arrives, it's that aware flow that we are looking for."

Some people don't have intense body pain from sitting in a meditative position. Others are able to let their thoughts relax right at the beginning. Those few have an incredibly flexible body, and their thinking mind is able to quiet and be calm. They have "success" the first time they meditate and are able to go right to awareness. This is common for many who have taken large doses of psychedelics over a long period of time.

However, this is not the case for the overwhelming majority of beginners. Most people feel like a freight train is about to crash into them, and they need to jump up and get the hell outta the way. ... There is a flood of thinking mind chatter going on inside. But we never noticed that inner dialogue before, and now Stoner Meditation is making us observe it. Sometimes it's difficult to get halfway through a breath before a thought takes us for a ride. The next thing we know, eight breaths have passed by before we notice we were thinking about what our girlfriend, boyfriend, husband, wife, partner, boss, stranger ... said three days ago.

Thinking mind's job is to keep us on automatic control. But this is not in our best interest. Thinking mind must learn that we are capable of dealing with the world without its constant advice and judgments. Thinking-mind will tell us that we have more important things to do than sit here and do this stupid meditation—we should find some sensual pleasure instead. It will constantly let you know about your pain, either physical or mental. Its main weapon is distraction. No matter how hard you are trying to concentrate on the breath at your nose, it seems basically impossible because there's so much input coming, so many distractions, interruptions, and sensations. This is actually a good thing, because we come to realize that the noise is just smoke and mirrors.

Typical thinking mind chatter: "This is hard; I could use a snack; I wonder what's on TV? I'm tired; only two minutes; damn, I wish I hadn't said that to my boss; did I put gas in the car? No matter which way I move that ankle, it still hurts. ..."

As with any physical or mental exercise, it takes practice to modify our muscles so we can sit in meditation. Also, at the beginning it's doubtful we have any real idea WHY we are sitting on the floor anyway. It takes some practice before body and mind have the strength to do what's asked.

Stoner Meditation is NOT *thinking of nothing*—although thinking of nothing is a valid meditation method, we don't think it will be effective for Stoners. Thinking mind's job is to think, just like it's the lungs' job to breathe. Instead, try to imagine (during meditation) that every thought has no importance.

In other words, if you think, "My boss treated me badly," and have an emotional reaction to it—then that thought has importance. If a thought fishhook snags you, then just like a fish, you struggle against the hook, only driving it in deeper. If you struggle against thinking, the emotional reaction has more energy. Once we are snagged, it cascades into the connected next thought, and then another thought, and another. It's a frustrating but not an insurmountable problem.

On the other hand, if we train ourselves during meditation to dispassionately look at "My boss treated me badly," no emotional energy arises and the thought naturally passes away. What we want is to let go of the struggle. Then a thought can arise, persist, and fade away with no emotional grasping. And like the hooked fish, if instead of pulling against the fishhook we relax, then the hook dislodges and falls out. This is how we Stoners should *think of nothing*.

Training ourselves to let go of the emotional reaction (attachment, clinging) silences thinking mind without struggle. It's a little like living in a house next to a train track. When we first move in, the noise from the trains drives us crazy, but after a while the sound fades into the background. The noise is the same, but our attention has changed.

Lao Two says: "Body and mind are one. Each moment is infinite, and space-time intersects like a river emptying into the ocean."

How long should you meditate? At the beginning, not more than fifteen to twenty minutes—but even five minutes is splendid. Some people like to meditate both morning and night for fifteen minutes. For working people, twenty minutes each morning will give excellent results over time.

There is a legendary Tibetan master by the name of Milarepa. He is famous for completely transforming his bad karma and transcending into highest nirvana. He is also famous for his magic, and his ability to constantly reside in Natural Mind. He spent many years practicing solitary meditation in caves. If there were a gold medal for meditation, he'd hold the record.

Milarepa said: "The lama (his teacher, Marpa) told me to meditate with perseverance. He provided me with ample supplies and directed me to meditate in a cave called Tiger Nak at the Southern Cliffs. Then I filled an altar lamp with butter, lit it, and placed it on my head. I meditated day and night in this way, without moving, until the butter in the lamp was exhausted." (From the Internet, author unknown; for more stories, search for Milarepa's name.)

He did this for eleven months without interruption!

When we ask, "What's the point of doing anything, why even bother?" we are discussing action and inaction. If we are at the mercy of our thinking mind, letting life pass us by, we are in the chaos of inaction. Doing mind is not just a busy lifestyle, mindlessly doing this and that—it's being aware, in control, performing life. The law of entropy is inaction; it is the natural force of destruction. The thing about entropy is that it takes care of itself: we don't have to help things rot, fall apart, and fade away—or in the case of Stoners, to lie around and do nothing. ... The danger is becoming entropic ourselves, living as mindless slugs instead of aware Stoners.

The world we live in is naturally aligned with creation and entropy—seasons arise, persist, and pass away. A storm forms, rains, and then clears. Time slips away, we age and die. There's nothing we can do about the nature of the universe to constantly destroy itself so it can build anew. I'm pretty sure this is what the Taoists call "The Way"—the universe unfolding on its own.

Born as human beings, we are naturally active. We are constantly in relentless change, until we die. We can be a creative force that is an active participant, giving us choice, free will, and productivity, or live a wasted, inactive, unaware life. Sitting still is actually impossible; we humans are in constant physical, electrical, and mental movement, which we usually just take for granted.

This is why we bother, and why we care—since we are alive and existing in this very movement anyway, we can either go through life mindlessly being swept along or use creative, aware actions to move forward consciously. We either use our life, or we lose our life.

This contrast between active and inactive also relates to our meditation. We have a thinking mind that is useful for analysis, but useless during our daily sitting meditation. Off the cushion, thinking mind has value, it helps us figure out this and that; but on the cushion, we want to use doing mind because it is not attached to the world's delusions, the world of our made-up storyline. Doing mind sees things exactly as they are—there is no analysis involved. An apple is just an apple.

Meditation is not something to think about; it's connected to your inherent nature, which is aware meditative silence. We might think that sitting in silence is inaction, but it's not—we are aware of all the movement in our body, like our beating heart, cyclic breath, and thoughts. We understand that aware silence includes all this action, and instead of ignoring anything, we are aware of everything. This intense concentration, eyes looking at the wall and mind concentrated on breath, is not involved with dualistic thinking—there is no good/bad, right/wrong—everything is just as it is.

At the beginning, don't worry that you can't calm your mind or sit perfectly, or if you miss a meditation day. Your goals are simply concentration and awareness. Just letting breathing come and go naturally is more difficult than you would expect. Don't expect happiness, joy, or bliss, because while you will have brief moments of great calm, you will also have brief moments of great distress—both are illusions, so keep meditating. When you're tired, angry, or distraught can be the best times to sit and meditate.

Single-point breath meditation is for developing concentration, and let's be honest—Stoners do need good concentration abilities, because we can get pretty spaced out. After you've been meditating a while, try to bring meditative concentration to the rest of your day. Try paying attention while eating, for example, observing as many things as you can. This is called mindfulness—instead of shoving down your food mind-less-ly, you are experiencing it with all your senses just by directing awareness. Doing mind watching thinking mind is another way of describing mindfulness.

Lao Two says: "Mind watching mind, contained in Mind."

Start becoming mindful of whatever is happening outside of your physical body, instead of letting all your thoughts be of yourself and your problems. Instead of letting life happen to you, become the aware actor of your life by being present in it. Take opportunities to depart from your old storyline; for example, instead of being quiet, speak your mind. Or instead of ignoring suffering, actively use compassion—give a smile and say hello to that lonely bum on the sidewalk as you pass by. It doesn't have to be heroic or huge, little acts can make a big difference. Our personality, our "us," is a unique presence, and each human is as different and individual as a snowflake. We all have a discrete electrical current and vibration that is individually us, a "presence"; it is part charisma and part awareness.

Our storyline, the constantly running movie that we keep in our thinking mind to help us navigate through our lives, is what we believe ourselves to be—and very often it's wrong. Here's an example: If we get pulled over by a cop for not coming to a complete stop at a stop sign, then maybe our storyline sees that cop as an asshole. He's being such a tight-ass, even after we argued (or lied) that we absolutely, did indeed come to a stop. We are also angry with ourselves for getting caught. Obviously ANY storyline is possible, and instead of thinking the worst about others, we can easily change the story to think the best about others—or at least think compassionately about them. When we can see people exactly as they are, our storyline has changed to awareness. To make up an entirely different storyline is the beginning of changing the way we interact with the world. Think of the possibilities. Maybe you got stopped by a cop who doesn't really want to write you a ticket. Maybe the district attorney told the cop that he's not writing enough tickets, so he sits at that stop sign because he knows there are a lot of accidents there, because people are not coming to a full stop. Maybe the cop saved your life. The point is, too often we write the storyline without facts.

Lao Two says: "Relaxing completely means letting go of who we are and merging into the universe. Ego must completely give up control and be silent if we are to walk through that door."

A goal of Stoner Meditation is seeing everything exactly as it really is. We can learn to rewrite the old, habitual storyline about our life. That's when we start to give up confusion, anger, and craziness. Wouldn't it be wonderful to live without pretense, fantasies, or judgments, and know what our body is actually feeling? Then we are not avoiding anything anymore, for example, experiencing disappointment as disappointment—not as frustrated depressive discouragement, but rather just understanding that we will never get everything we want—accepting life as it really is.

Many schools of meditation suggest we should mute our emotions, ignore our feelings, and dull our experiences into neutral equanimity and composure. Although this is a valid technique, Stoner Meditation wants us to live fully, actualize our dreams, and as they say, "live, laugh, and love." All the emotions and feelings that a human is capable of are within us—after all, we are not monks, we are Stoners. Stoner Meditation should be interesting, passionate, sexy, and fun.

This is why we are learning concentration in our daily sitting meditation, so we can be present. If you are doing some chore like washing the dishes, try to be present without wandering thoughts or tormenting emotions by opening up your senses and perceptions to the experience. Act with intention, purpose, and insight, and try to connect with the flow of your dishwashing experience. This is being mindful.

There might be very strong emotions like lust, fear, and anger that can affect your thinking. Emotions are not really "real." But our reactions to emotions are real: not only do we feel them, but also they profoundly affect our mind. Understand instead that emotions are temporary reactions to events.

The purpose of following the breath is to overcome and take attention away from thinking mind. You can do breath meditation while waiting at a stoplight, or in line to check out your groceries. We don't want to control the breath or thinking mind, but we do want control over our attention. Eventually you'll notice when you are letting the breath come and go naturally without working at control. Sitting spaced out, unaware, or falling asleep is not Stoner Meditation. Keep gently returning your attention to the object of meditation at the entrance/exit of the nose.

You are the only person who can get yourself enlightened. Maybe just reading about enlightenment will make you break through and boom—then you are out of the woods, looking at the world clearly. Enlightenment requires two things: emptiness and awareness (ego nonattachment and concentration).

Mind Set

Lao Two says: "We seek everywhere except inside our own heart to find the answer. Then unexpectedly we discover that the answer is right where we are."

I'm going to have to resort to some Buddhism here, because it's already figured out the cause and solution of the problem. The historical Gautama Buddha realized that human suffering is just a fact of our existence. But instead of using the word "suffering," he used *dukkha* (described below). Buddha laid out the Four Noble Truths:

1. There is suffering (*dukkha*).
2. Suffering is caused by attachment, and ignorance of our human situation.
3. We can change this suffering by awareness and enlightenment.
4. This is done by following some ethical guidelines (the eightfold path) and living mindfully.

The Buddha said: "Were there a mountain all made of gold, double that would not be enough to satisfy a single person; know this and live accordingly." *Samyutta Nikaya* 1.156

Dukkha: The Buddha spoke of suffering as the underlying cause of all our bummers. Actually the word used is *dukkha*—which is really the unease we constantly feel from our suppressed distress. No matter what happiness we find, it eventually goes away because we can't hold on to it, it's transitory. *Dukkha* is not natural because it's based on illusory dualistic thinking, but it's how we humans live night and day. We erroneously think that our existence is solid, stable, unchanging. What we see with our eyes seems frozen in time.

Experiencing nonordinary reality, on the other hand, shows us that the real world is impermanent, incessantly changing. As you look out your eyes, you can't determine whether what you see is reality; there's no way to be sure the chair we see is not a holographic projection instead. Obviously there is a big difference between stoned and not stoned.

Certainly we're not going to get everything we want. We don't want pain, sickness, or death—but we will inevitably experience these wretched miseries. Life is short and imperfect. It's not your fault that the world you are born into is imperfect and has suffering. It is what it is. Part of the cure for *dukkha* is seeing things as they actually are.

Dukkha is knowing that life won't always work out the way we want it to, and too often the shit hits the fan. It's also not embracing and accepting failure, aversion, or apathetic resignation—stuff is happening, and we can get past it to take positive action.

We can't escape the world we are born into, and it's not pessimistic to accept the true facts of life. But we try to avoid them anyway: we make up a storyline that has no reality—everything will be fine if I do so-and-so, or have this much money. It's our *dukkha* that causes negative habitual thinking and acting, and we can become our own worst enemy just by our negative thoughts. Some people consume so much food they are obese, and other planetary citizens have so little they are half-starved, or starving. Compare a woman who has four children because the offspring are an ego extension like owning a pedigree dog, or a display of wealth—or even worse, because of religious belief or cultural pressures. This would be much different from a woman having four children because she expects three of them will die from malnutrition. It doesn't have to be depressing to acknowledge that our world has hate and prejudice, war and natural and man-made disasters—suffering. Being able to see a problem exists, instead of ignoring it, is the first step towards fixing it. *Dukkha* shows we have a kind of fake, baseless happiness that we acquire by our meaningless search for pleasure and ease. Stoner Meditation says we can have true happiness based on understanding reality.

There are the (Buddhist) Five Hindrances that keep us in *dukkha*: misunderstanding and craving sensuality, holding on to anger, being lazy, constant worry, and our inner voice putting us down.

Jiddu Krishnamurti said: "It is no measure of health to be well adjusted to a profoundly sick society."

Since our life is so short, we must prioritize and actualize our dreams. As the Zen folks say, "our hair is on fire," because there is not a moment to lose. With the urgency of wanting to get rid of suffering and learn how to live creatively instead, our daily meditation takes on a different flavor. Now we want to help ourselves, instead of continuing the same old habits that don't seem to get us anywhere. And then, after we've helped ourselves, we can help others.

If you want to meditate sitting outside now and then, by all means do so. Don't worry what people think. Consider that you are setting an example of what everyone could be doing. Feel and experience nature—the wind against your skin, the sounds, the visual feast, and your location in the universe. Use closed or open eyes, but notice distractions as they happen. Of course, if a swarm of mosquitoes or a rainstorm appears during your outdoor meditation, move.

In the context of this crazy world we live in Stoners, don't let anyone tell you not to get high. Do not feel bad about yourself, or hold on to anger, or live without love. There will always be people telling you not to believe in yourself, to shut up and sit down, to keep your abilities quiet, or not to dream. So if you have to, do things in secret and under wraps if necessary, all the while working toward your goal. Keep seeking Truth, speaking your Truth, and realizing Truth—you'll know it's Truth with a capital T because it strikes a chord in you. The sun comes up each morning and everyone breathes the same air; above us the Milky Way spins across the universal sky. Our galaxy is so large, and Earth is so small—no alien race is going to come to save it. No Christ or Buddha will come to tell us what to do. We have to realize that this is our brief moment. Everyone has the right to express his or her life's dream if it doesn't restrict anyone else's. Be high. Know. Get in touch with your flow. Even after enlightenment, physical pain and death do not go away—there is pain to experience in life, it's inescapable. But with enlightenment, pain is understood for what it is. It becomes different because we realize physical pain is just body signals. As they say, 'pain is necessary, suffering is optional'.

Lao Two says: "The human body is a fragile spacesuit. If punctured, ripped, or abused, the life inside dies."

Sometimes, seemingly from nowhere, we feel bewilderment, fear, or anger arising. No matter how socially skillful we are, we slip up and obsessively question our actions. It's like suddenly discovering the solid ground we're standing on has become swamp muck and we're falling into the deepest holes, wandering almost blind, confused and lost. But we need to keep our perspective—the world is a harsh place, it's important to survive. Meanwhile, no matter how much we try to ignore suffering, it seemingly gets worse day by day on planet Earth. We can see the side effects of humanity's denial and greed—overpopulation, climate change, economic inequality, starvation, and constant war, bringing us toward extinction. *Dukkha* is even in our meditation practice, where we compare our progress to the Buddha—"Why aren't I enlightened yet?" Or we can fall into what's called spiritual materialism—using spirituality to appear better than others. *Dukkha* can also be our hiding out, living alone, being defensive, instead of letting down our barriers and allowing other people into our lives. *Dukkha* can keep us from loving ourselves, or loving another person, or appreciating life.

And maybe the worst part of being off balance is, we can't seem to see how messed up we are while it's happening right this very minute. We think we can put off meditation, dating, finding a job, or doing those household chores—but we can never replace the time that has passed. Although time is never really lost, it's often not used effectively.

Emotions

You wake up in the morning and for no reason at all you are in a bad mood. In the kitchen you get burnt toast and cold coffee. Then the bus breaks down and you have to walk to work in the rain, with your shoes leaking and socks full of freezing water. Somebody says something and it affects you the wrong way, and the next moment you are trying your best not to explode with angry words. Or, too late, you give an ugly grimace and they read your body language. Nothing at all was said, but the vibes turned sour.

Stoner Meditation to the rescue. We have the ability to realize that no matter how bad life gets, we don't have to react to our body's emotional stimulus. Emotions are not real inasmuch as they can be ignored, redirected, or changed. Right now do an angry scowl, followed by cheerful laughter—you can feel the emotional changes going on as it's happening. Most often our emotional body signals are an illusory storyline we create, misreading our emotions. Instead, we can let the emotion complain all it wants—we just listen with the volume turned down.

The Stoner Meditation trick is, if we are annoyed, we can simply focus on our breathing instead of our emotional thoughts. Through meditation practice, we can reenter calm at will. We can physically change our mood almost instantly. Discordant emotions are simply funky, habitual electrical vibrations created by our bodies. Angry? Change the emotional anger to compassionate understanding instead.

With breathing meditation, we can learn how emotions work. Noticing our breathing throughout the day can be magical, spiritual, and powerful. When someone we love enters a room, we start feeling loving vibes, our breath slows, we relax, and endorphins are secreted into thinking mind. We can use that same loving breath when involved in an anxious situation—seemingly magically; we turn anxiety into loving calm.

It's obvious that our body has the ability to raise our body temperature. When we have a fever, it can climb because we are sick. Apparently there are monks who can raise their body temperature through meditative training and sit naked on the snow. They are somehow turning on a part of our body that raises their temperature. It's the same with our emotions: we can experience a loving breath when our lover walks in, so we can change our emotion at will. It might seem we are using wizardry, but it's just knowing how.

Thinking mind's intellect keeps our concentration and awareness on the material world only, preventing us from fully experiencing all of life—and too often we become emotionally crippled. Our emotions are habitual reactions to learned expectations of good or bad. We are either grasping at good emotions or displaying aversion to bad emotions, but there are levels of emotions that we keep from feeling, out of fear and repression. For example, when washing dishes, we might not even be aware we are angry, resentful, or annoyed at having to wash the dishes, or about whatever happened earlier in the day. We perform our actions with our mind shut down, our body stiff, and afterward get no satisfaction. There's a lot of sleepwalking through life with thinking mind.

But if we wash dishes with doing mind, we are connected to a higher viewpoint where everything is connected. Every action we perform in doing mind is linked to the constant change all around us. We feel connected with both inside (self) and outside (other), moving through space. All the individual aspects of washing the dishes become part of our experience—the dishes, the temperature of the water, the dazzling colors of the soap bubbles, the itch on our neck that we scratch with a soapy finger, our emotions, body fatigue, our thoughts regarding past, present, and future filtering through the mind (but not grasped), gravity pulling our feet to the floor—all this flow and more is constantly going on around and in us. In emptiness we are mind watching body/mind, as presence. Try a dishwashing when righteously stoned, and pay attention!

During a psychedelic trip, in deep meditation, or stoned on mind-blowing marijuana, you might reach an emotional breakthrough. This is like a dam bursting open. Don't be afraid to scream, cry, roll around, or let your body shake uncontrollably. This could completely release and transform you, changing your meditation practice to calm abiding.

Where do our emotions come from? We believe it happens like this: stimuli, mental observation by doing mind, electrochemical development of emotion, followed by a reaction or judgment by thinking mind. It's this mental reaction to our emotions that we are trying to "control" in meditation. Love has a different emotional flavor than indifference, or even hate. But all emotions are created from a cause that affects us strongly, until we stop and see the process happening during sitting meditation practice. There we learn to see emotions as signals, communicating something to us. Does that mean we should be emotionless? No, it means that if we can be aware of the mental reaction and then consciously experience the resulting emotion, then emotions are just our way of being human. It's the emotions we are not aware of that screw us up—that's why we keep saying it's important to feel what is happening in the body during meditation. Many meditators think it's only concentrating on breathing and watching thoughts. But there is a second aspect to meditation which is noticing what's happening in the body.

Taking a good, honest look at your life, realizing that you've done some good stuff and some bad stuff, you feel the emotions of anger, jealousy, love, and bliss. Accepting that we will make mistakes keeps us respectful for the inevitable storms. Our goal is not to become saintly, our goal is to be fully, passionately human. To be able to express emotional love to everyone equally, without any exceptions—it's more difficult than we think.

Lao Two says: "Laugh along with the cosmic joke—we exist! We could just as easily not exist."

Ego Death and Emptiness

New smokers, please be aware that marijuana is not always benign. Investigate the term "psychotic break." Strong marijuana makes people take an honest look at their true self, and some people can't handle the truth. They prefer the made-up story of their lives instead. When this narrative crumbles, it's meltdown, ego death. Stoner Meditation wants us all to experience ego death but not be frightened by the experience. After all, ego death is temporary; afterward we remain the person we were.

We want to learn about how our world is divided up and how our perceived separation from others makes us lonely and unhappy. Part of the ego's job is to consider itself separate from the world outside, to protect us from physical and mental injury; "I" doesn't have room for much else. Ego also does not want us to die, or even think about our death. If our physical body or mind dies, ego dies, and ego will fight to survive. We know what made us happy or sad in the past, so ego keeps us analyzing, weighing, and formulating what will make us happy in the future. We can even become obsessive because we had traumatic pain in the past and want to avoid pain in the future.

Ego's real problem is that it doesn't know where to look for stable and healthy happiness. We cling to erroneous ideas and beliefs, such as that material things can make us happy, because they've become ingrained in the culture. We buy a new car, but a year later the newness is gone, the tires are wearing, the paint needs washing and waxing—and it will never again be the idealized car we had a year ago. So ego starts to badger us to buy the newest idealized car instead of the perfectly serviceable car we already own. Ego even draws our attention to the newer, shiny model driving by.

We're not saying material things are evil, but our relationship to material things is pretty messed up on planet Earth. We want to find a responsible middle ground when it comes to money and material things, because ego is so tied into the material universe it can imprison us. We don't have to renounce everything we own, and we don't have to chase after money neurotically either. On the planetary scale there is no reason for poverty anywhere on Earth, but greed, the desire for power, and wars cause endless problems for both humans and all other life. Why? Because ego keeps people separated from feeling their emotions authentically—they've chosen to ignore their feelings so their "I" can remain satiated. We suspect Post Traumatic Stress Disorder (PTSD) is caused by suddenly facing powerful emotions, after ignoring and suppressing them. The point is that emotions are powerful and deserve exploration in meditation.

Ego death: Unfortunately, this term, and concept has taken on some rather confusing meanings, but ego death is so important and central to Stoner Meditation it needs honest discussion and clarification.

Our ego is who we are and our personal identity, but a lot of who we are has been culturally created over time. Ego, in the sense of ego death, is what we consider ourselves to be, our "I," our unconscious social image, and the storyline we create around our life experiences. Ego will stay blissfully unaware of others' pain to remain self-centered and seek pleasure.

Eventually we really do have to let our body physically die—and this truth of our mortality haunts ego. It's especially disconcerting because when our physical body goes, ego disappears, and because we all die alone There is nothing more important to ego than "me first." This is why many people fail at ego death: they have become their ego image and can't let it go. Ego is so strong in them that it will not relinquish conscious control for even a moment. Ego is not self-identity; it is the unrecognized sense of entitlement.

Thinking mind is tied closely to ego. Never silent for a moment, our inner dialogue keeps "I" foremost in our mind. I want, I fear, I'm hungry.

Although we are in denial and don't think about death that much, someday, maybe near, maybe far away, the "I," "mine," "me" will be gone forever, along with the shiny toys we purchase. Ego wants us to feel good, so instead of taking LSD to sort out who and what we are, ego takes LSD as a pleasure boat ride, and anything that makes ego confront itself is a "bad trip." And instead of a life-changing learning experience, we say that we had bad acid.

Ego death occurs on psychedelics when we allow ourselves to let go. I like to think of it as a mile-long water slide. We can let ourselves slide along with the gravity, or grab on to the edges and stop the flow. Ego-death is not a comfortable experience, and takes great courage and trust.

To engage this experience we have to let our personality go for a few moments, and then we can overcome and confront our fears and face our ego death squarely. We have to lose everything to gain everything. We can either experience real death at the end of our life, which of course is not much help, or experience ego death now. Stoner Meditation wants us to experience ego death because it is so life changing, and it awakens a sleeping part of us. Afterward we are the same person, but with a new perspective on who and what we are. Stoner Meditation also wants you to have ego death safely, so it will be a big part of our discussion.

Lao Two's theory is that when we physically die we come face-to-face with the power of universal vibrating love. This experience of love is not the purring soft-kitten variety, it is overwhelming, passionate bliss. Unless we have experienced this love in an ego-death experience, we will fear the power of manifest love at human death. And without this, our death-awareness evades being drawn into the love light, falling into darkness (and rebirth) instead.

The word "ego" includes everything we are (self), separated from the world around us (other). Imagine an experience so overpowering that your "I" disappears for some moments, during which you merge with cosmic consciousness. This can occur during meditation or while smoking marijuana, but especially on psychedelics. This disassociation from our "normal" sense of being can be frightening, unexpected, as well as joyous and insightful—but in the end, on some level, we're reborn. Just for a moment, imagine that you aren't who you thought you were, maybe because of amnesia. You have no identity, body, or social life. Lastly, there is the physical aspect of ego death where we feel happiness and bliss like never before.

If you embark on the symbolic Stoner Meditation journey up the mountain, as we discussed earlier, then there will be a time you are tripping on a psychedelic that will tear your world apart. Either ego will clench in fear or it will move out of the way and disappear for a few moments. The person you were in the valley before you hiked up through the forest will be gone, and the forest that was benign is now freaky. If you can let your old self fall away and your new view emerge, you can transcend that sense of individualism—letting the "I" become "All."

You've become a forest person when you can completely let go of the valley person. In that forest you develop a new confidence and become self-assured. We want you to keep that self-assurance, but you also need to intuitively know that you can become even more insightful once you pass tree line. Your life view will be completely changed from what was once your perspective on "what is."

Ego death sounds like a damn scary adventure, but on the positive side, you will hear phrases like "universal oneness," "connected to nature," "out-of-body," "timeless void," "harmony and endless bliss," "meeting beings of light," "filled with energy or good vibrations," and "seeing in all directions." Linear thought is replaced with holistic and unbounded higher consciousness. Ordinary thought is transcended, thinking mind will be suspended, and its interrupting thoughts will disappear. Instead of seeing one thing at a time, we see the whole with all the parts connected. During ego death our opinions and judgments are eliminated, and the experience falls into the realm of "just is." Thinking will seem to come from a deeper portal (sometimes referred to as a fountain), and rather than being preoccupied with superficial thoughts, our mind grasps, penetrates, and discerns the nonconceptual. Ego death will be so life-changing that it will take months and years to accept and absorb the experience. Yet it can happen more than once. Ego death can happen anytime in our life, and it doesn't have to come from psychedelics. Many people in meditation confront ego. Some music can also let us float away enraptured.

During ego death there can also be scary, "negative" events, especially if we are not able to face our fears. We might experience our own death in the abstract (not dying in reality) or come face to face with the confused, deluded person we have become—the person we hate inside of us. All our insignificance in the grander universe, personal insecurities, and doubts surface, all of our physical ugliness and poor body image confronts us. We might cry, have body spasms, vomit, and feel chills. We might wonder if we have gone insane, and hear frightening sounds and voices. We might grasp at our old self, timidly thinking we will never be able to be who we were again—and feel the terrible loss of our personality, possibly resulting in a panic attack.

By resisting ego death on a psychedelic you might stiffen up, be controlling, and refuse to let the drug do its work. This is like swimming upstream against the current of a river, instead of flowing downstream with the direction of the current. Ego death will only be productive when you are ready to accept this "little death." It's possible you will completely miss ego death because you need to keep it together, hold on to your inhibitions, not let yourself go, and because you are attached and fearful of real death. Letting go can be very difficult, and our meditation practice is designed to give us concentration, knowledge of how the various minds work, and understanding of what is the right frame of mind that lets us flow with the experience. Logic will not help us here. Many people feel like their mind is floating away and fear that they will be left crazy after the drug wears off. The thought of letting the drug carry them downstream makes them freeze up. We just want to let you know the possibilities beforehand, so you can recognize the positive and negative aspects as they arise.

Facing our fears has nothing, and everything, to do with real end-of-life physically dying. As you would expect, it's crucial to ego death too. Ego is distracted, clinging, always demanding, and frightened. You might notice tension in the stomach, and the body will feel stranger than ever before, but at some point we realize we are not our body, or our thinking mind, and then we can let go of both and still have attention remain. We're temporarily leaving body and thinking-mind by entering into attention of doing-mind.

Ego death is a change of perspective; it's a growing up and evolving on our metaphysical journey. Afterward, you will resurface as the same "you," but you will have developed your presence, and the storms of life will not affect you like they used to. The past will seem unreal, as if your life experiences happened to someone else. Your future will be completely open, and everything that happens in the future is mind blowing, new, adventurous. Some people have even been cured of various diseases and illnesses after ego death, but we make no claims and scientific research continues in this field.

Briefly, ego death is the destruction of the mental picture that we construct about ourselves. All of a sudden we see ourselves as not having a personality, so we can let go of games like success and failure. Our hidden inner pain will surface and must be confronted. Unfortunately, it's a very unsettling, disorienting, confounding, and overwhelming experience. Usually we are flat on our back, unable to move a muscle while our mind transcends itself.

Ego death is the first step of leaving behind ignorance—the ignorance of not seeing reality correctly. We'll notice that we are not as solid as we thought, and if on LSD, we might merge with the entire universe, where there is no up or down, right or left—but it feels fine to be liberated. Once ego death has passed, and we've learned the lesson it wants to teach us, euphoria and bliss can occur in our daily interactions. Our emotions and physical sensations expand to a loving state; we can let go of all our hurt, because we now see it as illusory. We become kinder, more loving and open—to others, and to ourselves.

We create our world through the lens of ego, but it's a world of images, not a world of reality. When we get stoned, meditate, let-go, or use critical analytical reasoning, the ego comes face to face with reality. For a very small minority, the depersonalization of ego can be terrifying. There is loss of sense of self, floating, falling into a void, as the unreal ego world crashes around them; they lose their sense of self and worldview. It is a type of splitting, feeling separated from the identity constructed from childhood.

To put it another way, thinking mind is ego, and doing mind is our innate and natural personality that is our true presence.

If you are suffering from depersonalization (freaking out), it's important to change the way you think about things. You might take a thought as true when it is not. For example, in our imagination a piece of rope can appear as a snake, or we can imagine ourselves as ugly or unwanted—all kinds of depression and self-hate is part of thinking mind's toolkit. You don't have to believe the words that pop up in your thinking mind.

Stoner Meditation wizards seek ego death on purpose. If ego is set aside, doing mind can accept the flowing hallucinations and insights that arise. To have any success with the enlightenment exercises that are coming up, you must temporarily set ego aside and become invisible. In other words, put aside the person you cling to and let go of everything. There will be nothing to hold on to—after all, it's ego death. Just like real death, there is nothing to grasp because we will have no body, no conscious mind; we will be invisible in a world of emptiness, except for our attention. We must come to realize that our real existence is attention as nirvana, not ego.

Of course, ego death can't be turned on and off like a light switch, so for beginners use your imagination in the exercises, as preparation for the actual experience. But try to feel what is happening with all your senses, including your sense-of-mind. Experienced trippers however should have no problems with executing ego death at will.

Ego death is figuratively breaking down the wall that we consider our skin. Merging the inside of us (self) with the outside of us (other), letting the clenched knot of "I" relax into the constantly changing environment surrounding us. Instead of existing in a world of past and future, we discover we are here, now. With ego death we can become the flow of the universe.

Lao Two says: "Keep your sense of self. Ego death does not mean you become someone else, or less than you are. Learn to see everything exactly as it is. Scary can be scary without being truly frightening—it's just the illusions and musings of thinking mind."

There are ways to help quiet thinking mind, the source of ego. Here are some wizard tips:

At the top of the list is compassion. It is essential to understand the power of compassion and how it affects our own life, and of course, the lives of others. After ego death, our slate is washed clean. If we don't meditate, the daily problems can reenter creating an even stronger ego. Then if we are caught up again with an emotion like anger, we can become vengeful, resentful, and uncaring. Our tripping will reflect these issues. We will have to have an anger-death to overcome our new and more powerful ego attachment. On a higher level, we fall from tree line back into the metaphorical forest.

Life can be a self-imposed trial of swimming upstream against the current—fighting our parents, teachers, and the police, and crashing on a downward spiral. Only by relaxing with the flow can we be free to guide our course, like having a rudder on a boat. Instead of agonizing and straining to "find enlightenment," relax instead, and you'll see much better results.

When will you be happy? Tomorrow, six weeks from now, twenty years from now? Take a breath and realize that happiness is right now, right this minute! Quit negative thinking and emotions—how? By watching your negative thoughts and emotions arise in daily sitting Stoner Meditation. You will eventually come to realize that all thoughts are illusions. There is amazing power in "changing your mind." Changing the way we think changes the way we act. When sitting, notice how meditation flows; this flow is important. When we understand we are not our ego, we can be fully alive, aware, and wise. What happens when our clinging to body goes away and thinking mind is silenced? We become aware presence.

Just sitting in silence, just "being" with no expectations—you can look at your worst, most horrible memory and understand that it's just a dream, an illusion. There is absolutely nothing you can do about problems from your past; not even guilt or remorse helps. The only thing you can do is act differently in the present—to create your future.

After ego death, look for these positive results: physical bliss, a new wisdom (clarity), expansive and focused awareness, and compassion.

We fill our lives with constant sounds, visual stimulation and entertainments—but we forget the power of silence where peace and insights arise. When you get Stoned take 10 or 20 minutes to close your eyes and relax in a space where there is no TV, no advertising, or need to struggle against your 'problems'—give yourself the gift of silence.

After meditating for a while, many of us go through a very introspective, self-conscious phase, trying to reconfigure our methods for dealing with the world. These changes are a type of, and part of, an ego death and growth. During this period, be very kind to yourself and let your friends know that you are changing some of the ways you live your life. When you are ready, put childhood behind and become an adult. If you ignored your own *dukkha* (suffering) before ego death, you will now notice it—along with the suffering of the world around you. There might be some crying involved. This is a good sign: to cry because you feel another person's suffering and pain is an opening up.

We grow up learning to work for appreciation or applause. If a problem appears we might ignore it, repress it, think it's forgotten, or obsess about it. Inside of ego is a repository of these physical, mental, and emotional injuries festering.

There will always be events that knock us off balance. In sitting meditation we find balance and peace, but off the cushion we face the inevitable storms of life. If we find ourselves being sad or angry, we can turn it around immediately, just by saying something like, "Nope, I'm not going to get caught up in this sadness, it's still a beautiful day, and I'm not going to waste my precious time being bummed." This is the wizard way of having control over our thinking mind and emotions.

We can change a lot of life experiences. We don't have to remain in a protective shell, never speaking or contributing what we know. Maybe we have a real solution, an insight, or some helpful compassion—but ego has us locked down so tight we can't open up to the world. For example: if your friend had the hood up on his car and was looking for something wrong, wouldn't you tell him if the fan belt were broken? Or would you stand there in silence?

The point is to experience our emotions in the raw, as they are, without any labels or narrative. When we start to see everything as just life events, instead of thinking, "This bummer is happening to me," we are becoming balanced and free of ego. This is a sign we will soon be breaking through tree line.

We only have the ability to change ourselves. Let's say a person is angry, biting your head off—there is little you can do to fix them. But there is a lot you can do to fix yourself. Smile inside, knowing that your time is precious and you don't need to get on their emotional roller coaster. Be polite, be the positive example compared to their negativity. This takes a strong heart and supportive self-image, because you are shutting down the emotional reactivity of thinking mind. It's not being cold, or better than the other person; it's acting with dignity, self-respect, and presence.

Don't be hard on yourself. If your interior monologue, thinking mind sounds like this: "You are a stupid asshole who never gets anything right, you are ugly and nobody likes you," you need to immediately stop these negative put-down narratives. Change your mind. If anyone else said those things out loud to you, you would be furious. However, we often say these mean-spirited things to ourselves, usually not even noticing, because the voice inside our head has been "talking" that way since we were children. Changing your interior thinking will change your life.

To conquer thinking mind's assault, we need to develop in meditation: insight, concentration, mindfulness, and emptiness. In every moment there is enormous energy that we can make use of – this energy arises from emptiness.

Emptiness: First, please understand that there are several definitions of emptiness and positions on how it is explained. There are even opposing groups that claim their viewpoint is the correct one. So Stoner Meditation is saying right out front that it's enigmatic—and although we think we understand emptiness correctly, we might be right, wrong, mistaken, visionary, or perhaps we Stoners have discovered an entirely new type of emptiness experience.

If we ever needed paradox, it is here in describing and comprehending emptiness. Let's start with an empty cup. What is it empty of? Maybe it's empty of water, but it's not empty of air. The void of outer space is empty of air, but filled with all sorts of energies. Then, there is the arcane emptiness, that's empty of emptiness, but it's not nothing, or a void, or nihilism. Emptiness is also cause and effect, and it is this very moment of here and now. Another description is the emptiness that views what's inside of us and outside of us as ONE—not separate from each other. Emptiness doesn't mean we disappear into nothingness, it means we merge into everything, letting ego go. It can also be the connection and correlation between the most tiny element and the largest multiverses—as above, so below. It is the connection we humans have with every leaf and every star—what Zen master Thich Naht Hanh calls "interbeing." Nothing is independent, as all things have no inherent existence and are always in the process of evolutionary change. Emptiness can also be a viewpoint that sees (ascertains) existence as empty. We exist in/as profound emptiness, and emptiness is also in the most mundane event. It's not possible for everything to eternally exist, or for nothing at all to exist—it's the paradoxical combination of the two that works. Everything arises, persists, and falls back into emptiness.

Another problem is that we are already in emptiness, but all we see is dualism—it's not like there is someplace we can go to experience emptiness. However, the awareness of emptiness seems to make all the difference. So, when I say, "Standing in the experience of emptiness," I also mean "I'm in the awareness of emptiness." Also, emptiness awareness is not a thing, it's what arises as "view" when ego is transcended. Whew!

There'll be lots more, less abstract and more practical information on this stuff.

Note: even though it might be confusing, it's worth paying attention to our discussion on emptiness because doing-mind's awareness of emptiness will arise every time you are very stoned. Start looking for it.

Tibetan Master Nagarjuna said: "Misunderstanding emptiness is like holding a poisonous snake by the tail, or messing up a magic spell."

Nothing is independent, but rather, everything is dependent on everything else, as the ongoing causes and conditions that make up our world. Emptiness is possibly the most confusing concept of our existence—ever. That's because we tend to want to label everything: that's a tree, that's a cloud, that's the ocean. In Stoner Meditation, emptiness is being in the same space as the tree, cloud, and ocean without any differentiation.

At Deer Park in India a guy named Gautama sat down to meditate under a tree, but he didn't sit in meditation for twenty minutes like we do. He had had enough searching, and said he wouldn't get up until he had the answer. So he sat for days and nights in intense concentrated meditation until one night Gautama entered enlightenment, but that wasn't enough. He kept at it until he was absorbed into the highest emptiness of nirvana. In that process from enlightenment to nirvana he dissolved his Gautama ego and became fully immersed in emptiness as experience. He realized that by letting go of every thing, concept, label, and belief, he could enter the ever-creating flow of the universe. In emptiness, he realized, a type of wisdom arises that is pure, arriving before and untouched by thinking mind. As far as he was concerned, everything that was Gautama was gone—he was now Buddha, the awakened one.

In my meditation training by Lao Two I bumped into the emptiness of nirvana too, but in a much less stable way than Gautama did. What happened to me is called *kensho* in Japanese (*samadhi* in Sanskrit), just a glimpse of nirvana emptiness (breaking through to tree line). Many people on psychedelics have this experience, but few realize what's happened. I opened a door and walked inside, but everything was overwhelming and unfamiliar for me, so after a while it ended. Because I had not done the meditative preparation beforehand to understand what and where was occurring, it was too intense and foreign. My in-here and my out-there, and both together, were emptiness and there was only the merging of everything. There was no ego-based me, no solid world outside either—together they are just awareness (or view), ever-creating, lingering, ever-destroying each moment as a flow.

Gautama not only walked through the door, he conquered all his fears and stayed inside emptiness. With dedicated practice, we too can reside continually in this primordial emptiness. He awakened not by some magical ability, but by human ability. Emptiness is not magic, it is just clearly experiencing the actual nature of the universe.

I don't think anyone can really understand compassion until they've known emptiness. The situation we are all in, adrift on this small pebble of a planet, without any answers, is really overpowering. Denial of emptiness isn't helping us solve our fears; it's the cause of our distress. Our primal fear is death, yet what is death? Emptiness.

We constantly reify our reality because ego wants the world to be real for us. Psychedelics show other realities and possibilities of existence. Just because we take this three-dimensional reality for granted doesn't mean reality can't be changed—like walking through walls or flying. Of course, these can only be possible if an enlightened person uses emptiness to "change" the shape of the illusion of reality, to a different illusion. Might be possible, might not – let the mystery be... Do you understand? The possibility is not important, the stretching our imaginativeness for far-out ideas is.

There are some events that can only be called magical feats or extraordinary experiences. Sometimes things happen that seem magical, there's no other word that will do. I think in the far future, it will be possible for humans to change their reality by "thought." Why fly to Mars in a spaceship when you can think yourself on Mars, and then you are there? What once was considered magic will become science fact. Don't limit your imagination. Remember, no magic is practical without compassion and love because of the karma involved. Bad magic equals bad karma. We like to think anomalies arise from emptiness – unknowable, unpredictable and magical events.

In the West we think of emptiness as separation, nothingness, a vacuum, nihilism, and a condition of being crushingly alone. A person who is empty is apathetic, deserted, and unaware of their surroundings. Stoner Meditation has a completely different definition.

Lao Two says: "Emptiness is, and is not empty. It is the continuing energy of the universe, without beginning or end—even our existing is empty. Everything we are is contained, absorbed, and occupied by emptiness."

Stoner Meditation recommends Stoners study the Buddhist philosophical view on emptiness (*anatta*) because it's an excellent tool that will open you up. Emptiness can be a fresh way of looking at the world, where insights, coincidence, and hallucinations become signposts on the pathway to enlightenment. The material things we see become intangible, ever changing, and it's as though the space between objects blurs together—we might even get telepathic. Unfortunately, describing emptiness is like going to a city that has no street signs and no names on the buildings, and trying to give a stranger directions to the grocery store.

Lao Two says: "Everything exists, and does not exist. We are evolving Mind consciousness."

The example usually given to help explain emptiness is a wave on the ocean. The wave is born, is present, then dies—but all the time, the wave is still ocean. When we apply this to ourselves we discover that, like the wave, we have no permanence; even our thoughts will fade in time. What we are then is a persistently changing body and mind—a presence, not separated from the ocean of Mind.

When we experience emptiness our ordinary logic is of no use, but it's such a clear and obvious realization that we wonder how we didn't see it sooner. We'll be saying this throughout the book: we exist, and we don't exist—at the same time/space. This understanding lets us know emptiness directly, without thought, concepts, with all delusion gone in an instant.

Lao Two says: "Possibly the most important teaching in this book is 'soup'—like a hot bowl of vegetable soup. Fish swim through water soup. Humans swim through air soup. Stop thinking of the air that surrounds us as imperceptible—it's not. Reach out to air soup; fill your attention with it. Our physical bodies are made of various densities of soup, we are a different soupiness than other stuff. Everything has a different soupiness, and the container is the entire universe. Awareness of emptiness means to see the soup for what it is. Emptiness is soup."

Remember, we lead a divided, dualistic life—"self" is our physical body to the outside skin, and "other" is everything outside of us, from outside the skin to infinity. Thinking mind created a wall between the two as a way to deal with daily living. At the very least, thinking mind wants us to know not to bump into sharp stuff. But in an awareness sense, this way of regarding ourselves and the world around us keeps us separated and stuck in thinking mind. Stoners briefly get unstuck by smoking some marijuana, but even though it's chipping away at thinking mind, it's not enough. If we want to be enlightened and in higher Mind, then we have to understand that this view of separation of self and other is erroneous. There really is no separation, and if we can take that leap of understanding to bring them together, our world will never be the same.

Sometimes the only way to describe something so ineffable and ghostlike is to tell what it isn't. The Heart Sutra does this better than anything else that we're aware of, and I suggest you Google it—it's very short reading. There are several interpretations, the Hindu, Buddhist, Tibetan, Zen, etc.

For the backstory of the Heart Sutra this is one version. Basically you need to know that Gautama Buddha was teaching his assembly. But many of those students just couldn't make the leap into Enlightenment, so as an example, he entered highest nirvana in front of them. One of Buddha's disciples asked a god (Avalokitsvara) who was passing by to describe what the Buddha was experiencing. As I said, in highest nirvana, words and concepts, logic and intellectualism have no meaning, so Avalokitsvara described what it isn't. Many versions say it was Avaokitsvara that was meditating, not Buddha.

The Heart Sutra is very powerful and deep, so don't be surprised if you don't understand it right away. At the end it says, usually in Sanskrit, to keep going—even if you have an enlightenment experience, keep going further, then further, and further yet. The wisdom of nirvana is endless.

After reading the Heart Sutra, you might wonder what's happening to our perception when we get stoned and meditate. Of course, we notice that everything is dreamlike. You feel the weight of your body pressing into the cushion below, or maybe the floor hurts your ankle—simple things suddenly take on new meaning. In our daily meditation that uses concentration on the breath we realize that air is not nothing—air is tangible, life giving, manifestly full. We "watch" air being drawn in and then expelled out of our nostrils with every breath.

On the smallest scale, we've learned that even atoms are filled with more "empty" space than matter. As a matter of current scientific understanding, the material world only makes up five percent of the universe. The other ninety-five percent are peculiar things like dark matter. On the largest scale, what used to be called the emptiness of outer space is now said to contain things like dark matter, and energies like gravity, and even antimatter—so in actuality, there is no such thing as empty space. Since I'm not a scientist, this is as I understand it—this describes the way the universe is set up for us, it's just what it is ... but in the end, no matter how small or how big, it's just different kinds of soup. Aware soup, Mind soup, material world soup, star and galaxy soup.

We can say we truly exist in emptiness when we drop thinking mind's concept of feeling we are solid and separate, and merge with (exist as, become absorbed into) what's outside of us. Existing in emptiness is not some mental analysis, or thinking a certain way—it is direct experience of the world as it really is. Emptiness is not nihilism or nothingness—emptiness contains self/other in unity.

Sometimes people mistakenly think that emptiness can't be empty if solid form is included in the definition. In other words, the universe can't be emptiness, void, without any solid form, if we are physically standing there, perceiving with our own eyes that everything is obviously solid. If it weren't solid, we would fall through the floor or walk through walls. This is solved with the paradox that everything exists and does not exist at the same moment. It's not always either we exist, or we don't; sometimes we have to transcend logic to see the picture clearly, that both are happening at the same spacetime.

To explain this paradox, we try to find any one thing inside of us that is unchanging, and we discover there is nothing actually existing that is "us" at any one moment. If there were, we would all remain babies—but since we are ever-changing, we grow. The bones you have now are not the bones you had when you were three years old. We can also look for that ever-changing body, but the change happens too slowly for us to recognize it. When we get enlightened, we can experience ourselves as change. We humans have nothing we can point to that has any substance—even the chair you sit on is in constant change.

Yet paradoxically, we exist too. We are in our body, but it's like being in a moving car. We're in our moving body as it changes, and this constant change is part of our nonexistence. It's okay that reality is a paradox. But to say that emptiness is only change is not accurate. A closer description is awareness within change.

Once experienced, emptiness comes and goes in material life, and it takes time to fully recognize it in everything. There will be some exercises coming up to demonstrate emptiness in several different ways, not as an intellectual study like we've been doing, but as an experiential process.

Albert Einstein said: "Reality is merely an illusion, albeit a very persistent one."

Because of impermanence, we can say that all activity in the universe is emptiness—devoid of intrinsic existence, everything connected. Emptiness is also seen as a creative flow that includes all activity, action, and origination in the exact here-now. Emptiness is not separate, it is the interdependency among everything that exists. Again, it's not enough to understand emptiness intellectually.

Lao Two says: "We exist in emptiness; Mind is all that we really are. Nothing exists outside of Natural Mind, and everything exists in relationship with something else. Even though material existence does exist, it is fundamentally emptiness."

This is what we are looking for when emptiness is realized: the body and mind will transcend their separated independent solid state. We become aware that we are both in our body and not in our body, and our body and mind occur together as an aware presence. There will be a rarefied sense of wonder as we connect to this primordial insight that is beyond both time and space, beyond body and mind, as it seems we are "seeing" from outside of our body. This is becoming one with the universe, but it's more too. ... You will realize that all material form appears empty, and this surrounding emptiness creates and shapes the world we live in. Emptiness becomes for us an ever-expressing creation, but that creation has no attachment, grasping, or clinging—it's the eternal fountain. This creative aspect of emptiness results from all the previous causes and effects that brought us to this point in time and space. Another way of saying this is, when logic and analysis finally realize that there is no logical solution to be found, they hit a wall of opaque glass. We know something is on the other side so when we shatter the glass (ego), we apprehend reality. We have to let go of logic and just experience. When thinking mind hits that wall, no more thoughts can arise, and explanations or judgments become useless. Thinking mind can't figure out non-ordinary reality, so we slip into doing mind and see everything as it is.

When the balance of meditative emptiness is reached there will be a joy in life, gratitude, and empathy. Struggles seem workable, and there is inner peace.

Emptiness is not about astral projection, losing your personality, being out of your body and unable to get back, psychosis, or anything dangerous. It's our own fear and ignorance that are dangerous. Emptiness is not negation, nor is it dependent on eternalism. However, to experience emptiness is to experience enlightenment, and requires a strong sense of self.

The fabricated persona of thinking mind fears emptiness. When thinking mind is replaced by doing mind, we can conquer all fears.

Lao Two says: "If humans never existed, emptiness would still be universal reality. It doesn't matter what emptiness is called—it would still be reality."

Safety First

Lao Two says: "All this talk about letting go of ego, becoming invisible, losing the 'I', emptiness ... scary stuff. Instead, realize that there is a presence you were born with that is 'uniquely yours,' and it cannot be extinguished even by death. Take comfort in knowing that you can let the attachment to 'I' go fearlessly, and still retain that presence."

Some of you are brand-new to both meditation and smoking marijuana and curious what the fuss is all about. Why not just get high and enjoy ourselves? Because marijuana has two levels: getting high, and getting stoned. Meditation and getting stoned can produce a nonordinary state of consciousness, ego death, and other shamanic situations. Being prepared is prudent.

We're aware of our responsibility to discuss safety because some people don't follow instructions, leave out steps, and take foolhardy risks. On the one hand, marijuana is usually so benign, any "bad" side effects will only affect a very few people, and no matter how stoned you get, after three or four hours everything will be back to "normal." To those people still confused about the breakthrough into emptiness, we dedicate this section on safety.

Marijuana can be very strong, especially when made into products that we can eat (edibles). It's very easy to overindulge by eating two brownies because of the munchies, and then we are overdosed, becoming overwhelmed by an intensely uncomfortable high. We all have different tolerances—some marijuana smokers get zonked on one hit. But they notice that after smoking the same marijuana for a month it takes two hits.

The upcoming sections discuss some **advanced** techniques for realizing enlightenment. The experience can be disorienting, life changing, disturbing, and sometimes nightmarish. People who have smoked marijuana and taken psychedelics successfully for a long time have already faced some of their fears without any major problems. It's obvious to even the beginning smoker that the hallucinatory mind has both joyous and dreadful images. Experienced trippers understand that all hallucinations are temporary and harmless, so if something scary comes up, it's just part of the experience. We need you to take the same attitude to the sudden enlightenment experience.

Remind yourself about the first time you drove a car. You had an instructor, but basically you learned on your own. It was scary having all that mechanical power, and unleashing it made you cautious. Once you learned how it all works, it seemed commonplace.

Lastly, some drugs are lethal, so know what you are putting into your body. Research before you ingest anything. For example—belladonna, ecstasy, methadrine, and various herbs and mushrooms (amanita) can sometimes be deadly. Most any drug can be overdosed. Be prudent, smart, and aware.

Never, ever dose someone, or give him or her any drugs without their knowledge—especially psychedelics. It's dangerous, and not fair. Lao Two says: "Marijuana is a psychedelic."

Marijuana can bring about profound visual, auditory, and tactile experiences. It can bring hallucinations that can affect every sensory level. Marijuana enhances and intensifies inner-perceptive mental experiences, bringing on nonordinary reality. Our research shows that nobody has ever died from smoking marijuana. If you overdose on marijuana you usually fall asleep, or cope with the intensity by knowing it will pass in a few hours. Coughing from smoking marijuana is common, while throwing up is rare. Some people get red eyes, and dry-mouth. The munchies are a wonderful side effect, making food taste amazing. Most people smile and laugh a lot, cracking stupid jokes, and marijuana is awesome with sex! Marijuana is not physically addicting, although it might be psychologically addicting.

Psychedelics like LSD, 'shrooms, or cactus will dramatically change your life; they are not like any drug you are familiar with, even marijuana. Do not take psychedelics if you are mentally ill, severely depressed, or just taking them for fun. Psychedelics are serious business, and since we can't know what's in underground pills, I suggest only taking naturally growing psychedelic drugs. I love LSD, but anything that comes in pills is suspect—know your supplier, ask questions about what you are buying, talk to people that have taken it.

Don't trip alone on your first psychedelic journey.

Investigate Tim Leary's "set and setting," and be sure you take psychedelics in a safe, comfortable situation and surroundings. Don't do psychedelics when you have obligations; don't answer the phone or call anyone. I know some guys who took LSD in prison; they said it turned out to be a bad idea.

Marijuana and psychedelics can, and do, warp the status quo of our mental universe, turning what we once knew for certain about life into scrambled eggs. In other words, they change the way we think about everything and make us question our assumptions. Also, they make us question authority.

Realize that every small anxiety is amplified on drugs, but by the same token, joy and bliss are also amplified. You must understand that thinking mind and will never go away, but as we said, we can turn down the volume on thoughts. Our mind is very flexible when we smoke marijuana or drop some LSD, it will happily accommodate new experience. When you trip you might have anxiety, bad thoughts, or awkward feelings of distress—but remember; much of it is just plain nonsense, and must be dismissed as such so it will become a learning experience instead.

After you've been practicing meditation for a while, you will find it is an amazing aid to tripping and will help you face your fears. Not all tripping should be enjoyable; crying your eyes out can be liberating.

Medical marijuana has become a standard for helping cancer patients, people in pain, insomniacs, and depressed or anxiety-filled individuals. Medical marijuana is benign compared to many harsh pharmaceuticals with their horrible side effects.

Please be aware that marijuana edibles can injure pets if they eat them. Stoners should also be aware that chocolate is poisonous to dogs. Call your vet for instructions if your dog or cat gets inadvertently stoned by eating your marijuana brownies.

Warning: Some of this psychedelic stuff can be scary for a few people unaccustomed to mind exploration. As we've said, Stoner Meditation is not for everybody. If you are determined to smoke marijuana for the first time, please only inhale a small amount and see how you feel about the experience after a half hour. The same goes for any psychedelic:

take less the first experience. Go slow; don't be pressured by others—only do things when you are ready.

If, for any reason, you ever feel *suicidal*—do not wait to try to figure it out; spending hours, days, or weeks in paranoid analysis, depressed angst, or other delusional mind games. Serious and prolonged suicidal thoughts are the brain's equivalent of a heart attack and need immediate counseling. In the United States, call 1-800-273-8255—the suicide help line.

Suicidal thoughts are WRONG thinking, and suicide is NOT EVER acceptable—suicide is WRONG reasoning, and WRONG action. It is of vast importance that you fulfill the time allotted for your life, and that you learn that both love and suffering, pleasure and pain are necessary parts of human experience. You do have a purpose and are not here by accident, and you are not in anybody's way. There should always be hope for tomorrow because it gives us another chance to change, set things right, and improve our circumstances.

If you need help, even if you are stoned on LSD, call the suicide help line and talk to someone, call a friend, or knock on a neighbor's or even a stranger's door—but seek immediate help, then get long-term help if you notice suicidal thoughts. If you have a history of mental distress or anxiety, or any other serious psychological problems, again—get help.

Note: No human has permission to knowingly take "poison" or other dreadful actions that will harm him or her, just because it is a "choice." We all must understand completely that suicide is absolutely counter to the Universal Stoner Law—we believe that "every breath is to be venerated"—and the breaths with which we inhale marijuana are magical, spiritual, life affirming.

Once again, choose drugs carefully, and be wise, aware, loving, happy, and a little paranoid (due to drug laws) to stay safe. Do not let delusions rule your thinking mind, and do not believe all your thoughts.

Thoughts, or the inner dialogue, can be just plain wrong, misleading, or hurtful.

The drugs we put into our body alter our perception of body and mind, and every drug has side effects and dangers. The amount of a drug that works for one person will seem imprudent for another. Each of us needs to know where our comfort zone is.

Onward, Psychonauts

Lao Two says: "People find it strange that I smoke so much marijuana. I find it strange that they don't."

This section is for the dauntless and clear-sighted psychonaut Stoners, those folks who sometimes like to push the envelope and go for totally mindblown psychedelic transcendence and multicellular disintegration of their erroneous assumptions. These are the folks who will smoke until they can't get any higher. We acknowledge your quest and appreciate your journey, for it is our journey too. We also appreciate the sacrifices you've made and understand what you are reaching for. There are different kinds of Stoners—some who like to sneak up on getting high and others who like to dive right in. An ounce of weed will easily last me for months. I have friends who would smoke up an ounce in two weeks.

Lao Two says: "What I'm doing is not accidental, and I resent people assuming I'm purposeless or lazy, just because I smoke marijuana. My life has definite objectives, and I've seen positive results with my methods. Smoking marijuana works for me."

Many of us are politically active Stoners without even acknowledging it. We might not think we are making a political statement just by smoking marijuana, but every time we light up we are outlaws. We won't accept the limitations of incredibly stupid drug laws, and the mean-spirited actions of those who enforce them. We refuse to wait for the interminably slow changes toward legalization, and many Stoners have become activists who won't sit down and shut up any longer. To make real change in policy, we will need a few brilliant people who are willing to speak up. And we need more and more people willing to keep breaking the law. (Can I get put in jail for writing that? Oh, well—I'm 68 and won't live too much longer anyway.) Someday marijuana prohibition will be history, and then Stoners can create an aware, magical world hand-in-hand with the straights. No, we're not so naive that we think marijuana will solve all the world's problems, but we do believe that people acting from higher Mind are bound to make better decisions than those controlling our current world paradigm.

Lao Two's way, and my way, is not your way—your way is your way. Within reason, amid the current restrictions, make your own rules. Try to live as free and wild as possible. We hope that whatever drugs pass through your lips won't take you down a dark road of bummers, and we hope the angels and gods protect your search and journey along the way. We particularly hope that all your drugs are high-quality psychedelics with no additives or bad surprises.

Lao Two says: "Our brain and consciousness—take it off the pedestal. It's just another sense organ. We have a sense of consciousness, just like we have a sense of smell."

Figuring It

Being a Stoner can be awkward. Sometimes marijuana can affect job performance, and not every job is marijuana friendly. It's a good idea to stay a little paranoid and alert, don't leave marijuana lying around where it might bring trouble. Be extremely careful when you travel. Use your common sense, stay in touch with your instincts—don't get busted.

Tripping on psychedelics is tricky, and surroundings are important. Sometimes the mood is for music or concerts; other times a walk in nature is called for. Neither marijuana nor psychedelics will fix all our problems; they are just tools to help us see clearly and open up a new world. No one can make you change, and maybe you don't need to be changed. Only you know if your life is working the way you want it to, so create your own mystical journey.

All we're asking, is to do the work necessary to realize your full potential. Get rid of your fears. Be grateful that you have marijuana in your life and have the opportunity for the magical. Dedicate yourself to a daily meditation; take the time for your inner development.

Our short lives are for living, but most of us only wet our feet in the raging river. Some hide away in lonely prisons of our own making. They end up alone, paying for safety in their rocking chair, slowly waiting to die. We don't know about you, but we want more out of life, we want the mysterious, the unexpected, to feel passionate emotions, explore, and have crazy, wild, and unpredictable adventures.

Lao Two says: "Walking the razor's edge—is the willingness to accept that you might fall and be split into two instantly."

Learn to surf the waves of life, balancing work and relationships, becoming stable, humble, sincere, loving, and wise, and participating as a part of the human community. There is a stark difference between risk as consciously choosing to do something - and recklessness as mindlessly blundering forward.

Think about all you do during any five-minute period. How many times do your hands touch your body to itch and scratch without even noticing? Do you ever observe things like whether the water you are drinking is warm or cold, or feel it going into your body? Are you mindless when eating munchies, or when walking, sleeping, or at work? As they say, do you ever stop to smell the roses? On a more subtle level, can you become calm and quiet enough to feel your heart beating?

None of our heartbeats will ever come again. In that five minutes, so much is happening—perhaps a massive giant star exploded, sending out the raw material for new stars and planets to be born. The spinning Earth flies around the sun at about a thousand miles an hour—and on Earth we call that zero. We are so incredibly, infinitesimally small; we might forget the mystery and the extraordinary variety that surrounds us. The awesome universe could just as well have not come into existence at all, with no Big Bang or laws of physics ... yet here we are with an uncountable number of material phenomena. This is why Zen says the whole universe is in a single blade of grass.

Really, it's a miracle just being alive—right here, right now—this book in your hands or on your computer screen, sick or well, cold or comfortable, mellow or stressed out. You are existing in time and space, the web of the entire universe emanates from you because you are at its center.

Lao Two says: "Discontent is produced by wrong thinking. Expecting enjoyment to last, we discover that the Earth spins through space whether we are happy or not."

The Buddha said: "If there is no awareness of the body, there will be no awareness in the mind."

Compassion: Without compassion, it is not possible to maintain enlightenment. First we have to be able to feel the love in our own body. Next we have to feel the suffering of others, at least intellectually. And finally, we have to be able to love everyone and everything equally. Then, because enlightenment is such a powerful experience, we must be able to be selfless and be willing to give up everything during the breakthrough experience itself. Remember, we do not have to give up all our material possessions, our personality, or every waking moment and head out on the road as a penniless beggar—that's not the renunciation we are discussing. We need to be the person we were before we put the layers of ego on.

If, on the other hand, we want to achieve enlightenment to have power over people, to be cool, or for personal gain, then it will remain elusive and unobtainable. It's one thing to have confidence, but quite another to be a jive shuckster manipulating people. It's just as bad to be an ineffectively naïve shmuck at the mercy of the world around you. Stand up for yourself; be aware, humble, grateful, and fully alive. At some point in our meditation we should feel love arising for the person we are, and acceptance of the person we are. We should be able to look into a mirror and love the reflected image.

Aldous Huxley said: "Maybe this world is another planet's Hell."

We can get high and enter into a blissful state and feel compassion for the entire universe. We can also get high and hold on tight to our anger, fear, and confusion. Any inside or outside stimulus can knock us off balance. We had an intention to be compassionate when we woke up this morning, but we got angry instead. ... We can't attach or cling to compassion; it should arise with a cause, so compassion can be the effect we use. Everything changes day-to-day, moment-to-moment, and compassion should arise when it's needed, in the here and now. Compassion can be learned as a mental exercise, but then a real-life opportunity will present itself for us to act. As usual, awareness is the key, and seeing people as they really are is the second step of compassion; loving them just as they are is the next action. After we've meditated for many years, a type of love emanates from within us, and it's possible that people around us will feel that. These techniques give us power, but the smallest negativity or anger will destroy positive growth.

Lao Two says: "At my job I did ninety-nine things right. But I did one thing wrong. What do I imagine people remember about me, the ninety-nine things right or the one screw-up? The replay of our memories is emotional."

Bring compassion to the political world around you, become involved in the process of humanity struggling toward peace, security, and justice. Don't ignore the political world—it's okay to be engaged in positive change (as you see it). Our personal inaction breeds disaster, evidenced by the real possibility that humans could become extinct in the near future. When you smoke outside, you come to understand the value of being an environmentalist. It doesn't need constant political bickering; it takes positive acts that respect Mom Earth. Remember, Earth bats last.

Consider the relationship between loving partners: you are not in a "committed relationship" unless you can talk honestly about everything. I'm not saying we need to divulge secrets told in confidence, but we need to overcome any fear and know that our partner will treat us fairly. A technique I often use with my wife is to start with, "I don't know how to say this very well, so I'm just going to say it the best I can." Tell your partner what you need sexually, emotionally, and mentally—because it's unlikely your partner is a mind reader.

Make your own life choices in your relationship instead of clinging to your partner, and give your partner permission to make their own life choices too. Compromise when necessary, but don't allow anyone to control you—be compassionate toward yourself too, self-loathing is not the Way. A relationship does not mean giving up the life choices you love; for example, if you get high and your partner constantly gives you a bad time about using marijuana even after you have presented facts, then it's possible you might want to think about moving on. Or instead of leaving, you can choose to compromise somehow. Choice is power, and it's your choice that determines how your life unfolds. So you have a responsibility to empower your life by doing what you want, because the only rules in a relationship are whatever rules you two agree on together.

People enter relationships with inaccurate images of their partner's characteristics. We see the person as all good, but eventually their faults become known to us. If we find disappointment in our thoughts about our partner it will turn into resentment, because we are attached to the fantasy image we had of that person. We need to always try to see the real person (this can be fun when we are really stoned because what we see gives us more information). We must accept our partner's faults as we see them, and love them for the person they genuinely are. We call this "being real."

If we sincerely care for the other person, we should be finding joy in doing things for them. There should be no resentment. A real relationship is fifty-fifty, but since no one is perfect, you might find yourself doing something that gives you no pleasure, like picking up your partner's dirty clothes from the floor. You do it anyway. Don't expect applause. Do it because it fits your world construct to see the floor clean.

The compassionate gift of a relationship is that you and your partner are sharing and giving the gift of time. Since time can never be retrieved, our time, and how we use it, is perhaps the most important thing we own.

Parents are not one hundred percent responsible for how their children turn out. Children are not one hundred percent responsible for how their parents turn out. We are each responsible for our own life. When you have children in your home, treat them as children, but respect them as you would an adult. When you leave home, treat parents as adults. Be compassionate.

Lao Two says: "Compassion is more important than enlightenment. We can use compassion starting right now. Enlightenment has its own schedule."

Compassion is not standing on a pedestal, helping a poor unfortunate below us. We, and the person suffering are the same because we all face the same universality of suffering—we all age, suffer pain, and die.

Enlightenment is a different part of our training. It's typically difficult for anyone to realize enlightenment, and at the beginning we see it as a goal. After we become enlightened our actions have more power, and that's where compassion truly becomes necessary. Since enlightenment is active, not passive, it's a force in the world. When an enlightened person loses their mindfulness and becomes angry, they pay a higher price, and suffer directly from it.

The Buddha said: "Holding on to anger is like holding on to a hot coal, which only burns your hand."

Are you angry with anyone right now? Have you held on to hate for years? If you can let go of this anger and hate, it will free you. The other person probably doesn't even know you are angry with them—it's like you've been holding on to that hot coal burning your hand for so long that you forgot what it's like not to hold it. Let their ignorant mistakes and past actions go, throw that hot coal away, and let your hand heal with forgiveness. The past is an illusion. Yes, we lived it, but it's only a memory now. In meditation we discover that memories are flexible, changeable, selective, and not carved into stone.

Mahatma Gandhi said: "The simplest acts of kindness are far more powerful than a thousand heads bowing in prayer."

An open heart is necessary to transcend our anger and insecurity, and face our fear with a more appropriate response. In our search for enlightenment we tend to use our brain, logic and analytical mind to try to figure it all out, instead of relaxing into it. One important thing we've buried and forgotten is the amazing physical bliss that lives inside of each of us, waiting to be released and shared. Our daily sitting meditation will help us notice such subtle body energies, and when we feel that energy we will compassionately want to share it with everyone.

Guard against sharing your enlightenment, insights, and realizations right away; if you do, people might think you are insufferable. Hide your wisdom away, and only reveal it when it's necessary or requested. Be careful what you say: practice mindful speech.

Sometimes we light up a bowl with the express purpose of trying to figure out what the hell is happening in our life—why was our spouse, or boss, or why were we, a jerk today. We hope that by getting stoned we can analyze our situation from a higher perspective to try to transcend the sense of right and wrong. When stoned we are not holding as tightly to our position. Sometimes getting stoned helps us to see the situation through someone else's eyes, feel their pain and suffering. Smoking this way is compassionate if we change our behavior. We certainly can't change the behavior of anybody else. ...

Anytime you say to yourself, "I hate that person," or "They are such a jerk," you might as well be saying, "I hate myself," or "I am such a jerk." The mirror of our life is right in front of us, and that mirror is the best teacher we have. What we hate in another person is what we hate about ourselves—we are seeing our habits, failures, and judgmental reactions exhibited in the behavior of our "enemy." It's exactly the same with prejudice, as the separation that sees "them" as different from "us."

Any event that happens to us is judged, processed, and forgotten—or, if the experience is emotionally compelling enough, stored for retrieval. As we said before, we have stimuli, then observation by doing mind, next emotion (probably chemical), and lastly reaction and labeling by thinking mind. When thinking mind picks up on the emotion, it initially becomes aware of the event. All this happens. Lightning fast, so thinking mind takes the emotional content and decides whether fight or flight is the best response. Lust, for example—do we confront it (act) or run away (repress)? Yet another reason to meditate—to learn the mindfulness necessary to see this process in action.

Think about the power this gives us, to be able to control anger or fear by putting a different label on the emotion. Instead of an anger label, we can change it to a compassion label. Right now we might be angry and have a clenched stomach without even feeling or noticing it. But if we practice meditation, we can learn how to catch emotions at the very first body signal, knowing that emotion is just a brief feeling passing through our body. Unfortunately, too many of us are completely separated from feeling these emotional signals and need to reconnect with our bodies.

When we scan the world with our eyes, we take in a million details—but most of what we see is a blur. Our physical body is also scanning everything, feeling everything, producing defenses, keeping safe—but it's a subtle feeling. Learn to feel this subtle body energy, as the sense of touch also includes the sense of subtle feeling. The slightest movement is noticed physically and emotionally—colors, sounds, and vibrations are processed and irregularities noted. These are physical traits we've developed for survival.

We absorb negative body tension, so we constantly live with discordant energy, attached like a parasite eating away at us (sometimes literally). We keep our pain silent rather than admit anything is wrong; culturally we do not complain. When someone asks us how we are, we are not supposed to give a true answer. We never speak of our anger, dissatisfaction, and pain. We don't talk about the secret time we cried, or even about the time we felt so much joy we thought we would explode. Inside most of us are hidden stored anxieties that, after so many years, we consider normal—but they're not normal. Maybe you have headaches, or anxiety in the pit of your stomach, or you act out with bursts of anger or impatience or are troubled by restless interrupted sleep at night. In meditation we can release anxieties by facing our fears and letting the "hidden past" memories surface, where we can look at them directly and honestly. When strong stored emotions return in sitting meditation, face them as you would a mirage, a memory-dream, and look at them dispassionately with no attaching emotion. The memory-dream no longer has any power if it doesn't carry the emotional baggage – it's just a life event. That's why I keep saying to feel your body when meditating. Some people practicing this type of meditation say silently, "I'm feeling anger about my mother," for example, to note and describe the emotion. The answer to emotions is always compassion—but sometimes that means being compassionate to you.

When someone flips you off on the freeway or treats you mean, you get angry. But that person has gone, and now the anger is yours. That person did not make you angry—you made you angry. You reacted to your emotions, then thinking mind amplified your emotional response instead of accepting the situation for whatever it was. It's gotten so I laugh when someone flips me off, because I'm glad they are able to express their anger a little, hopefully releasing it for them.

Anything that happens outside of your skin is open to interpretation; you are the interpreter, the perceiver, and the judge who makes the decisions. Our life (karma) is decided by our input and how we react.

We are taught to constantly overreact to our emotions, or suppress them—very conflicting messages. Once we let mindless emotions take over, we have lost balance. We all know the results of overreacting, or acting out—lack of respect, possibly getting punched, fired, or divorced. And suppressing emotion has a huge physical and mental cost. Our job is to immediately try catching our body signals, feeling what is happening. Instead of entering the spinning nosedive and the inevitable crash, we take control. Inaction, instead of reaction, is an amazing capability, and it's part of being compassionate.

Are you going to remember this anger because someone flipped you off on the freeway, two years from now? Is this situation really that important? We can do ourselves a favor and do an angry stranger some good by simply not reacting to our anger signals. Recent research is showing that compassion equals happiness.

Lao Two says: "Sitting meditation on a cushion is preparation for moving meditation off the cushion. We carry our breath with us all the time."

I've discussed compassion and particularly anger because anger is the very worst enemy. Not only does it destroy those around us, it destroys us too. You might win a battle, but you lost the war—your heart rate, blood pressure, constricted breathing, tight muscles, and immune system all suffer—and let's not forget the anger is also being imprinted on our karmic memories as cause and effect. Get in touch with your body.

Then get in touch with another body and have joyous sex, fall in love, grow old together, and share an aware, adventurous lifetime. Live a rewarding and conscious life, and you will be in harmony with the natural universe. If a seed falls on a rock it won't grow, but if everything is in accord with the flow of the natural universe, the seed will fall into fertile soil and bloom. Be kind to yourself: bloom.

Lao Two says: "What do we all want? We all want peace, love, and happiness."

When you are angry, your thoughts replay the events over and over. What if you just said to your mind, "Stop!" and refuse to let the cyclic thoughts and body emotions take you down that road? That's when meditation becomes rewarding, because you learned to give yourself permission to not dwell on useless thoughts and feelings. You can become competent in ignoring negative thoughts when you realize that many of them are just habitual thinking or lies you've made up, and not worth your attention.

Three Minds, Again

It's our theory (or depending on how you look at it, a hypothesis) that we have three minds at our disposal. Remember, we only actually have one mind, Natural Mind. The other two terms are just descriptions of how we use mind. To expand, and recap:

Thinking mind: This is the habitual, emotional, survival mind that carries on with few restraints. It's good at running the operation and likes to be behind the steering wheel. Thinking mind makes up stories, analyzes situations, labels, judges, and mindlessly runs the show. Thinking mind has memorized the "rules and regulations" imposed by others, and wants to play things safe and not get into trouble. This is also the negative part of our mind that puts us down, is confused, and selfishly rules as ego (the "I"). Although it knows the rules, the thinking mind hates rules, and that can create built-up anger, body stress, resentment, and long-term hate, resulting in negative, dangerous impulsive actions. Thinking mind is our "inner-judgmental voice."

Doing mind: This works quietly to move us through the world—it is the mind that observes everything without judgment. Doing mind observes thinking mind but doesn't interfere. Through daily sitting meditation, we learn to direct doing mind to take over the steering wheel. There is no inner dialogue, but it is the voice of insights and ethics. Doing mind bangs the nails, cooks the supper, creatively invents, performs concrete actions, and is willing to take a risk. It's doing mind's awareness that employs and appreciates our senses when we notice them. It allows musicians to play notes flawlessly. Most scientists, intellectuals, craftspeople, artists, and musicians get their inspirations from doing mind. When Stoners are peacefully tripping along, coming up with those "awesome ideas!"—these come from doing mind. Doing mind observes, seeing things exactly as they are, and it is our proficient, competent mind.

Natural Mind (notice, capital N and M): This is the mind in which both thinking and doing mind reside. After ego death, body death, or enlightenment, we slowly begin to consciously inhabit Natural Mind, contained in nirvana. Inexplicitly, we reside in Natural-Mind right now, but without awareness we can't recognize it. Our residing completely in Natural Mind is not the final destination—Lao Two says there are several more levels of a highest nirvana mind, which surpass absorption in Natural Mind. Lao Two likes to jokingly promise to report back on this theory, about the levels of nirvana mind, after he's dead. Natural Mind is our true reality of aware emptiness

Lao Two says: "The world surrounding us is phenomenon because we sense it. Our brain senses the world surrounding us."

The next time you find you are becoming angry, or afraid, depressed, out of balance, etc., take a step back into doing mind and observe the events dispassionately as they happen. Suspend the content of thinking mind; pretend the scene in front of you is a movie unfolding, and don't try to change or react to anything. Try to feel and sense what is happening moment to moment in body and mind. This is a critically important exercise, so really try to find out what's happening with anger, fear, anxiety, or other negative emotions.

Anger is our most dangerous emotion. Some physical symptoms of anger: body warmth, especially around the face; hand clenching with arms feeling like they want to move on their own; also neck and shoulder pain. Possible headache, or eyes averted from the object of anger, and an inability to speak on the one hand, and feeling compelled to verbally yell or emphasize on the other—or even physically strike out. The face hardens, taking away your smile.

There are also more subtle signals during the onset of anger, such as losing mindfulness, feeling like we are not standing on the ground (loss of gravity), not feeling like you are in your body, or claustrophobia, and thinking mind completely takes over from doing mind for survival (fight or flight).

Anger must have been an instinctual survival technique in our primitive days, but has become a self-destroying, and planet-destroying liability in modern times. We might think our body and mind are not damaged by constantly carrying anger around, but the damage is happening on a lot of levels. Anger will destroy us, set us back on the path (like a Monopoly "Go directly to jail" card), and make years of our hard work turn into nothing in an instant. To body and mind it doesn't matter if there was a good reason to be angry—the feeling is affecting our body.

Lao Two says: "Anger causes all the horror, destruction, and negative karma of humanity. I recommended a detailed study on anger."

With practice, anger will go away replaced by compassion. Anger doesn't exist on the level of doing mind or Natural Mind.

Lao Two says: "The only cure I've found for runaway negative thoughts is to ignore or discredit the inner voice of thinking mind."

Our modern-day thinking mind is defective, stuck in social conditioning, and has bad judgment—just look at how ineffective the governments of the world are. The mess we are in is complicated by angry, lonely emotions running amok. And thinking mind is at the steering wheel, habitually driving humanity off a cliff.

In prehistoric times thinking mind helped us stay paranoid and alert so a lion didn't eat us. Our anger might have kept others from trespassing on our territory or allowed us to survive by trespassing on someone else's territory in a threatening way. Thinking mind is very me-first. But our continued dependence on thinking mind's deluded decision making has messed us up. Unevolved human-monkeys still desire power and promote the delusion of 'us' against 'them' – an obviously failed system. A successful system, on the other hand, would be cooperation.

Mr. X

Lao Two says: "Breathe in in calm silence, and let go of body/mind—that's emptiness. Breathe out in calm silence, and let go of body/mind while remaining mindfully aware—that's enlightenment."

Here's a conversation Lao Two had recently—paraphrased for clarity:

X says: "What if you let go of things in meditation and you lose contact with reality?"

Lao Two says: "Not sure what you mean."

X says: "I mean psychosis."

Lao Two says: "Psychosis is loss of insight into reality, and mistakenly thinking that emptiness is all there is instead of remembering the paradox—things exist and don't exist at the same time. Or to say it in another way, empty and not empty at the same time. Sounds like you entered emptiness and freaked out. Here is a Zen koan I recently read:

Master Sekiso said, "You are at the top of a 100-foot-high pole. How will you make a step farther?" Another Zen master of ancient times said, "One who sits on top of a 100-foot pole has not quite attained highest enlightenment. Take another step forward from the top of the pole and throw one's own body into the 100,000 universes." Mumon's Commentary: "Should there be any who is able to step forward from the top of a 100-foot pole and hurl their whole body into the entire universe, this person may call himself a buddha. Nevertheless, how can one step forward from the top of a 100-foot pole? Know thyself!"

X says: "Sounds like this Mumon character is being dangerous with his words. If you try pole-jumping suicide, you are called a buddha?"

Lao Two says: "Momon (and the other masters) are saying that we have to push ourselves beyond our conceptual ordinary mind and see the world accurately, allowing ourselves to have an ego death. It's not suicide; it takes intention, fearless perseverance, and determination to climb the 100-foot pole in meditation. Then it takes everything we've got to go past that into emptiness.

"Few of us have that courage to completely let go of our 'I,' our 'identity,' to merge subject and object, and become one with nonduality. It also takes awareness of knowing the paradox that we also still continue to exist, even though we've become emptiness."

X says: "The danger I see is that people can lose touch with reality in meditation, because they forget where they are anymore, their identity gets lost. They get caught up in this ego death and loss of themselves and become psychotic. I got so confused in meditation that I lost myself and felt like I was splitting in two, didn't exist as the person I was. I injured my body and attempted suicide. I gave up meditation, because all I saw were these separations from who I used to be, and now I have psychotic episodes from which I'm recovering."

Lao Two says: "Um ... seems you are blaming meditation for your situation, and under your circumstances that's entirely understandable. On the other hand, many bipolar people have used meditation to stabilize their situation. I'm guessing you did all this without a teacher or guidebook?

"No matter how damaged we are, life is not over, or useless, unless the body has gone over to death. You can still come to understanding if you find a compassionate teacher or read about tried-and-true meditation techniques—so suicide is out of the question. There is no giving up, because karma follows us even past death. So your psychosis is also part of the illusion your thinking mind has created.

"The Buddha tried all kinds of austerities and realized that wasn't the Way—neither was his cushy life as a prince the Way to get enlightened. He eventually discovered that meditation follows the middle path; it's not a U.S. Marine training camp designed to break your spirit. No one is asking you to leave your personality behind, or give up the person you are—that's not the purpose of meditation. Even monks remain the original person they are, although they do consciously change identities (from lay, to monk)— but their personalities remain. But in meditative emptiness the context changes; the inside and outside of us is transcended to become One. It might feel like we have no body and mind because we enter into emptiness, but we never truly leave our body and mind. It's confusing to discuss, disorienting like in your case, and like driving a car for the first time; fun, exhilarating, overwhelming, and scary.

"So it's essential to still have a strong sense of self at that 100-foot stepping-off point. Ego death does not mean the loss of who we are, it means we understand that we don't have to identify with 'I' during that emptiness experience. It's fear that has captured you, not wisdom. I'm sorry to be so blunt, but sadly, you have missed the point of Enlightenment.

"Consider that the thoughts that bubble up in your mind might be wrong. I used to believe every thought that arose was true and in my best interest. But not all my thoughts were true; many thoughts were habitual and tied in with my emotions. Quite often, negative thoughts and bummers only bring us down. Do not believe those negative thoughts to be true.

"Meditation is designed to look at those thoughts, not believe those thoughts. Remember doing-mind sees things exactly as they are. Look at Buddhist (and other) masters: they did not change the way they essentially were, they changed the way they looked at the world."

Quite often people meditate without first reading books like this one, studying Buddhism (or a similar meditation-based tradition), or finding a qualified teacher. Lao Two has always been mostly fearless and willing to "let go of life," or have a "metaphorical death," if necessary, during meditation and psychedelic experiences. The people who cling to their personality have the most problems, and unfortunately turn meditation into something mentally uncomfortable—even psychotic. Again, unfortunately, this is a cultural perspective we westerners have.

Shamans see these breakthroughs differently than we do. The shamans understand that there is "the other side," and for some people in the West, entry into the other side contradicts everything they understand as reality. Since this is a book for Stoners, many of you already understand that there is more than one reality. People discovering that can become bewildered, and feel overwhelmed.

Of course there are events like a spiritual crisis; there is no reason to deny that honest introspection can bring about bummers and negativity, and can even trigger a psychotic breakdown. Does that mean we should fear what's inside of us? Everyone has stuff inside them that they would rather not look at, and stepping off the 100-foot pole is indeed scary. This is why we're writing this book, so people can know that there are cliffs they can fall off, but discovering and revealing emptiness shouldn't be misunderstood. The point is that we, our body and mind, are already in emptiness. But we are stuck in the isolating duality of self/other.

For most people a spiritual crisis is a temporary experience, part of the drug acting on us, or a momentary experience during sitting meditation. We get through it, and afterward we reflect on it; in this way we learn some insights from our "bad trip" and grow from it.

Having a community of trippers, or at least a group of friends who are tripping on the same psychedelic or discussing how their meditation is going, can be helpful. It's important to be able to ask, "During that LSD trip, did you experience a really down, bummer part after about two hours?" and have your friend say, "Yeah, I was crying like a baby for a while, but I learned a lot about myself." The same goes for having some friends who meditate, even if they are on the Internet.

When we took ayahuasca in Peru recently, the session was guided by a qualified shaman who had been taking ayahuasca since he was a young teenager. I was suffering physically from the drug interacting with my digestive system and was very body-uncomfortable. Although I had physical discomfort, I was tripping fine in my mind. Several times during the night the shaman came over and blew tobacco smoke around my body. One time he massaged the crown of my head with one finger, blowing tobacco smoke at the same time. Each time he came over, my bodily distress went away for a while and I was able to trip without digestive problems. Sadly, the next day I was so physically uncomfortable I felt I had to discontinue any more ayahuasca ceremonies—something I now regret. Lao Two had no problems and enjoyed his ayahuasca trips tremendously.

I didn't understand that I was blocked, unable to release my attention to my body. Even if it was for good reason, I might have overcome it with meditation. I also had fear that I was too old to process the chemicals in ayahuasca, and thought I might physically die if I continued. In my younger days, I would have definitely kept on.

These negative energies must be removed, ignored, and discarded. They are unreal, of our own making, and do not help us trip or meditate. It's okay to ignore and try to transcend negativity. If, in meditation, you feel like you are losing control and you fear the experience is too much—that's the time to find a teacher, or at least read some books, or if necessary, get some therapy. Unless we are confident about taking the shamanic leap into the other world, we should not try to break through. I'm not going to kid you—it takes courage.

Enlightenment

In the first paragraph of the introduction, we promised instructions for enlightenment, and here we finally are. I know it's been a tough climb through the forest of concepts, but we have been gaining elevation, learning things along the way.

Lao Two says: "What makes some people successful is their ability to employ risk, and a willingness to attempt what other people won't."

The following sets of exercises are designed to let you step through the door to the other side. The exercises are similar because people learn things differently. In some ways, this is a new type of awareness, so keep in mind the conversation between Lao Two and X. Remember the first time you smoked marijuana? That was also a new type of awareness that took some getting used to, so just enjoy the exploration.

Lao Two says: "I prefer to describe myself as someone on a spiritual path. To describe myself as an enlightened this-or-that is hubris."

Enlightenment requires concentration, emptiness, ego death (nondualism), and compassion—and lucky for us, some good weed or a psychedelic. Don't worry if you don't "achieve" enlightenment from these instructions—you should know enlightenment is just a new way to view reality. It's what we do after enlightenment that is the most important. At the very minimum, Stoner Meditation wants to show you some new possibilities that will get you high that you might not have experienced, or might have held back from because they were too freaky...

Lao Two says: "Don't get caught up in nihilism, or in lazy indifference. We have to do the work and learn how to intensely focus, and engage our awareness while in sitting meditation, where we sit and watch change happening."

"Sit and watch change happen" is good advice for both meditation and passing to the other side into enlightenment. All these detailed exercises lead to the same result—sudden enlightenment as nondual awareness (self/other as one). Lao Two and I want to share the various techniques that have worked for us.

Lao Two says: "The Buddha gave some 80,000 teachings, and never spoke a single word. To really understand teachings like the Buddha's, we have to know the other side."

Again, don't be discouraged if you don't become enlightened on the first try—it could be that our instructions suck, not you. Even if you are successful and have a sudden enlightenment experience and become aware, you will still have to continue daily meditation—there is no point at which anyone is "finished." Also, after such a breakthrough, we need to really know how the three minds work and become comfortable with emptiness. Once enlightened, we still have to carry out the garbage, clean the toilet, and live effectively and wisely. Remember, sudden enlightenment is just breaking through above tree line. There is still the rest of the mountain to climb.

Lao Two says: "If you need permission, then we give it: get as stoned as you want."

The question is how can you get enlightened anyway? Do you need to sit in meditation for a gazillion years, or have a Zen master or the Dalai Lama make you enlightened? Do you have to be a Stoner? Who is it that wakes you up to enlightenment? When the student becomes the teacher, where is the teacher?

All these types of questions don't have exact answers, because they must be answered through your own experience. And it's all right, because we are no longer analyzing what is happening. We are just "sitting and watching change happen," letting the experience happen to us without resistance. All you need is some courage and faith in yourself to open the door and walk through to the other side. Or in Stoner Meditation, let the other side join with and contain you. ... The path is to understand what reality is, because it's not what we normally think. Enlightenment can also let us release the heartfelt presence of compassion. Sometimes this will be felt as ecstatic body bliss. Pay close attention to what is happening with your body, even if it becomes invisible—meditation is not only using mind to analyze and figure out what's going on. This is one of the reasons we sit in meditation, to feel the interaction between body and mind dichotomy, and ultimately realize there is no separation. Ultimately, there are no answers, so if everything becomes mysterious, then we can accept unusual events, magical experiences, and manifesting wizardry.

It's quite useless to tell people they are already enlightened (although this is true), as we often read in meditation and Buddhist books. So how do you know when you've reached enlightenment? In Buddhism there are the famous "pointing-out instructions" given by the master to the student, sometimes called the secret word-of-mouth teachings. But guess what? The pointing-out instructions are always done after the student has already become enlightened—as a way of confirmation. We want to end all this confusion by being the ones to walk Stoners up to the door, give them the key so they can open it, and then encourage them to walk inside. To partly answer the question, though—you will know you are enlightened when you open to the world around you and feel included, expansive, visceral, alive, your thoughts and emotions surpassed, wholehearted, intuitive—and you can "sit and watch everything change." Again, the Heart Sutra describes emptiness using negatives, or, what enlightenment isn't—but it's still the best description ever.

Calm Abiding

What we are doing is sometimes called calm abiding meditation. It starts out focusing on a single point, then moves to emptiness; next we realize that there is nothing inside of us or outside of us that has independent nature, and finally that we have nothing to stand on at all except our attention (awareness). These are the stages of meditation, and of realization. Here is the progression with our metaphors:

1. Breath concentration at the nostrils to learn mindfulness. Leaving the comfortable valley and hiking through the forest trees. Monkey mind is most active here, and we are noticing what is there because we have stopped our busy lives to meditate.

2. Experiencing emptiness. Using single-point meditation and expansive presence. Breaking through, past tree line to clear view. Monkey mind has quieted enough for a breakthrough into silence for a short moment—turning down the volume on thinking mind. This is opening the door and peeking inside.

3. Experiencing enlightenment. We observe Natural Mind creating the universe. This is living meditation at tree line, active participation in view. Monkey mind has become an inner voice far in the background, with no grasping at concepts. This is walking through the door, absorbed in the other side.

4. Stabilization. This is the rest of the path up the mountain, into spaciousness. This is continuous participation from the other side. We are awakened in Natural Mind with clarity and view in the here and now—there are no interruptions, and we watch, and live life arising and manifesting naturally.

Warning: Stoner Meditation does not paint only a rosy picture; we give you information, and advice for dealing with potential negative experiences (bummers). The next bunch of exercises can make an extremely small minority of people lose their "sanity" if done wrong. Please take this warning seriously.

Remember, there is no place you can go inside your mind that you can't get back from. Hallucinations are not "real" and are temporary. The negative thoughts produced out of fear by thinking mind are not "real" and are temporary.

Keep your "sense of self," of "who you are." You were born the person you are for karmic reasons. Ego death does not mean that you really disappear, or that your mind won't work anymore. Remain aware of paradox, particularly existing and nonexisting as it applies to ordinary and nonordinary reality—we can exist and not exist at the same space-time. To say it another way, we can be stoned, tripping our head off and hallucinating, but still realize that our body is comfortably real.

Also, please remember that we are using words and concepts to describe something that can't be described using words and concepts. Our goal is to bypass, overcome, and quiet thinking mind.

We then enter nonordinary reality, using awareness of emptiness to break through to enlightenment.

If anything becomes uncomfortable, quit. Try again after you get more experience with nonordinary reality by smoking marijuana and sitting meditation.

Exercise 2: Get into your normal meditation position. First, close your eyes and take a very deep breath, then give an equally deep relaxing sigh. Then feel yourself completely relaxing your body. Next unclench your mind, unleash all your burdens, all your guilt, stress, remorse, and worries—just let them go like smoke up a chimney. Then let your identity go, as if you lost your wallet in a land where you don't know the language. Have no idea where you are; become like a seed, floating on the air released from a flower. Forget that you were born or will die; as far as you know, you are in eternity. Forget that you have X job, X partner, or X car and become like an invisible, unknown, surrendered presence. Imagine you are a just-fed infant with all your needs satisfied, open and curious. Imagine, and feel, that you have a warm blanket of love, bliss, and joy wrapped around your entire body.

Continue concentrating on breathing, but keep the breath in the background; open your eyes and let your eye attention become expansive. Relax the focus of your eyes and expand your field of vision to include peripheral vision. Sometimes I like to focus on a single point, while seeing the sides of my peripheral vision included too. You might feel this visual opening up happening as if your skull were lifting off.

Don't identify with thinking mind, let all thoughts pass by without any regard to their content at all—don't react to or ignore them. Let thoughts be neutral, like you're sitting in a car watching the scenery pass by and not being grabbed by the roadside advertising. Remind yourself that ego (thinking mind) is like the billboards on the highway, and always wants something—your attention. Ego even wants to get enlightened, imagining enlightenment to be something big. Ego can't understand emptiness, or nondualism. As far as ego's concerned, "self" is ME, what's in here, and "other" is whatever is outside there.

But we are going to turn the tables on ego. Instead of being stuck inside the confines of "self," we are going to let our presence and awareness move out of our physical body to "other". So we do this by using our eyes, then without moving, fill the whole room with our presence. You might get some visual hallucinations at this point. That's good, because we want to consider the world outside of us to be a hallucination.

Using vision, see the outside as not only surrounding you but also including you. It might help to imagine that you are made of air, and your air and the outside air are merging. It's all right if everything in vision blurs together, as long as you feel you are more than just inside your body. You should be feeling that your presence fills the room. You might feel a floating sensation with your peripheral vision open.

Next imagine yourself as if you were on the ceiling looking down at you meditating—not looking with eyes but with your presence. You might feel your third eye, or feel the top of your head tingle—these are good signs.

Lastly, expand your awareness to see everything, including your-self, as just a flow of arising aware energy moving through space-time. Remember soup? Everything inside and outside is made of different soup ingredients, yet both are contained in soup. There is no skin, mus-cles, bones, or organs right now—you are just conscious energy exist-ing as awareness. This is where fear can arise, and you might feel that in the stomach area, or as physical pain, or even skin itching. Breathe slowly, giving compassion (positive, loving feeling) to that area to relax it—then, after it relaxes, put the attention back on the breath at your nose. Then reopen your presence.

If possible, persist in this state of self and other merged as one. It's okay if it seems no thoughts arise while you are in concentrated expansive attention. After you get up, you should notice that you are in an elevated state of acute mindful awareness.

End of Exercise 2.

Exercise 2 is moving beyond the intellectual understanding of becoming enlightened to "being" absorbed into enlightenment—self and other are absorbed into each other to become doing mind. Enlightenment is not analytical understanding, it is active—a doing or being. Nothing is seen as separate, but rather it is just the action of being wherever you are, moving through time and space. In other words, you and your outside have merged into a singular world of no boundaries. Expand your senses to feel the vibes around you, and feel as if your body has energy coming out of every pore. Use Exercise 2 to bring Oneness back over and over again. Each time you should be finding it easier to expand your mind. The world outside of us and the world inside of us, are constantly changing, although mostly too slowly for us to notice. We should keep in mind that we are nothing but constant change.

Consider that the Big Bang created movement. From that central point of 'explosion' creation-stuff was thrust outward to become stars, and us. That movement is still happening as constant change, and we are a part of that drifting current. If we pay attention we can see that flow happening.

View

This is the groundwork. Our human existence has several components—the inside of us to the skin, and the outside of us that is the entire universe. We describe the universe as a flowing, luminous, loving energy. Although we like to think we are separate, we aren't. We humans are also flowing, luminous, loving energy.

We tend to keep these two "realities" separated out of misunderstanding. True reality is the seeing the merging of self/other. We have to temporarily twist our outlook to be part of the universe, instead of being disconnected from it. In the instructions that follow we will learn to put dualism aside and first become aware, then become part of the universal flow.

Lao Two says: "These exercises have an element of risk, similar to skydiving or solo backpacking in the wilderness. Stay alert—we left the valley a long time ago, but now we see a path in the trees on our trek up the mountain."

This is an advanced, complicated, free-form, yet disciplined practice. Think of this as mental and physical multitasking, keeping your attention on several things at once, like juggling while walking on a high wire.

Reminder: Enlightenment is just the first opening. It is the beginning of a longer, more aware path that has no ending. We expect that you have been doing a daily sitting meditation for a few days at least. Enlightenment is an opening up, an "aha" moment, also known as awakening, satori, kensho. Thoughts are stilled (not forced) into quiet, and wisdom arises in the profound silence where no ego exists—only presence. If the slightest distraction of ego arises (sounds, words, physical messages, thoughts) then we return to dualism.

Lao Two says: "Enlightenment requires emptiness, concentrated attention, absorption, and the courage to let go."

Exercise 3: Have your smokes ready, and keep them nearby—take a few hits. Have you ever tried to juggle? Once learned, it's fairly easy to keep several balls in the air. At the beginning, though, you're mostly learning how to get the rhythmic movements and timing necessary to make it work. Exercise 3 is a long exercise that teaches mental juggling, so try a little, take a break, retry, and continue later if you get fatigued... but since it is also like a recipe, it's helpful to read it through completely before you start cooking.

Sit in your normal meditation posture with eyes closed. Spend a few minutes in quiet breath meditation, just relaxing body and mind as discussed in Exercise 2. Continue breath concentration, and then add arising thoughts. Remember that both breath and thoughts have a cycle—arising, persisting, then fading away. After each breath or thought ends, there is a little space or pause that we call coasting, then a new breath or thought begins.

It takes a kind of split concentration to notice both breath and thought together. This is why we emphasize learning concentrated breath meditation so often, so we can use it during these highest levels of awareness. Remember, we are juggling concentration, so be ready to move awareness to different focuses at will.

Now that your attention is on thought, notice the circular flow of each thought while disregarding the content. Pretend each thought is a voice coming from a different room. You can hear the words, but since the voice is not directed toward you, it's just the sound of a human voice—in this case, it's our inner voice. By not paying attention to the thought content, we are leaving thinking mind and entering doing mind—as mind watching mind. When you are comfortable letting thoughts pass by like fluffy clouds in an expansive blue sky, move your concentration back to the breath like a searchlight focusing.

When thinking mind starts fading into the background, put complete attention on the breath. If you are stoned enough, your breath will become like an important movie, where we want to catch every detail possible. A single breath cycle can be amazingly intense when we are using concentrated focused attention. We might automatically feel the stomach rising and our chest moving in concert—this is fine, but keep the majority of attention at the nostrils. This vigorous concentration on breath without attending to thinking mind is the silence of doing mind. Doing mind is just sitting, not talking (no inner dialogue); it's observing and neutral, carefully watching the movie of breathing. Doing mind doesn't think, it acts. And in the case of doing mind that action is insight, hallucinations, wisdom and awareness. No inner dialogue is necessary because doing mind just sees "what is": it's in the flow of events as they are happening.

If you can't keep track and thoughts keep entering, try deeper, slower breathing. Most people in the West have chronic shallow breathing, so if your breath is shallow, start taking deeper, longer, slower breaths. You should start to feel relaxed immediately because more oxygen is in your bloodstream. Slowly take ten or twenty relaxing breaths until you start to feel calm and alert. Note: don't take fast in and out breaths—it will bring in too much oxygen causing dizziness.

Eyes open. You should be staring at something specific, as we discussed in the instructions for single-point breath meditation. Lao Two uses the burning ember at the tip of a stick of incense. I use a spot on the wall as my focus. Do not deviate from that focal point. It takes years of practice to become unshakable using single-point meditation. It demands that your eye not waver from that center of attention, not even allowing blinking to distract you. Don't worry too much if you can't keep focus constantly, it will come naturally over time. While keeping attention on the single point, return to breath concentration. Notice thinking mind is trying to interrupt concentration. In any case of distraction, return to the breath and just stay with it; don't be stiff, try to feel your body, your nostrils—and unclench. If you feel like starting over, fine. If not, just stay with the breath till the end of your meditation session.

Next, we'll add more conditions, or juggling balls in the air: first, primarily keep your focus on breath at nostrils, not allowing arising thoughts to distract you. Next, move your attention to your single-point focus away from breath. Give your "spot" the same attention you previously gave your breath and feel breath fading into the background. You should feel some initial exertion, but the tension in your shoulders will automatically relax; go with that relaxation. Hold your focus for a minute or two. Now it should be easy to switch back and forth from breath to single-point meditation, then focus on them together.

Next, as in Exercise 2, unfocus your visual field to accept everything to the edges of your peripheral vision. You should be still focusing on your spot, and seeing the larger picture at the same time. Everything in your vision should have an equal value—let the world become "just stuff." Again, you might feel as if your skull is lifting off your head; that's fine. Do this as long as you can.

Continue into the view of doing mind's triple focus of breath, single point, and peripheral vision. You might notice that the lighting is brighter while you're in "three-focus." You are seeing correctly, it's called luminosity.

Let go of all stimulation, do not scratch an itch or react to chills up your spine or body tension—let concentration stabilize as nothing else but the triple focus. Everything will start to take on equal value, as if everything surrounding you, and everything inside of you, is a flowing river of energy. Lao Two likes to imagine that he is facing this flow of energy like being naked in a rainstorm, feeling it hitting the skin as he moves always forward. You should be feeling a little invisible. This invisibility feeling of the equality of everything is a type of emptiness. Everything around us is constantly forming, persisting, and fading away moment by moment in space-time. Take a break and just breathe quietly without the intense triple focus. Just sit without concentrating on anything for a few moments and become a puddle of whatever's happening.

Let's take a moment to step back and try to understand why we feel invisible when we focus like that. It's because we have dropped thinking mind and are looking through the eyes of doing mind. We can see (intuitively understand) that everything existing in the universe is this invisible emptiness. Our feeling this invisibility when we are involved with intense focus closely echoes emptiness. In actuality we (and the entire universe) are illusory, void, empty of actual form, unsupported in time or space—if we are anything at all, we are only constant change. As the Heart Sutra says, "Form is emptiness, and emptiness is form." The material world is form, and at the same time everything in the material world is empty, changeable, and impermanent—absolutely nothing exists on its own, and the bigger picture connects everything. We don't get to see the connection until we get high, concentrated, and focused enough.

We are just a conglomeration of awareness or existence, clumped together as this or that body (soup). It's as if we came into existence exactly as we are right this moment; whatever happened before is just a dreamlike illusion—gone forever. The future is only potential, full of possibilities, not even guaranteed to arrive. All we have is this moment—and damn, it's already changing into the next moment ... the reality is we are "sitting and watching everything change." This would be a good time to take a couple more hits on that reefer. ...

Okay, let's go back to the triple focus on breath, single point, and expanded peripheral vision. We are moving into concentration on our body. First, notice your negative or positive emotional feelings, and any physical pain or pleasure. Try to really pay attention to anything that arises—thoughts, emotional feelings, or physical sensory input. Notice how these events are temporary; like a mosquito bite. Each perception will soon pass into having no importance at all. Label everything as neutral, without judgment, as just experience. Accept pain as a signal. Accept your inner voice saying that you screwed up big time as a signal.

Keep all your triple-focus juggling balls in the air, but now add how breath moves parts of your body. Feel your stomach, chest, and torso in rhythmic movement. Release any body tension—your legs, stomach, or the shoulders and neck. Your body should feel pleasant, calm. We just switched from being invisible to feeling our physical body. Also feel gravity pressing you down toward the floor, and feel the floor under you.

You are probably completely in your body now, and the triple focus is gone—that's okay. Stay with body concentration and after a few minutes your breath and thoughts should slow down, unless you are grasping at or controlling your breath and/or thoughts. If so, try to imagine you are a weightless cloud and let your body be, floating, just passing through the sky.

Do not count breaths. It's more important to notice the slow-motion world going on inside your body with each breath. Try to delineate the beginning and end of each breath cycle. This is where we can notice how powerful breath concentration is, because it draws us back to the present moment and often shuts down thinking mind. Continue to ignore any interruption, judgment, or message thinking mind gives you—tune it out. Your spine should be straight but not rigid, body relaxed but not drowsy.

Thinking mind does not like to be ignored and knows all our buttons. But here we are, actually taking control away from thinking mind and giving it to doing mind. Thinking mind will do everything it can to get its toy back, because thinking mind is the ultimate spoiled child.

Thinking mind has been running the factory since our birth. Now doing mind is hired as the new supervisor. The tables are turned, and instead of doing mind sleeping, its awake and thinking mind has become the employee. We have to sit thinking mind in a chair while we show it how to run the factory correctly, as we want it. We know we can't discuss these new procedures with thinking mind because it will be endless discussion—thinking-mind thrives on words, concepts, logic, and analysis. Doing-mind is action, confidence, wisdom.

Right now as the supervisor you are busy with breath, single-point and peripheral visual concentration, and feeling your body, —you are juggling four balls in the air. This is doing mind.

Intermission, Exercise 3

All of Exercise 3 so far is preliminary, so now we are coming to the essential point.

What we're describing next is the classic enlightenment emptiness experience—but since the experience is such that it's beyond words or concepts, all we can do is point you toward the view. Enlightenment is in some ways similar to having a sexual orgasm, inasmuch as it is a complete letting go, a releasing where there's no thinking about it. If anything, it's like waking up clearheaded in the morning from a deep fitful sleep filled with dreams and nightmares. Except for normal breathing and other body functions, there will be no movement—this is yet another reason we learn to calm and stabilize our body in meditation.

If we're able to teach this effectively, you will be able to open the door and step inside. Being able to stay inside (on the other side) is where the real work begins. It's one thing to walk out of the trees and cross tree line, but you can't climb up farther without learning mountain-climbing techniques (serious meditation). What I'm describing is entry to enlightenment.

We're sure we can agree that guys like Gautama Buddha are transcendental human beings who showed us by their own example the Way to experience the various levels of enlightenment. Our contention is that lots of people who use meditation and psychedelics have had the samadhi experience. They have opened the door and walked inside, but were drawn back by the life they led. Guys like the Buddha, on the other hand, spend all their time on the other side of the door, looking back at us. They are floating above the highest mountain peak.

Lao Two says: "In all of time and space there cannot be found anything that could be called 'nothing.' But emptiness can be found everywhere."

This is not describing concepts like zero, or nihilism; what Lao Two is saying is that the other side is also this side. There is no dropping off into a void; it is just the opposite: we absorb into emptiness inside of us and outside of us. The consciousness that we are using inside our brain is not ours exactly; it's more of a sharing with the greater consciousness around us. We tend to believe that every thought we think is golden, but during Exercise 3, it's just the opposite—every thought is a distraction, and the volume must be lowered so we can concentrate on what 'this' is.

No words, teaching, or philosophy can guide you. You will be "undone," if you can release your attachment, clinging and grasping at who and what you are. I'm not fully enlightened, perfect, and fully aware, but I've had a few insights from meditation and psychedelics that I would never have received from just reading or even getting personal instruction from Gautama Buddha. These have to come from letting go of ourselves, by ourselves. We are moving our awareness into silence and emptiness.

Return to Exercise 3

Find the strongest marijuana you can and get zonked. Sit in your normal meditation posture. We'll start again by taking a deep, slow in-breath, then letting it out like a big accepting sigh. Close your eyes and calmly relax into your breath. Let your body become comfortable, but try to find the natural straightness of your spine and then quit moving, letting your skeleton support your muscles and organs. You'll instinctively know when you've found the balance. Relaxed is more important than rigid.

Open your eyes. Reestablish the four focus components: breath at the nostrils, single-point focus, expanding focus to include peripheral vision, and feeling the rhythmic movements of the body.

Once you have established these fairly well, let go of all four of the focus components—not by ignoring them, but by relaxing into each, or turning down the volume on each. If you've quieted down enough, you should be able to hear and feel your heartbeat. Let your heartbeat fall far into the background with everything else. There should be no struggle or forcing, you should feel stoned and peaceful.

Whenever anything intrudes like thinking mind, body pain, noise, or sleepiness, very gently go back to breath. Breath should be your comfort focus.

Now we are going to do some games. Your breath, eyes, and entire body have no substance. Up until this moment you have believed yourself to be real, solid, with a specific storyline—but instead the truth is it has all been a constant hallucination to which you have become accustomed. In reality we are just the awareness of ourself, just stuff moving through space, where there is in reality no time. We invented time, but it has no reality—the "now" is just our position in moving space. The past is the space we've traveled through, and the future is where we will go. All the "controls" are in the here.

We have nothing to grab on to except our awareness. We can't exactly locate where this awareness is, so it's helpful to keep our focus on the breath. Thoughts might happen, body pain might happen, but they are now events happening in this particular movement through space. The outside of us is happening like this too, and there is really no up or down anymore. Let your awareness expand like a bubble around you, intuitively feeling the room you are in. Being very still is as important here, as is letting go, because we are changing how we normally think of reality.

What we are is just floating awareness. Within that floating space is silence that is not silent, and stillness that is not still. It's the changing movement of our environment that we are noticing. We thought our environment was in the metaphorical trees, but now that we accept everything in our "field" we realize that the trees limited us. We couldn't see around us, and our perspective has gotten pushed inward. Now you step out of the trees into an open area and can see with no restrictions. The visible world is life in the trees, the invisible world is the other side, where your mind opens too. You are safe here, so you can even step out of your body. ... This is a good time to take another deep breath and let out a long exhale, then be completely still. I like to hold my breath for a few moments, then let the next breath come slowly and very high, very stoney.

You should experience the flow of the space that surrounds you, always pushing you forward even if you can't feel it. You haven't noticed this before. Merge your intangible awareness with the hallucinatory world outside of you, becoming just vibration. To put it another way, let your electrical vibrations merge with the vibrating universe outside of you. If everything turns into a hallucination, you know you are on the right path.

This should be a very high place to review your body. Is there any tension, anxiety, or pain? Any of these is a reaction to fear. Courage is the opposite of fear. Let go of everything you are, except awareness.

When you are getting it right, your vision will turn luminous, like someone turned up the light on everything a little. You will also start to have a blissful body feeling, as if there were joyous energies flowing in, then erupting out through each skin pore and nerve ending. My palms sometimes feel like they are pushing energy out from my body.

Feel that you are floating through space and become completely quiet and still. Do you hear a background sound, a hum? It should sound like a continuous OM—OoooooMmm. Our vibrational presence gives off a pulsing vibration; our individuality is like a plucked string on a guitar the moment we are born. The universe also has a vibration—a different guitar string. When enlightenment is realized, the two guitar strings are played together and we have harmony—OM.

Or, if the release from 'I' is especially intense along with the opening of bliss, you might experience tears and similar emotional outbursts. Also a good sign.

But the most important part of this experience is when you feel like "you" have disappeared and become the same as outside of your body. Relax into it. Let go of who and what you are, and become just presence experiencing the flow of the river—the space surrounding you, and including you, is moving. Everything that is brought to the experience is part of it—there is nothing to distract, because even thinking mind is part of this moving through space, it's just what's happening. If you are extremely stoned, comfortable in your body, and super aware, then you have stepped through the door to the other side. The location of "you" might be gone for the moment, but there is still ongoing experience. Emptiness is filled with flowing space as awareness. Enlightenment is emptiness with this nondirected, nonclinging aware attention, and no attachment to "I"—just presence. BE-ing.

Okay, let's come down—by first paying attention to your breathing again. Feel the area at your sternum—it should have a pleasant tingle or light pressure. Experience that feeling centered in your lower chest for a while. Your entire body might be tingling, even down to your toes. Reclaim your storyline, be the human being you are, but also be the vibrational presence you are.

There is no longer dualism, there is only "who you are" moving through space. What an adventure life becomes when its just events happening, experiencing them connected to the mysterious present. Now the learning really begins because you have view. Now your every action becomes important, and you must find some ethical grounding. Use Exercise 3 often. It's especially effective and fun with rock-and-roll music by bands that are aware of nonordinary reality. I'm very fond of bands like Pink Floyd. If you use this exercise with a psychedelic, expect even higher levels of enlightenment to occur.

End of Exercise 3.

On the other hand, if your thoughts did not quiet and are still dragging you away now and then, that's because thinking mind naturally resists letting go. This should not be seen as a problem, but rather as a learning experience. If this were a book teaching tennis, would you expect to be going pro after the first lesson? If the volume (focused attention) is loud on thoughts, breath, body sensations, emotions, and grasping at ego, then you are probably just getting used to listening inside. If you get stoned and just sit there, at the mercy of your monkey mind running amok, no attention on breath for more than a few seconds, then you are just spaced out. Don't get me wrong, I think spending time being spaced out and high is absolutely a learning experience—just listening to whatever comes along and letting thinking mind go is good for everyone. But that's not the intent of this exercise. As we said in the beginning, it requires intense concentration learned through daily sitting meditation—to achieve the results we have to put in the work.

Practice, meditate, read about various techniques from other authors, lead a good life, and keep at the quest. Keep experimenting and find some methods that work for you to transcend thinking mind and experience awareness.

It took many years of meditation for me to understand what it was teaching. I didn't learn to completely let go for twenty years, but during those years, my meditation practice was sporadic. I would quit for months and then start up again, usually because life would take a nosedive and I wouldn't be able to calm myself. But even though I wasn't meditating daily, I would read books and magazines on meditation, Buddhism, philosophy, science, and psychology. For many years my thoughts screamed, finding devious ways to interrupt my attention on breathing—and sitting for more than ten minutes was unbearable at the beginning. One day, Lao Two mentioned how calming he considered his daily meditation. For me, my daily meditation was a vigorous struggle, so instead of sitting stiffly and at strict attention, trying to fight thinking mind, I let my body relax completely. I gave up the struggle and let thinking mind chatter about this and that, and put me down without the usual reaction. I noticed how good my relaxed body felt, and then did the same thing with my mind: I unclenched, and it was like letting all the water out of a dam at once. Since I wasn't giving my attention to thinking mind's content, the volume started going down. For a while thinking mind would regroup, but now panic had set in—"I'm not my thoughts!" The rug had been pulled from under my feet and I had nothing at all to stand on. It turned out that this was exactly the invisibility of body/mind that I was looking for—this knowledge and acceptance that we have nothing at all to stand on.

After some practice with not fighting between concentration at my nostrils and interruptions by thinking mind, everything got peaceful, quiet, and aware. I just succumbed to letting go and fell into emptiness. Now I can write about it, hoping my experiences might shortcut the struggle for you. Stoner Meditation has been a great path for me, a journey with amazing events along the way. It also changed my relationship with Lao Two as I was able to hear what he was saying – deeply.

At some point of having doing mind watch thinking-mind, I realized that thinking mind was giving me thoughts that were wrong. Looking deeper, I noticed thinking mind works from habitual past experience and is controlling. That's when I started completely ignoring the content of most of my thoughts. Eventually I realized that I could ignore all my thoughts when I was in meditation; then I experienced calm abiding, and discovered stepping off the 100-foot ladder into the void, where all that is left is aware presence.

I look back now understanding the role psychedelics played in this great gift. I learned how to turn the high on or off, depending on circumstances. I could work a straight job, drive a car and operate machinery, raise a family, invest in the stock market, and live completely stoned. I'm not saying that I was smoking all the time, but in the end Stoner Meditation is living with this very high knowing awareness, of moving through space and existing on several "levels." After those experiences, meditation took on a different flavor. I was able to sit more days in a row, and I increased my meditation from ten minutes to twenty, then thirty, and every once in a while an hour or two. The more years I spend in meditation, the more insights I receive.

Stoner Meditation becomes, paradoxically, stillness that is filled with activity. Being stoned is being centered, balanced, and aware amid the hustle and bustle surrounding us. This is living in doing mind, and the juggling is gone, replaced by a kind of wisdom voice inside. It's not the voice of untamed thinking mind, and honestly I'm not too sure where wisdom voice comes from. ... Sometimes I feel my whole body is one big vibrating smile.

Extra Credit: Imagine that you and everything in your immediate environment are nothing more than atoms. Inside each atom is a great deal of space, so there is more space than stuff. Everything outside is made of ever-changing, ever-moving atoms filled with space.

Now imagine that you are a single atom, and what makes up your atom is an even smaller, more microscopic world of only vibrations in the shape of infinitesimal, short vibrating strings. Each separate string is held together only by the glue of their collective vibrating energy—and the type of vibration determines what kind of atom you are. Each string is shaped differently, colored differently, and vibrating at a different tempo, all joining together to create group pulsations. Zillions of these strings make up your atom; some make up the solid, material part and others make up the separating space. So all the space between atoms now is a type of vibration. The atom's matter is vibrating, and the atom itself vibrates. We humans are just vibrations. Blur your vision and imagine disappearing into a world of vibrations.

If Exercise 3 worked for you, you should now have an intuitive understanding that ego is a fabrication and our senses and emotions are illusions. Logically, if there is no "me" and there is nothing outside of "me" except emptiness, do we end up with nothing? It can't be nothing, because something is obviously there. So we fall back on the original paradox—we exist and we don't exist, at the same time. But now we've seen the other side, and enlightenment is no longer a word—it is an experience. This nothing left is emptiness, where our eyes are the universe seeing itself—enlightenment. We are awareness, being at just this moment without past, future, or individuality— even the present moment is emptiness. Since space is constantly changing, formless, "empty," without ego, Exercise 3 should result in an experience with no reference points at all—only pure awareness.

Clear

What if you knew that the next ten breaths would be your very last breaths on Earth? After that tenth breath there would be no next one. Maybe you didn't realize the importance of breath meditation before, but now can understand just how much power this current breath has. We are always breathing our last breath—we only have this breath.

In your breath meditation, get right down into it, notice every infinitesimal moment, as if this current breath is the most valuable breath you'll ever have. Become nothing other than your breath—no thoughts, no pain/pleasure, no past/future, and nothing solid—you will have completely disappeared, except for your breath. Each new breath will feel very welcome, and we can become grateful for the cycle inside and outside of us—the magic of life itself.

If Exercise 3 was successful your body is now gone and you sit in a kind of awareness or presence, invisible. Even your thoughts have changed; your "I" is gone and your storyline needs looking at, because you are not that person anymore. You feel as if you are spirit, a ghost swimming in a kind of universe soup. Merging the inside-of-you with the outside-of-you, and there is no boundary at all, –just this present breath, existing, floating along as awareness without an existing body.

This invisibility should feel good, natural—maybe for the first time you realize Natural Mind is all you ever were. Then it can get really heavy when you consider your birth and death. ... If space is moving and I'm connected to that space right here and now by my awareness, an awareness that doesn't even seem to be localized anywhere in my body—then maybe I was awareness before I was born, since a body doesn't seem to be required. And maybe I'll be awareness when I die. Strange stuff. In essence, we've transcended birth and death.

At some point we must think about death, but too often we figure it's way in our future. But we never know just when we will be dying; perhaps it's today. In the meantime we seek pleasures and distractions to keep from thinking about our current loneliness, and eventual demise. Exercise 3 helps us face the oblivion of our body now, instead of later. We can understand the eternity beyond the boundaries of birth and death.

Your conscious self is just a tiny fraction of the presence that is really you. There is no reason to freak out; it's a realization that we are aware presence. Remind yourself that you have always existed as this paradox—we do exist as a body with a brain-sense, but we also exist as the other side. We are so much more than just a body.

Enlightenment is not something that we intellectually understand— it is something we are. Again, paraphrasing from the Heart Sutra: in Natural Mind there is no body, senses, emotions, thinking mind, or doing mind—there is only neutral, observing awareness as Natural Mind. Everything is illusion, even birth, sickness, and death. It is a paradox that there is dualism, because all possible manifestations are experienced in the oneness of the here-now. If nothing else, remember that we are of the Earth, and Earth created us.

Some other names for enlightenment are: calm abiding, no-mind, *satori, jhanas, shamatha, bodhi*. I'm sure those enlightened humans of prehistory, the wizards and shamans, had their own names.

Let's see if we can clear up any remaining confusion. We exist in an electrically charged body, which is a kind of floating mass of extremely complex energies that began at our birth. At that birth moment, our body was pure enough to exist as Natural Mind because our thinking mind was undeveloped. As infants we used only doing mind as our learning tool. With socialization, mechanical and verbal skills, and as a defense mechanism, thinking mind was created. Eventually our

Natural Mind was pushed far into the background and became foreign to us. Our oneness became ego-labels where everything—stereo, chair, ocean—has a name. As we were growing up we also learned about dissatisfaction, so we seek constant pleasures, trusting our emotions and passions because we have grown to see these as solid, reliable, and real. Yet deep down we feel unfulfilled dissatisfaction (*dukkha*) and physical pain (is your neck tight right now?) because we are disconnected from feeling our body. Most people say they do feel connected to their body, but unless they meditate or get stoned, that's really not true. For example, examine how you drink water—do you even taste it, feel the temperature and the sensual nature of water, and feel it all the way from your lips to your stomach?

Some of us were lucky and found that marijuana opens up doing mind again. Mostly we didn't understand what was happening, we just enjoyed the feeling of openness. Maybe marijuana made you realize that all dysfunctional relationships, and anger, angst, pain, and negative emotions are just signals—but probably you just didn't know that thinking mind likes to focus on those issues.

If you want to change the world around you, be the lit match that lights a candle for other people. You don't have to say anything special, just your presence can be a light at the end of the tunnel for a suffering friend. If you smoke marijuana, you will naturally develop love, awareness, compassion. When the volume on thinking mind negativity is turned down, we can experience what our body is really feeling, and you will come to know that all negativity bummers are illusions.

Indra's Net is the ancient Hindu archetypal metaphor of Natural Mind. It describes each of us pictured as a large reflecting diamond, connected at a position on an intersecting multidimensional net to an infinite number of other reflecting diamonds. Each of us, as a diamond, is the exact center of the net, reflecting all the other diamonds, like a vast spider's web.

Indra's Net is a very common hallucination for Stoners while on LSD. I hope you get an opportunity to encounter that hallucination - it's very high. Even as just an archetypal insight, it is an accurate description of enlightenment where ego has gone and all that is left is a pure, transparent diamond of awareness.

We've learned that the breath, heartbeat, and thinking mind do not need to be controlled. The only solution is to transcend the inner noise, letting it all drift by like clouds in the sky. We now understand that we are not separated from the outside world, and it's our attachment and clinging to our ego image of a separated "self" from "other" that causes our suffering and bummers. We can also understand that one of our goals is to keep our strong sense of self, so when we merge inside with outside, we can do so fearlessly, knowing that we still are what we are. We have experienced that we are not fully our body, and our thinking mind is filled with illusions. When we let go of grasping at each and every thought, we can accept whatever comes our way.

When someone yells at you, you can realize that it's him or her who is suffering, not you. It actually might have absolutely nothing to do with you; you just happen to be there, that's all. If you do not react to the emotional content of their outburst, you can step back into doing mind and realize that their anger is coming from their dualistic view of the universe. They believe the erroneous assumption of me and you, us and them and probably stuck on being right at all costs. They also don't know that they are stuck in the irrationality of thinking mind. We can now see their angry bummers without reacting to them. Suddenly life becomes the miracle it is—we get it. This is the arising of compassion.

Once we start to understand that almost everyone is suffering from their run-away emotions, we can instantly change our own vibes. Our wizard power is that we don't get sucked into their negativity, but instead keep our own vibe positive. This is part of having a strong sense of self. Since their distorted energy doesn't amplify in the way they expected (they didn't make you angry), it doesn't have the effect their emotions wanted. They immediately have to step back and question their situation again. It can be staggering, magical, and even breathtaking. It's like they threw a ball of fire at us, but instead of catching it like we used to, we just step aside and let it pass us by. How can we take it personally, when anger is illusory, nothing solid, just temporary passing emotions?

And yet, all our problems are not solved. The pain and suffering in the world still exist in a very real way. Your boss will have problems, your lover will have problems, and you will have problems. But when we see them from a higher perspective, we discover that these painful experiences are our teachers.

Lao Two says: "There is no enlightenment without intimately knowing and feeling heartfelt presence. The vibration that holds all of this together is love."

Wherever you are is the center of the universe, and the world around you is your mirror. How you react to your immediate environment creates your karma—if you send anger to your universe, the mirror will be sure to return anger—instant karma, or down-the-road. Karma becomes very immediate when we get stoned; it's almost like we can see cause and effect happening in real time.

Lao Two says: "Why does the universe exist at all? For its own reasons."

For a moment, see yourself as a pie chart. Your body is 50 percent, and your thinking mind and doing mind are 25 percent each. The room containing the pie chart is enlightenment, and the entire universe surrounding and including everything is nirvana.

To paraphrase the Four Noble Truths of Gautama Buddha: We are "not fully human" in dualism, because we reduce everything to judgmental opposites and disregard the human condition of impermanence. We ignore suffering by distracting ourselves with pleasures, but ultimately even the transitory nature of happiness is unsatisfactory, causing suffering (#1 and #2). When we realize that the separation between self and other doesn't exist, we give up our craving, attachment, and grasping—this acceptance is enlightenment (#3). Living in the activity of enlightenment is being "fully human." In the Buddhist model, this 'activity of enlightenment' is the Eightfold Path. But for secularists, most ethical philosophies like nonharm, intent, intuitive moral principles, logic, reason, and wisdom in each moment, are fine (#4).

Gestalt with Mind

Lao Two first heard about the concept of gestalt (synergy) in a no-credit night class led by Stephen Gaskin at San Francisco State University. The class was titled "North American White Witchcraft," which as it turned out, was more about psychedelics than about witchcraft. Gaskin went on to become one of the great psychedelic San Francisco gurus in the late 1960s, eventually teaching the "Monday Night Class". In 1970, he and many of his followers moved to The Farm, a huge thousand-acre commune in Tennessee. Lao Two didn't go with them, he stayed in San Francisco.

Gestalt is a German word meaning, seeing the whole as more than the sum of its parts. For example, the combined efforts of many individual instruments playing collectively produces a shared orchestrated sound. In Stoner Meditation, this Gestalt with Mind passes through thinking mind like lightning, moving instantly into doing mind—it's a mind-blowing, breathtaking, expansive "something" we can do, once we know how it works.

Those who have taken LSD or smoked marijuana for a long period of time are aware that we humans are much more than the sum of our individual parts. But we need to also understand that there are still more potential energies in us that are hidden.

Looking out the window of our eyes, we see a somewhat circular/elliptic field that stretches from our focus out to the peripheral vision. The entirety of that field is Gestalt with Mind. As I understand this (from the perspective of Stoner Meditation), we see the entirety first, and then bring our focus toward a specific object or objects. Our brain then filters out whatever isn't necessary for that moment's visual perception, and then the brain interprets—often filling in parts here and there. This is like seeing a stick on the ground, but the brain sees it as a snake until we focus clearly, realizing it is only a stick—labeling it.

To put it another way, we continually see the entire field. But we think all we see is what we're focusing on. We are seeing both, and more – using thinking mind to focus, while doing mind is seeing the entire peripheral field.

And both together are Gestalt with Mind, and the peripheral field never goes away, even if we aren't concentrating on it. In other words, even though we are focusing with our eyes, our awareness is informed of everything in our field – we see more than we think we see.

And after we learn Gestalt with Mind, we can take it further yet to the wizard realm. If we can loosen ego's grasp on how we color our world, we can have a transcendental realization (enlightenment) that encompasses the entire universe. Here's how it can work, for example if I'm looking for a friend in a crowd, I first relax my mind and let my vision take in the whole group of people. Somehow in the expansive movement my mind will automatically focus on my friend after a few moments. This "aha" moment is also common inside conscious mind as we take a shortcut from logical thinking and suddenly grasp and transcend right to the essential point. Many of us do this by letting the mind seemingly work on its own to solve a complicated problem. A common trick is to think of the problem before going to sleep, waking up with the answer.

Years ago Lao Two had the uncanny ability to find lost objects. He would go into a stranger's house and wander around, taking in the whole, only now and then looking at specific objects. Then he would let the object find him. I have no idea how he did it, but I have to attribute some of this magical skill to all the LSD he was taking at the time. Sometimes I can do this using this same mysterious Gestalt with Mind technique. Try it.

Gestalt with Mind has another important aspect called figure-ground. We can learn how to switch back and forth from focus to expanse—or from figure to ground (background) and ground back to figure. This gives us the ability to see more than the individual parts, and see patterns of the whole. Other senses do the same thing, like our ear sense focusing in on the brass section during a classical music performance. The rest of the orchestra is still playing, but we have simply amplified our focus on the brass, or even an individual flute. Also, consider the complexity of taste when we eat elaborately spiced food, tasting one spice and then switching to a different specific flavor, or to tasting the food in its entirety. All our senses, and especially our consciousness, use Gestalt with Mind. This is the ability to exchange figure-ground perception, but we want to push this further into expanded consciousness.

Optical illusions are typical examples of figure-ground where we can shift between two ascertained objects, twisting our vision into something inexplicably greater. Remember awareness, emotions, and our actions are all connected with the storyline and judgments of thinking mind trying to make sense of all the input from our senses. Doing mind, on the other hand, just perceives, feels, or does stuff.

Lao Two says: "What we fear is silence. Part of meditation practice is preparation for silence."

We choose what we want to focus on, and our thinking mind perception moves through the complexity by labeling everything. But we can take that focus up to the next level, when we arrive at mind-watching-mind (doing mind), and that's our shift between the figure and ground. Our goal has always been to push into Natural Mind, where perception exceeds the definitions of figure and ground. Then we are in the state of awareness that is not conceptualizing, not labeling, just naked perceiving.

Exercise 4: Here's an advanced (esoteric) guide on how to shift into Gestalt with Mind. To be honest, being stoned works better at first, but after this is learned it can be done naturally. We are going to use the ocean as our example, but a large forest of trees or sweeping growths of tall grass flowing in the wind are also excellent vehicles for learning Gestalt with Mind. We will be using the terms "figure" and "ground" to move back and forth between focus and expansive peripheral visual perception—and "Gestalt with Mind" when we transcend those both. Remember, figure is like the words on this page, and ground is like the white paper that is behind the words, and also surrounds them. Whereas Gestalt with Mind is everything surrounding the book, and including the book.

It's best to use an ocean, lake, or river, but this visualization can also be done taking a bath. Find a comfortable position that's physically relaxed, and a meditative state of mind. Lao Two prefers doing this exercise outside, in his sitting meditation posture. You can intellectually read this, but to make Gestalt with Mind work, head out to the ocean and physically experience the process.

Sit on an elevated beach overlooking the ocean. With eyes open, pick one small spot where you can watch individual ocean waves form (figure). Keep your vision just above where the waves are crashing on the beach, not far off toward the horizon. It's important that your eyes stay focused on one spot. Notice the ascending, duration, and falling aspects of a specific wave as it comes and goes. Ignore the surrounding ground for now. Open your senses, like the inner ear listening to the sound of your breath only (figure). Continue watching that small focused area, and listening, until your breath is slow and deep. Continue for as long as it's comfortable, or until your eyes start darting here and there. This is a very easygoing exercise, no stress, hurry, or figuring anything out. ...

Now, letting go of the focus (figure), see the larger ocean area (ground) and expand that out to your entire peripheral vision. You will notice the change of colors at the horizon where blue sky meets green-gray ocean. Notice any ships and clouds. Again open up your senses to listen to your breathing, but add the ocean crashing on the shore, the wind in your ears, feeling the breeze on your skin, and body temperature warm or cool, ... You might feel a pleasant tingling around your forehead as you fill expanded perception. Keep your head and body still so the scene doesn't shift, and try not to focus specifically. Feeling spaced out is a good thing. Without moving, notice everything in the visual field, but keep the broad focus on the totality of the scene. Stay aware of the breath.

Your focus has to be somewhere, so find your original focus spot where you watched the individual wave, but don't microscope it. We want to stay aware of how eye focus (figure) can be a little more generalized and larger than the intense focal point first described above. But now we have also added staying aware of the entire scene (ground). You might notice your eyes darting here and there after a while; don't worry about this at all. So now we've got both field and ground.

By not listening to any inner-voice comments or labeling, we can really start to relax. Feel any tension in your body and just puddle out. Lying down with your head elevated is cool too. ... This exercise only visually looks outside our body, so we can really loosen up everything else.

Specifically; To move perception into Gestalt with Mind, we have to first put our focus on the whole of the ocean, and put the sky, the beach, and the white waves crashing onshore into the background. There should be only a band of the full ocean in your primary field focus.

The tops of the waves should start to move as a rhythmic group, all contained in the circle of your visual perception. Hold your attention on this converging dance, and see the individual waves join together, rhythmically as a whole. Did you ever notice the waves synchronizing before? Keep your breath relaxed and calm, and try to not make the slightest movement with your head.

Lastly, bring together both figure and ground in your vision, being aware of as much as possible while still letting the rhythm of the waves happen. Include boats, clouds, sun, shadows, white foam on the beach, etc., not leaving out any details—all seen as happening within the whole. If you focus darts around at this point, that's all right, because the darting should be seen as included in the ground. If you are seeing all the movement as one unfolding event, you have moved into Gestalt with Mind.

Extra Credit: Stay aware of the synchronous waves, and the background (focus and peripheral) that includes and surrounds everything you see. Let's add our body to the mix of Gestalt with Mind. Keep your eyes steady. Feel the sitting on the Earth; feel the line between what is you and what is beach supporting you—there might be tingling in the muscles that you didn't notice before. Feel your breath moving your chest and stomach, but your eyes stay fixed, and yet expansive. You might notice some muscles relaxing on their own. Completely ignore any anxiety, just groove on being in nature.

While being aware of your body sitting there, let yourself "disappear," becoming a part of the surrounding area. Become an animal connected to nature. You are not separate from the beach; your presence right now is like a vibrating mass. Not only that, but your awareness stretches like a huge electric-vibrating bubble to the surrounding horizons. Perhaps you will now have the ultimate breakthrough where you will see with 360-degree vision, especially if you are on a psychedelic. This seeing completely around you, as if you had eyes that circled your skull is a valid experience. Hang loose and remember you exist, on the one hand, and are of the beach experiencing Gestalt with Mind, on the other.

Next, consider your vibrating essence of body/mind the field, and everything outside of you, ground. Your eyes are the connection between the inside and outside. Now experience letting go of who you are and merging with the ground—both you and the outside-of-you becoming Gestalt with Mind. What was you is now included in the surrounding area. This is the point when the flow of the crashing waves on the beach (taken together, as an orchestrated group) might synchronize with your breath. The sound of the waves, synchronized with breath, might become the sound of OM.

If everything is working as it should, there isn't much left of you except what's passing by outside, and a very nebulous feeling of existence remaining inside. If, at this point, you can just be view, or be the perceiver, you will find your awareness floating along in space-time from moment to moment. Your awareness will feel like it is centered just above your skull, but it will be seeing arising mind. This is where Gestalt with Mind will subtract the unnecessary—your body will not be sending signals, and the outside vision will become simply a group of images, nothing specific, while the rhythmic waves seem to mysteriously hold the visual attention. Your higher mind will reach out to become part of the surrounding everything. Everything you see might be luminous, foreign, otherworldly but still within recognition.

Let yourself be the rhythm of the waves.

There is a higher point where you will completely let go of your ego, forget about the past and future, ignore directions like up and down, and become absolutely nothing else but awareness. If you can achieve this level, don't do what I did: I started debating this amazing way of viewing the world—am I going nuts, or is this enlightenment? So I dropped back down into consciousness and let it all fade away. If you are able to reach this awareness, just relax for a while and groove.

To return from all of this, place your attention on your breath. Close your eyes and take deeper breaths. Feel your breath at your nostril, feel your body, move and stretch. You should be feeling very sensual, and probably have developed the munchies.

End of Exercise 4.

Lao Two says: "Mind once seen, is realized forever—Gestalt with Mind."

See Things Exactly As They Are

Lao Two says: "I've searched inside for anything that would be 'me' or 'I' and have found nothing solid, substantial, continuous, or what could reliably be pointed to as 'myself.'"

Every person we meet, everything we own, and every thought we think needs to be seen exactly as they are—temporary, without form. When we color an experience with our judgments or our habitual way of seeing, we are not IN the experience. When we fall in love, we idealize the person and don't see any of their imperfections, but after a few years their faults become evident. That's when we either are repulsed by their bad habits or continue to love them for their faults too. After all, we are all imperfect beings, in an imperfect world—the universe is the way it is.

Zen Master Shunryu Suzuki Roshi said: "You're perfect just as you are, and you could use a little improvement."

At the end of morning meditation, Zen masters give a daily talk. Sometimes the teaching is quite comprehensive and detailed, other times extremely short, or even silence—after all, there is no need to say anything if you have nothing to say. The monks and lay students sit on the floor cushions waiting, and then the master walks in, takes his seat in meditation position, and speaks. There is a story going around about Suzuki Roshi that goes something like this: he took his seat and said only, "Life is basically impossible." He sat for a while in silence, then he got up and left. He was asked the next teaching, "Yesterday you said that life is basically impossible. What are we going to do?" The master replied, "You do it. Every day."

Most bummers come from our inner anger and dissatisfaction with the world around us (*dukkha*). It's almost impossible to find our hidden-away anger buried deep in our memories, but we all know that anger is more than willing to arise—then, boom. Really, our only hope is to become self-aware so we can put out the burning fuse of anger before it explodes.

What Stoner hasn't looked at the complexity and beauty of a fallen leaf, a puddle of rainwater, or the clouds floating overhead above us? Simple, hidden events that would have gone unnoticed if not for our being stoned. The impossibility of life is countered by the living of each moment, and finding the ecstasy there. The miracle is available only if we show up for life, instead of mindlessly watching time pass us by.

Our six body/mind senses are: taste, touch, smell, vision, hearing, and conscious mind. Now we have a seventh sense—the ability to include everything in Natural Mind, emptiness, and Gestalt with Mind. These are not separate, they are One, but Stoner Meditation has broken them down individually.

When negativity rises, we can change it instead of being taken for a negative loop. When a thought says, *Man, that was so lame, you never get anything right,* we can ignore it, or counter with something like, *At least I tried, and it's okay to not succeed every time.* Don't let negative mind get away with it—argue if you have to and change it to positivity, or at least neutral. You might be thinking; *I don't want to lead a constantly happy, blissful, not-connected, passionless life.* We're not teaching that. Not letting negativity rule won't stunt your feelings or dull your experiences—just the opposite, you will be able to open up your mind, body, and awareness to higher experiences.

Zen Master Sesso warned: "There is little to choose between a person lying in the ditch heavily drunk on rice liquor, and a person heavily drunk on their own 'enlightenment'!"

Getting enlightened can be a little like learning karate. You've become proficient at a few moves and assume you can kick everyone's ass. Then a short, skinny person is chosen as your new sparring partner, and they kick your ass. We are all students, we are all teachers—never show off or assume!

Simply because we have high experiences on our path and we put some label on it (enlightenment) doesn't mean that our friends and family want to be hit over the head with our enchanted elation. For one thing, every experience we have is temporary—if you keep trying to duplicate an experience, you are carrying extra baggage. Any experience you are trying to duplicate is a barrier to moving forward.

We are presenting exercises, but each time you do an exercise it will be different and you will be transported differently. The train ride of meditation, and the supersonic jet of LSD go where they want, not where we want.

All the concepts and levels that we've been describing are ultimately meaningless. We're drawing a map so you can follow directions. Once you are at your destination, throw the map away.

Lao Two says: "If I don't feel negativity, and I'm noticing that my meditation is giving me more wisdom and love in my life, then I know I'm on the correct path."

There's no reason to get jaded and start "teaching" all your friends what you've discovered—always let your wisdom become known naturally, as it pertains to the moment. Everything in Stoner Meditation is just the very beginning—these are just a few mental/physical "tricks'" that we've come across in our short lives. Can you imagine the secret teachings of spiritual groups like the Tantric Tibetan Buddhists that they have developed after a century of intense meditation?

Even after enlightenment, we still carry negative habits and have to work to change. We now have to make careful ethical choices, because our vibrations have more effect on those around us. A danger is that once enlightenment is tasted it is never forgotten, and we want to talk about it. Unless you have friends on the same trip, I recommend you keep your enlightenment close in your heart of hearts, only giving up your wisdom when asked.

And remember, the fact that we use the word "high" is not accidental—it means we have that much farther to fall. Being in a very high place can become evil if love and compassion are not there. We've all heard of famous religious leaders who turn out to be incredible jerks—because of their bad habits, lack of control, or just plain greed. The idea is to develop strong principles and ethics so that we can avoid sticky karma. Our path is awareness, compassion, peace, and service to both others and ourselves. This is also called developing social awareness.

Lao Two says: "After we realize that we can let go of who we are and start paying close attention to each moment, life becomes the anticipation of whatever-happens-next."

Milky Way

Lao Two says: "Part of Stoner Meditation practice is preparation for silence. Silence is probably not what you think it is."

Once again we are leaping off of the 100-foot pole. ... This builds on the previous exercises, and is Lao Two's favorite. He says it works best "incredibly stoned."

Kahlil Gibran said: "And forget not that the earth delights to feel your bare feet, and the winds long to play with your hair."

Exercise 5: We find this is best done outside during a warm, calm, dark, starry, moonless night in a solitary location. Choose a place where you can stand and walk without interruptions or obstructions. Barefoot is best; and if possible being completely naked. It's important to con-sciously keep relaxing more and more, releasing tension and anxiety. Keep your body feeling very loose and comfortable. You might want to start with Exercise 1 to get into the mood. Note: anytime any of Exercise 5 gets uncomfortable, take some deep breaths and feel them inside your body. Then move your body around again like Exercise 1, coming back down to Earth. ...

Eyes closed. Lao Two and I always start with palms together at the sternum (breastbone), fingers pointing upward. Standing very still arch your back a little, and lift your head upward also a little. Release any tension in your neck and shoulders, and breathe slowly. When you are ready to start, put your concentration on your breathing for at least ten slow breaths so you feel connected and comfortable with your concen-tration. Your body should feel as if you have no bones, like you are sus-pended and supported by the surrounding air. Rub your palms together vigorously for a half minute. Pull your hands apart about four inches, bending the tips of your fingers, and either feel, or imagine, a built-up energy flowing outward from each palm. Feel this energy also at the tips of your fingers, and notice how it is flowing upward, away from your fingers toward the sky. Put your arms down at your sides, but keep feeling this energy from your fingertips, and imagine the discharging energy is going into the Earth. Feel the soles (souls) of your feet where you are standing.

Open your eyes, let breath go normally in the background. Now start walking slowly, keeping your eyes toward the horizon, not down at your feet. Choose an area directly ahead of you to focus on using the single-point method. After a few steps your head should be more open, both visually and mentally. Put your attention to your bare feet meeting the ground. Feel the texture of what you are stepping on and consider what you are walking on.

Add to your attention all sounds, lights, skin receptors, inner feel-ings, emotions, and subtle energies (psychedelic experiences). If you're not naked, try to feel the layer of clothing against your skin as you move. Remember that your physical body is always naked under clothing. Notice your breathing and thinking mind's thoughts, as if you were on the meditation cushion. But in this exercise, don't stress if thoughts won't quiet; it doesn't matter now.

The purpose of this exercise is being an entire orchestra: your breathing is the drum that keeps a steady rhythm, while all the other elements are various other instruments that all play with equal harmonized volume, intensity, and importance. At this point try to have your footsteps synchronize with the rhythm of your breath, even if you have to walk slower or faster. Without moving your eyes off the horizon, use your peripheral vision to take in as much as possible, all the while noticing the elements of the orchestra.

Those of you trying this exercise straight should slow the breath as much as possible, making all body movements into an ultra slow-motion movie. You want to exaggerate the slowness, using intense attention. Use microscopically precise concentration for each breath, body movement, input, and even the strain of moving so slowly. See if you can develop an orchestrated rhythm to connect, relax, and coordinate body/mind. Remember, the breath cycle is: in breath, short pause, exhale, and long coasting to the next breath.

Let your eyes fill with the whole sky, so include your peripheral vision—in other words, open your mind and space out. Notice how the stars twinkle, and see clouds moving across the sky, lit underneath by city lights. If in the country where it's dark enough, see our Milky Way galaxy yawning above. Notice the size of your body in comparison to the galaxy. A minute ago you were filled-up tall, and with one concept you realize how small your body really is. Be both amazed and grateful that you are walking on the Earth with your miracle pair of eyes. Now, opening to the peripheral, see the sky as a whole.

Since we've opened to the peripheral, let's now imagine that our body has become invisible, and everything we are doing, feeling, and experiencing is a hallucination. Your presence can be any size or shape you want, so explore limitless imagination—make yourself into a fifty-foot monster walking on the Earth for the first visit. Move your naked body like the monster would be moving. You just landed in this very strange neighborhood and stepped out of your spaceship. Your monster is open for everything, ready for anything, alert. Have fun with it, be silly.

Stop walking—come on back into your body. Open your legs a little for stability and drop your arms at your sides. Stand completely still and as balanced as you can, keeping your eye focus toward the horizon. Feel your feet pressing on the ground. Next, bring your focus toward your sternum; it should have a peaceful feeling. You feel it gently moving with your breath. Enjoy the pleasant feeling, keeping your concentration centered, as if the sternum is the dividing line that perfectly balances the upper and lower parts of your body. At that midpoint imagine an infinitely small, whirling ball of love. Your skin might begin to tingle at this moment. Each breath makes the whirling ball slow down on the out-breath and coast, and speed up on the in-breath.

Next let's go in the opposite direction. Expanding the small whirling ball inside your chest, fill your whole body with whirling ball presence. Then push the whirling ball outside to fill the area you are standing in. Give it a push on the out-breath and let it return on the in-breath. Lastly, take that whirling ball out to the horizon, including the farthest stars, from where you stand. The whirling ball of love is a signal to the stars that you send your love out to the universe on the out-breath. And as a conduit for universal energy passing through you, back to the Earth down through your feet, on the returning in-breath. Use your concentrated awareness, seeing, feeling, and reacting to everything equally. Instead of being your human size, become limitless, and let your presence dissolve into space—just vibrating, moving presence. You might feel physical bliss surrounding your entire body. Don't resist bliss, let it go wherever it wants. Hold this process as long as you enjoy it.

Whenever you want you can relax, take a smoke break, whatever moves you. ... At this point Lao Two likes to raise his arms and tense all his body muscles for a few moments. He tightens his fingertips, moving each shoulder up and down, letting his body move him wherever it wants.

He says the whirling ball exercise brings out his passionate feelings, and reconnects him with his human energy. He calls this "embracing the stars." It also reconnects him physically to Mom Earth. After all, the marijuana we smoke and the psychedelics we consume come from her.

The reach of our imagination is not limited by the confines of the human body. Even if you can't feel physical bliss or psychedelic hallucinations, your imagination can extend to the stars.

Extra Credit: Walk around very slowly any way you like, but keep your attention on your rhythm a little. Feel the naked soles of your feet, and the body weight they support, as they lift up and set down again. Try to feel what is happening on deeper levels, extending your senses to subtle energy. As you plant each step, you pass your personal vibration to Earth. Immediately Earth responds, sending energy back into your body. As you lift your foot, your combined energy flows up that side of your spine, to explode out of the top of your head to the stars above. If you can't feel it happening, at least try to imagine it. ... We feel it's very important to get in touch with Earth, giving all your attention to the feeling underneath each step. You should feel very euphoric doing this.

Now completely stop moving and stand up straight. While concentrating on everything around you, eyes open, take twenty-one slow, concentrated breaths. Then smile a smile that goes all the way from your feet up to the stars. Feel the whirling ball at your sternum again as love. This is a good time to let it all go. Become a human monkey—move, weave, or dance—your steps celebrating your existence on Earth. Think of the air as dense, heavy against you as you move. It doesn't matter if there is a breeze or not, because the air is our human water, we swim in it. Remember Lao Two's soup? Try to feel everything happening around you, and in you, as flowing in this heavy-air soup. You are the observer. Connect with any insights coming into your mind right now; at this high place you understand things intuitively, such as your presence is made out of the stars above, the Earth floating in space soup. ... Allow your presence to become this flow within the surrounding horizon, your energy going down into the Earth and up to the stars. You are moving through space-time, no past or future, standing on a floating, spinning and moving Earth—absorbed in the movement. Your skull might feel as if it were opening up (not literally).

You can invent lots of trippy mind games in this awareness. You can also enjoy this headspace, and heart-space at musical events. We are hoping that you just stepped "outside" your body into the surrounding Natural Mind—and enjoyed it. It turns out our attention on heart vibrations opens a new way of seeing ourselves. Eventually we can expand our consciousness like this wherever we are, and our good vibes affect those around us. No matter what happens, the silence of Natural Mind is there. The whirling ball of love is still spinning inside—this is heart-felt presence.

End of Exercise 5.

Love is the most radical concept that can be introduced to our world. Most of the people who have historically, openly promoted love got killed off—Jesus, Gandhi, Martin Luther King, even John Lennon. But if we take psychedelics, we can personally experience what love is. The truth is if you really get to know all the types of vibrations, you'll find the most powerful of all is love. Continue your concentration at the sternum area and you'll be surprised at what you find.

Lao Two says: "Unfortunately, our concept of love is mostly limited to the romantic feeling. I'm describing love as a tactile, underlying, ubiquitous, ever-creating vibration. I'm saying that love was the vibration that exploded the Big Bang and continues unabated. At the highest level, we exist as love consciousness, which is more intense and clear than all other vibrations. Love is the mind-blowing, intensely blissfully powerful vibration we enter into at body death."

Shamanic World

Lao Two says: "Participate in life with compassion, wisdom, and joy."

After smoking marijuana for a while, and especially after taking psychedelics, you might start to experience a transcendent, magical, spontaneous, blissful state of existence. You will have opened your mind and heart to a peculiar familiarity with higher mind. You will start to see through people's facial makeup, their falsity, and their games. You are seeing the world as it really is, and it's not always pretty. This can make you very vulnerable. What you thought was true before has turned out to be much different now.

You are caught between two worlds. Only a few of us will accept the call of the shamanic world, where we reside in that higher mind comfortably most of the time. Most of us will freeze when we enter, because it's powerful, strange, and beyond what we are familiar with. To return to the mountain metaphor—it's one thing to walk through the forest trees, but once past tree line, we are offered membership in the shaman's world. Gender makes no difference, but not everyone is cut out to be a shaman. And to choose the shamanic world is to pass on climbing much farther up the rest of the mountain, skipping the peak.

Lots of people quit taking psychedelics at this point and curtail their marijuana use, choosing to remain in the straight world and head all the way back to the valley. Don't worry, there are a sizeable number of people working in the straight world who have passed tree line. Not everyone who has taken a lot of LSD remains in the shamanic world. Actually, most people just go on with their lives. Good lives.

It's fine to remain in the straight world. Psychedelics are not for everybody, and quitting smoking or taking psychedelics is nothing to feel bad about. There should never be any peer pressure or judgments from anybody—and nobody should ever dose another person (give them a drug without their knowledge). We keep saying: make your own rules, don't be influenced, stand on your own two feet, make your own life decisions.

But even if you quit getting stoned, keep meditating—that's where the real power is. The mountain can be climbed by meditation alone. And meditation is stable like a train on tracks, instead of the rocket of psychedelics. ...

Basically we've been telling you to let your mind and body float away. Damn scary stuff. It's not for the timid, and some people aren't interested in a spiritual quest. No amount of magical psychedelic or mellow marijuana insights will want them to become a buddha or a shaman. No matter how hard we try, anyway, we probably won't become as advanced as Gautama Buddha was—it took dedication few of us have. The real gift we are receiving is setting out on the path in the first place. And although we discussed attainment, and a destination—it's really the path that is the destination. It's not a competition to see who gets "there" first; the path is a journey we are already on, since being born in a human body.

If some of you prefer these amazingly high places in Stoner Meditation, then welcome. Leave your fears behind, walk your path with confidence, and be very clear about your intentions. Practice concentration, emptiness, compassion, and love. You won't have to seek out experience; on the shamanic path, the universe gives you experience. When you get up in the morning, step into your shoes, fill your body with your aware presence – nothing else needed. Use your imagination, intuition, and wisdom. What I do is head out into the world pretending I'm a famous actor, known for my improvisation. I'm changeable, adaptable, and alert—that way, when I step through the door I'm pre-pared for whatever comes. The door of life that I walk through in the normal world is also one of the doors to the shamanic other side.

Lao Two says: "No one can judge you. Enlightenment is action. Meditation is not passive, it is presence. BE."

When you get a point where you have to decide about anything, I recommend taking some risk and going for your dream—get out of your comfort zone. After you start, the negative inner voice will inexplicably tell you that you can't do it. Don't believe it. Fight for your future by believing in yourself—fight against the negative inner voice. Stay in the present and be mindful.

If you have a dream, take steps to make it happen. For example, if you want a college degree, you know it takes four or five years. Start now, and four or five years from now you will have a college degree. Maybe it will take longer if you have to work at the same time you attend college, but live your dream. No one can judge you. You don't have to apologize for your path.

Lao Two had roommates who were going to UC Berkeley. All were nerdy, brilliant, bookish, and painfully shy. One was in a doctorate program and writing his thesis. One night he came into Lao Two's room and tried marijuana for the first time. As they were talking, he said how unhappy he was with his life choice and wondered if he had made the right decisions. He discussed his parents' expectations and how they were so strict with him. Lao Two asked him what he thought would be a cool job to work at just for fun, something he secretly wished he could do. The roommate said he always admired a bartender's ability to work so fast and keep up con-versations with people at the bar. He secretly wanted to be a bartender; he was sick of college. Summer break was coming up, so Lao Two told him to at least try being a bartender for the summer, and as he said those words, his shy roommate opened up like a flower. Never before in his life had he given himself permission to pursue a dream that was his alone. He had cut the umbilical cord between himself and his parents' expectations. He took the summer off and completely enjoyed the experience as a bartender. He later told Lao Two that the summer spent as a bartender gave him the confidence to finish his doctorate. He enjoyed the rest of his time at college, discovered he preferred marijuana to alcohol, and became socially adept, meeting the woman who would be his wife. Turned out he became a famous lawyer, family man, and civic leader in Los Angeles.

Lao Two says: "We need to be kind to ourselves. Living a happy life has nothing to do with what life offers us."

Wizard Tripping, Techniques, Totality

No, No Thanks, Nope

Lao Two says: "We are entitled to our 'NO.' Don't be afraid to use it. Saying no is not aggressive. We are allowed to defend ourselves."

Some places are physically hazardous, and since the politicians on Earth refuse to fix our ongoing problems like endless wars, pollution, and overpopulation it's easy to run into situations where we can get physically damaged. But in a very real sense we are never safe—death is always right around the next corner. The dance of life is also the dance of death – nobody can see the future.

We live in a very fragile body, and on the Stoner path we have to know how to avoid getting stuck on cactus. In today's world, anyplace can become chaotic and life threatening. If we can learn how to listen to doing mind, we can learn how to trust our intuition. We don't have to needlessly sacrifice ourselves because a situation around us is out of control—depending on a hunch, and being aware might save us.

Most importantly, we don't have to live our lives in fear. If someone is punching or attacking you, then defend yourself—or best of all, get away. Do not allow anyone to bludgeon you with words or hostile actions either. We understand nonviolence to mean that we are allowed to defend ourselves.

Does that mean we need to carry a concealed gun or other weapon? Just the opposite, we Stoners must be peaceful, unarmed, and open to nonviolence. It's up to us to be the example of how peace is possible. Work for peace, evolve.

Lao Two says: "After meditating a while, we develop a spiritual vibration. Letting this vibe emanate from our heart will sometimes keep us out of danger."

Lao Two has lived in unsafe areas, traveled to third-world countries, walked around bad parts of dangerous cities, and hung around some nefarious characters during his life—and I believe, because of the nonthreatening, compassionate Stoner person he is, he avoided being hassled. On the other hand, maybe in all these years it's just been dumb luck and it's all coincidence ... or, on the invisible hand, maybe there is a shamanic vibe in him that people respect. Over the years many bizarre people I've met because of Lao Two's teachings have given me magical experiences.

Inside of us is a center, and from that center our body moves—either gracefully or stiffly. When walking, try throwing your shoulders back a little, and keeping your head uplifted instead of looking down at the ground—try to feel for your center. Traditionally it's your belly button, but for me it's my sternum, and for Lao Two his center is outside his body. Once you've discovered your center, start noticing it when the world knocks you off balance. Finally, notice what's happening to your center when you are being messed with. We're not talking about good-natured deprecating humor that's done in mutual fun—we are discussing nasty putdowns, aggressive, controlling, mean-spirited, angry people, and even ready-to-fight violent people. You can easily see there is a scale of violence.

Teach yourself how to trust your instincts and your gut feeling. Don't be self-absorbed, open up your "feelers," your ears and eyes, and be aware of what's going on around you. Large groups of people develop a group vibe, and if you travel to different world cities you will discover a city vibe. People suffering in places under oppressive regimes carry a heavy burden with them constantly; even their laughter might be guarded. Learn how to feel the vibes of large areas, because with training we can feel when something's not right. If necessary, use your NO to stop violence by not giving it the energy it craves—walk away, refuse to argue. Don't react to anger with your anger—smile and be cool-headed, empathetic, and aware. Always try to see where the other person is coming from, and if possible say whatever is necessary to defuse the situation. I'm always willing to say it was my fault, sorry... I used to pat a person's shoulder with my hand, but I was told recently that some cultures consider that an invasion of their space—live and learn.

Do not accept abuse from relatives. Everyone, even the smallest child, understands what is fair. Sometimes, no matter how kindly you act, an abusive person will have a preconceived image of you they can't let go of. That is their problem; our solution is to either be positive or use no. Being compassionate to others includes being compassionate to ourselves. If you are an abused teenager, physically or mentally, seek help; don't be ashamed or embarrassed. All children and teenagers deserve a chance.

None of us can change the past; we can only be more thoughtful and respectful in the here-now. Very often we have incidents in our past that act like a ball and chain attached to our ankle. Let the past go, forgive yourself, forgive someone else, and do what you have to do to let go. Give yourself some credit. Believe in yourself. The future is created right now.

Lastly, don't let the negative, critical inner voice of habitual thinking mind mistreat you. The inner voice inside our head tells us lies and can be abusive. Part of meditation is listening to this voice so we can understand how it works. It's critically important to learn which voice to listen to, and when. A negative voice can be helpful when considering whether to take a shortcut through a dark alley in a strange city, or not—sometimes when thinking mind or doing mind's instinct says we are an idiot, it is right. When something happens to arouse your emotions, pay attention to what's going on in thinking mind, and what thoughts accompany the emotions. After a while we learn that emotions cause habitual thinking mind reactions; then we can react, or not.

You are already going to get stoned, or you wouldn't be reading this book. But in my opinion, that is only half the equation. It's entirely up to you to meditate. We could give you a million reasons to meditate, like scientific studies that suggest it makes people happier and more productive. Or we can explore all the people who have benefited from it throughout history, and discuss the power meditation has. But if you are still not convinced by now to start a daily meditation practice, then we wish you the best. Stoner Meditation is not interested in saving your soul or demanding that you follow some dogma. And remember, meditation is not a quick fix. Rather, it's a lifelong pursuit and path.

Our insistence is that you help yourself to crawl out of the hole you are in. Get rid of apathy and sloth and realize your life's dream. Marijuana will be legal soon, and we will no longer be excluded from participating in the political arena—get involved. There is no escaping the crazy world we live in; we all have suffering, pain, and too soon, death. If not a daily sitting meditation, then find another worthwhile way to deal with life and death, and particularly find a constructive way to use your short time here.

Lao Two says: "To the person about to die nothing stands out as special, everything is of equal value—mud and diamonds have the same value. No more thinking about the future, there is only here and now."

Chief Aupumut, Mohican Indian, said in 1725: "When it comes time to die, be not like those whose hearts are filled with the fear of death, so when their time comes they weep and pray for a little more time to live their lives over again in a different way. Sing your death song, and die like a hero going home."

In Exercise 5, we said to feel your body naked under your clothing. It seems human beings have such a strong sexual nature that we can't tolerate naked bodies. Well, the truth is that humans run the gamut from highly sexed to barely interested—what a curious species we are. Consider: humans are the only animals on Earth that wear clothing. Of course, it's been that way since forever, first for protection from the elements, and increasingly as a means of social and personal expression. So everyone culturally accepts that we clothe ourselves. Clothing is art, it's part of our expressing our outer self, and the art has changed over the centuries. But what doesn't make sense is that we think clothing defines us. We are still naked; we just forgot to feel anymore what's wrapped around our skin.

If you know how to look, you can see through people's disguises, as if their clothes were transparent. I'm not saying we have x-ray vision, but we are able to see their emotions when we get high. Our emotions are often written on our face.

The only ugly body is a judgment in someone's overcritical mind. Somebody said that if we have a problem with someone's body, take it up with the manufacturer. It's like saying a flower is ugly. Flowers, like people, go through stages of life, from bud to blooming; then they die, rot, and fall off to become new dirt. Is any particular stage more or less beautiful than the others? We commonly think of death as ugly, but on some levels it's really just another stage.

Try pretending you are visibly naked next time you are out in the world. Let everyone see all your hidden imperfections, the ten pounds you need to lose, and the animal you are—and you will liberate your body, and maybe blow your mind.

Lao Two says: "I came to a place where I no longer existed, yet there I was. Here I still am, and I still no longer exist. I don't know what shape I'll take when I'm dead, but I know this human body is not the end of my journey."

Buddha said (in the Jhana Sutra): "directed thought and evaluation. He regards whatever phenomena there are that are connected with material form, feeling, perceptions, fabrications, and consciousness—as inconstant, stressful, a disease, a cancer, an arrow, painful, an affliction, alien, a disintegration, a void, not-self. He turns his mind away from those phenomena, and having done so, inclines his mind to the property of deathlessness, and says: 'This is peace, this is exquisite, the resolution of all fabrications, the relinquishment of all acquisitions, the ending of craving, dispassion, cessation, unbinding.'"

Nirvana is, and is not, a place. More accurately, it is a state of mind so profoundly vast that no words or human thoughts exist—nirvana is pristine awareness where our own thinking is replaced by an indescribably different way of not-thinking, and instead of words, intuitive images appear. Nirvana is boundless, filled with, and standing in ever-creating wisdom. It is beyond our human body, human senses, and even beyond thinking mind and doing mind—to be in nirvana we have to let nirvana run the show. Nirvana feels empty, but there is no emptiness there—everything is there, and nothing at all too. Many of you have experienced this type of nirvana by taking psychedelics.

But no matter how stoned we get, we can't seem to stabilize the high, it comes and goes. Since we can't be that high on psychedelics all the time anyway, we have to learn how to re-create that experience differently. The first thing we do is take a good look at the person we've become. It's rare to find people who are happy with themselves, secure in their choices, content and grateful for what they have, and not overly concerned with wanting this or that.

We can break away from most of our harmful habits by creating new habits to replace them. No one grows up perfectly adjusted or finished; we all have flaws and live in the same lunatic asylum. These flaws are only bad because they hold us back, don't let us know the truth of our situation, and make us blunder through life like a pinball bouncing from this pleasure to the next disaster. Just as there is no perfection, there is also no failure—so don't dump on yourself because you can't break a habit. Life just goes. It's our choice to live with awareness and compassion, or be a creature of habit.

Accept that your life might include a little neurosis. It can exhibit as anxiety, insecurity, or being too lazy or too driven—only you can decide if you need to change. To break a habit, we need to make a different decision in that moment it appears. Compulsive behavior is persistent; we can only catch it when we are paying attention.

Like we said, don't expect applause just because you know about enlightenment or have had various higher levels of insight. The world will not swoon at your feet—being humble is where it's at. Our good actions do not come from religious beliefs or because of outside imposed rules—if something needs to be done and it's the right thing to do, then there is movement and action in that moment. For example, I wouldn't have bothered to write this book unless I thought I could offer some help for Stoners. Now that I'm old I understand some shortcuts, and if I can give an honest account of Stoner Meditation, then maybe others can form a new worldview. Wars haven't changed people's worldview, it can't be forced—it's new ideas that make sense that change the world. I have no need for success in a material sense, but it's worth spending my time if Stoner Meditation becomes a worthwhile methodology.

Plants

Arapaho Indian saying: "All plants are our brothers and sisters. They talk to us and if we listen, we can hear them."

If you have a pet, you are probably aware of human-to-pet communication, mostly by subtle facial gestures and body language. When we think about it, our pets are as alien as any creature from outer space, but here we are having interspecies comprehension. The strange thing is that dogs and cats understand our human words better than we understand their more subtle communication. I hope someday we develop a technology that lets us truly communicate with our pets.

Very soon we will be meeting intelligent aliens who travel around the Milky Way, and we'll need to be able to communicate. I hope we don't miss our opportunity because of our limited skills and self-absorption. Certainly we should be able to do better than playing music together (as in *Close Encounters of the Third Kind*). Fortunately we have a highly intelligent species right here on Earth that is trying to communicate with us, using a different form of conversation than words, gestures, and concepts.

Plants communicate with us, especially psychedelic plants. I'm specifically discussing the psychedelic plants we've tripped on: marijuana, mushrooms, peyote, and ayahuasca. But even LSD belongs on this list because it originates from rye mold (ergot fungi). From personal experience we believe that these plants are using interspecies consciousness. Not in the same way as dogs and cats; it is a very different form. When we smoke marijuana or trip on psychedelics we might think we simply smoked some bud or ate some vegetable, not really connecting with the cycle that created the plant itself. Our conjecture is that these plants trip along with us. First the plants become absorbed in us. Then they wake up—and the plant takes over our body and mind. Then the plants start to communicate—not in words, but in pictures, hallucinations, and insights.

Every single plant we eat communicates and interacts with us. In our diet, meat interacts even more, but I won't get into that. Remember there are thousands of types of living bacteria inside of us, each microorganism performing a different function, requiring different food. The miracle of our humanness goes on and on, but we are what we eat, and smoke. Can we even consider our human body "ours," when we share it with thousands of other living organisms?

Part of Stoner Meditation is being able to talk to and listen to plants. Psychedelic plants hold up a mirror so we can see our true selves. If we are fearless, we will look at the mirror. The fearless Stoners will not only look into the mirror but also demand to see the secrets behind the reflection—peering into the hidden.

Essentially everything we ingest is Earth, and Earth is whatever fell on it from outer space, from the first impacts to the shooting stars today. Earth did not evolve separately from the universe, and the universe didn't go away just because humans arrived. The universe is still intimately involved with Earth, which is intimately involved with everything growing on it. Could psychedelics be part of a universal Mind, or maybe an Earth Mind? Psychedelics seem to teach us that Mind wants to help us evolve, to teach us in ways our linear mind can't discover. Plants are the conduits for that alien communication that plugs us into what could be called spiritual insight. We have to learn the language of plants. The only way I know to do this is to ingest psychedelics.

Stoners should respect psychedelics, because psychedelic plants are great, wise, and formidable teachers. Taking psychedelics should be wondrous, special, and big fun. We should have a grateful frame of mind and a loving heart, and be in a location that keeps our body safe while mind-to-Mind communication goes on.

Extreme caution should be used with all psychedelics. Tim Leary's 'set and setting' should be prepared beforehand. Set is the mental construct that describes the person you are and the attitudes you are bring to the trip. And setting is the tripping location. There's lots of information on the Internet about a normal dose, so there's no need to eat too little or too much. With pills, try to find out the purity of the substance.

Timothy Leary said: "A psychedelic experience is a journey to new realms of consciousness. The scope and content of the experience is limitless, but its characteristic features are the transcendence of verbal concepts, of space-time dimensions, and of the ego or identity."

Your trip will last for hours; some strong LSD formulations can last up to twelve hours. Imagine yourself in a good mood, tripping joyously, carefree, riding the mind-blowing roller-coaster and laughing. Now, imagine yourself in an unhappy mood, thrust into a hell world, insecure, falling into bizarre images, screaming inside—both emotional extremes intensified by the chemicals rolling around in your body. Think about how many mood swings you have each hour. You are happy for some moments and unhappy for other moments. Or you spend time tuned out, mindless and self-absorbed. Every day you are watching a movie of your life and are swept along by the emotional content—you are the copilot. Psychedelics work best on those who are pilots, mindful, with concentrated awareness.

You must accept at the beginning that not all hallucinations are going to be benign. Some parts of tripping are heavy, intense, and vivid because we are reacting with our base emotions or thinking mind. As I've been saying, thinking mind is incapable of letting go on its own. We must transcend thinking mind and get to doing mind while traveling at these supersonic speeds.

There are different kinds of hallucinations. Some are inside of us with eyes closed, and look like visual cartoons, or mandalas. There is intense appreciation and perception of sounds (your favorite music is very effective). Other hallucinations are outside, where the familiar world changes into unpredictable shapes, lights, and dimensions. While we are watching the hallucinations, thinking mind is desperately trying to label them—good, just okay, bad, happy, scary, sensual, intense, etc. Stoner Meditation recommends learning how to stop the labeling of psychedelic events. Let the hallucinations be unpredictable and let moods come and go.

We all have "bad" trips, but if you have an exploring heart you'll be fine. Actually we quit labeling them as "bad trips" because the tough ones are often the best learning experiences. There's a lot to learn from psychedelics, but we've noticed that once a lesson is learned during a bad trip, it doesn't recur.

Our cosmic joke is that we live on this insignificant planet, toward a far edge of the Milky Way. The distance from our sun to the nearest star is 4.24 light years; one light year is about 6 trillion miles. Certainly there must be a way to travel these immense distances, and if we survive as a species, someday we'll eventually know how. We are smaller than small compared to our universe. We don't often think about how amazing our existence is. But when we do, why should plants that want to communicate with us be so strange? There's certainly a wizard in marijuana who will speak to you if you learn how to listen.

For now, we are basically stuck in our little puddle of a solar system. We struggle to learn, fight our stupid battles, have some fun and shed tears, we hate and love, get old and sick, and then die. Up to now humans have had it easy on planet Earth, imagining that they have divine importance. On the greater scale of things, we are in truth not especially important as a species. If we don't change our ways with all our wars, overpopulation, self-importance, anger, and denial, we are absurdly unworthy of surviving. We've listened to medieval ideas for so long that we believe them true—now it's time to listen to the plants, who are telling us to throw away our anger, live in cooperation with Mom Earth, and evolve. It's time to use psychedelics to teach us how to mature as a species.

When humanity is connected to Earth in symbiosis, we become important to the host, Mom Earth. Remember Earth is a self-regulating system, and if we push the parameters too far, Mom Earth will shrug her shoulder and humans will be gone. We Stoners have to be the ones to reconnect to the plants. Use Stoner Meditation, create new myths, and become the shamans of the modern age. Mother Earth will welcome us again. Earth gives us marijuana as an interface. Stand on the Earth naked and feel gravity pushing you toward her.

Forest for the Trees

Dakota Indian saying: "We will be known forever by the tracks we leave."

Get to know Earth before it's all gone, or before you're all gone. Start to hike, run, bike in nature, even golf, sailing, or spelunking is good. I like to trek because walking with a daypack or backpack slows me down. Walking seems to be the ideal human activity because we are designed for it. It's okay with me if others want to use various mechanized equipment (such as golf carts, or bicycles) to visit the outdoors—just get outside. Reconnect with your senses, the majesty of nature, and the awesome miracle of the process of life. There is absolutely no place better to get stoned than the outdoors—spiritual, in the true sense of the word. Therefore, support environmental causes. Learn how to camp in a tent under the stars. Take your children.

Lao Two says: "Backpacking into the wilderness is sublime—learn how."

Backpacking is an excellent way to reconnect with and appreciate our unfathomable world. Lao Two is an experienced backpacker and has learned after much experimentation and training to backpack alone. He started out in groups, took courses from the Sierra Club, and learned outdoor first aid, navigation, and survival. Do you know how to self-arrest with a climbing axe, or how to use crampons, or safely cross a river? Don't go solo camping until you are very experienced. Rent equipment at the beginning. Don't forget about national parks, car camping, and day trips. Always, always, always take the Ten Essentials (even for day hikes)—compass and map, multitool knife, high-energy snacks, space blanket, water, warm clothing, flashlight, first aid kit, fire starter. We also add signal mirror, flint-type lighters, some dryer lint in a baggie, a wax candle, and extra marijuana joints. Stoner reminder: look at your compass when you start hiking from your car, and jot the general direction down.

John Muir said: "The clearest way into the Universe is through a forest wilderness."

Lao Two says: "Reality is—there is no inside you. Expanded consciousness puts reality outside you."

Story: Many years ago Lao Two camped alone on Mt Shasta at Horse Camp. Mt Shasta is in the northern California Sierra Mountains range, and is considered a spiritual power-place like Machu Picchu in Peru. Driving from the San Francisco Bay area to Mt Shasta takes about four hours, so it's easy to get to the parking lot trailhead at Bunny Flat with lots of daylight left. The parking lot was empty except for what seemed to be two abandoned vehicles, covered with snow. There was already thick snow on the ground, but he was between storms so it was a fun hike to the camp in snowshoes. Since his backpack was extra heavy, when a foot sank unexpectedly into a snowdrift, the backpack would propel him awkwardly into a tumble. He made his camp just above tree line, a little higher than the Sierra Club cabin, avoiding the avalanche zone. He specifically picked a midweek cold fall night, with no moon for his snow camping trip.

He made his camp in the open on a slight rise, knowing that cold air collects in valleys and depressions. It was unlikely anyone else would be backpacking this time of year for fear of being caught in an early snowstorm, but Lao Two was willing to take that risk to have the mountain all to himself. He had camped on Mt Shasta many times before, and in an emergency could find the downhill parking lot with his eyes closed.

Daylight ended early and darkness started filling the sky. He was rewarded with a perfectly clear, star-filled night. He looked toward the horizon, past the tops of the giant fir trees below him to the small cities in the far distance. As night came he felt that the legend of

Mt Shasta being magical and sacred might be true. It also felt ironic seeing the electric lights so far below. People would be cooking dinners, watching TV, comfortable in their warm homes. Meanwhile, he stood in front of his tent naked except for down booties, his wet clothes hanging up to dry. The cold wind whipped his tent and the trees around him, making him wrap up in his sleeping bag for warmth. Snow lifting from the treetops would travel on the wind, looking like crazy birds, and it took some moments for Lao Two to figure out what was going on. It was so spooky being in the darkness able to see with his night vision. Looking up, he saw our local planets appear one or two at a time, then the highway of the Milky Way filling the sky. Not too far away he heard the growl of a black bear, perhaps appreciating the same freedom and serenity of the mountain, or perhaps appreciating a potential meal of backpacker food.

The sleeping pad was upside down, acting like a hood on his head, but unzipped. With one hand he was trying to keep it closed, with his other hand he pulled out a metal container with prerolled marijuana joints from the sleeping bag pocket. Lighters don't always work at altitude, so he'd brought wooden strike-anywhere matches. With the wind starting to gust lightly, he carefully struck the match, knowing that if he set the tent or the sleeping bag on fire he would be in for a rough night. The wind quickly blew out the match, so he covered himself with the sleeping bag to block it. Awkwardly he struck a match, got a flame, and the joint was aglow. But the sleeping bag over his head quickly filled with smoke, sending Lao Two into a prolonged coughing fit. That led to a laughing fit at the same time. He quickly took the sleeping bag off his head. He figured all that noise would at least keep any curious bears away. As soon as he thought this, there was a rustle in the brush below him; he could see definite movement. He turned his flashlight on the area and was relieved to see a striped skunk digging in a patch of ground where the snow was sparse. The skunk turned and ran away, leaving a little odor on the wind.

The joint was still lit, so Lao Two took another hit. The wind picked up, sending sparks flying off the ember—the evening chill was arriving quickly. Constantly aware of the danger of starting a fire, he moved carefully. He inhaled four more deep, long hits then put the ember out between his thumb and first finger.

Lao Two is legendary for his ability to meditate standing up. He immediately connects to his environment and adjusts his body so he is balanced and centered. Since he was in such a powerful environment, he picked a star to enable single-point focus and quickly expanded his consciousness into the entire field of vision. He let go of his body and then let go of his mind, becoming awestruck awareness.

His sleeping bag slipped off his head to his waist, leaving him half naked in the cold wind, but his attention noted the cold then ignored it, so he was unaffected. He chanted three AOMs slowly, always a reliable way to get even higher. He felt the vibrations moving throughout his body, through his feet into the earth. The sleeping bag fell to his ankles— he stood naked. He took a slow breath, arched his spine, and relaxed his shoulders. His third eye expanded his perception and he filled the horizon. His body felt solid and invisible; at the same time, he felt like he would explode his entire body into the stars above Earth. He had tried to ignore the cold before on other backpacking trips, but this night he succeeded in turning up his inner thermostat. For a while. ...

A colder, stronger wind picked up and Lao Two felt the beginning of a shiver, but instead of allowing it to roll through his body on its own, he directed it up his back, setting off the chakras along his spine. As he looked upon our galaxy, he felt very small and insignificant, yet at the same time felt the galaxy and the Earth were all inside of him as he now stretched to the stars. He laughed, feeling that if he wasn't careful he would fall into the dark starry sky and leave the Earth altogether.

His vision was more than just his eyes, similar to being on a boat looking out on an ocean and seeing to the horizon, knowing the ocean stretches far, much farther away.

Laughing at the now splendid mental and physical situation he found himself in made him realize the absurdity of his own thoughts—and at that moment the marijuana really kicked in and allowed his thinking mind to quiet, and he started to hallucinate.

Lao Two watched the glittering colors that only exist in the darkest starlit night when you're stoned. After a while he brought himself back into his body, relaxing his gaze. He became conscious that he had been standing naked in the cold wind for quite a while. Lao Two felt a dislocation between being so incredibly stoned a few moments ago and now just feeling high.

He hobbled away from his tent, sinking into the snow and filling his down boots with cold snow . Gingerly walking downhill over the snow-covered rocks and brush to a huge fallen tree nearby, he found a spot to urinate. Lao Two was amazed he was able to manage so well without using a flashlight, but he guessed his eyes had become completely dilated. Walking back uphill was more difficult, and for several moments he couldn't find his tent. There is a kind of panic when camping alone that only lasts an instant, but things like momentarily not being able to find a tent in the dark bring it on. That, and realizing he would be lost naked, wearing only down booties.

At the tent he quickly took off his soaked booties, wrapped the sleeping bag around him and put on his headlight for some last-minute organization. Suddenly the other side of the coin hit him. From surfing the heights he was thrown into a negative wave, and the feeling of being completely alone and lonely hit him like a whip. An emotional-physical reaction followed, pulling him back into his body and ego thinking mind. He could feel the tears coming down his cheeks, starting out warm then turning instantly cold. He felt sad and depressed, thinking about his relationships, his job, his whole life—nothing was working out. He muttered how he always ended up camping alone because his friends were too busy. Thinking mind was returning, bringing up the fear of ego loss, and fear of bodily harm. Now fully back in control, thinking mind was merciless, completely bummed, muddled, and emotional.

But Lao Two had been here before in his mind. He knew that thinking mind uses logic and analysis, so he consciously argued with his negative thoughts that he had planned to be alone; no one forced him to be there. And if he had brought someone along, they would have spoken or distracted him just when he wanted to let himself go into nonordinary reality. Lao Two knew it took intense concentration to do what he had just done; he had been practicing for a long time to be able to let go. It was always that way, either loneliness, or friends speaking at the wrong moment, asking questions, and never understanding Lao Two's shamanic quests. He had to give a little laugh at his predicament—after all, he was dating three women, he had a steady straight job and extra income from dealing marijuana, and his health was excellent—he was actually thriving as a longhair hippie in a crazy straight world.

Almost immediately he started feeling much better in his head. Then the munchies struck. As usual, munchies took precedence over all other concerns. He grabbed an altitude-pressure inflated bag of potato chips, which made a loud pop when he opened it, and mindlessly ate the whole bag, still staring at the stars. He started to feel much better, more loving, and reconnected to a night of camping on Mt Shasta. Then he ate the leftovers from dinner, and the sandwich for tomorrow's lunch—rationalizing it would keep him warm at night.

After he was completely done scarfing everything, he remembered his resolution to only eat slowly, consciously, mindfully. He reflected on his now botched plan to eat less and chew his food completely—he was skinny, but wanted to be more "spiritual." He erupted in laughter—then he howled as loud as he could into the moonless night. Lao Two was mindblown when several human voices howled back from across the sweeping valley, then again from another location—other people were camping on the mountain! A howling contest had begun.

He finished cleaning up his camp, which generally meant throwing everything into a pile in the vestibule of the tent, climbed into his sleeping bag, and lay on his back with his head sticking out of the tent flaps so he would be able to continue to look up at the starry night. He opened a candy bar, then took a few more very careful hits on the roach, feeling the Earth spinning under him, moving around the sun at 1,000 miles per hour. ... He drifted off to sleep.

Lao Two was startled from deepest sleep by the loud growl of a black bear close by. It was an enormous noise, and he swears that he could feel the bass vibrations through his bones. He had ignored the rule and forgotten to hang everything edible on a tree branch, out of reach—would he pay the hard way, with a bear visiting? For that matter, he still had trail bars in his coat pocket that he was using for a pillow. He took out his Swiss Army knife and opened the largest blade. He had his ice axe in his other hand. He stood up, shined his flashlight all around his campsite, but saw and heard nothing more. Then the black bear growled again, closer. Lao Two had an epiphany at that moment.

He remembered reading about American Indians and Buddhist monks being sent out to forests to test their resolve to nonclinging and nonattachment to life. The goal of the monk was to remain centered and let fears manifest, reside in awareness, and remain calm—even if they faced death—or in this case, bear food. He knew he was in a bad situation, for he had chosen to camp alone and had been sloppy in his habits. He also knew that Mt Shasta is the habitat for the nocturnal black bear. His car was several hiking hours away, the other campers were too far away to help, and there was nowhere to go and nothing he could do at this late moment. He resolved to relax and only defend himself if necessary instead of banging pots together and yelling like he was supposed to. He returned to his sleeping bag, carefully placing the open-blade knife on one side and his ice axe on the other side, and strangely, quickly fell back into a deep, peaceful sleep. The black bear never did visit his campsite that night; everything was untouched the next morning. After cleaning up his campsite, zipping up his tent with everything inside, Lao Two headed up the mountain for a day trek on the glacier.

End of story.

Zen Master Basho said: "Do not seek to follow in the footsteps of the men of old; seek what they sought."

Smile

You must relearn how to smile (not optional).

Exercise 6: Part 1: Sit in a comfortable chair. Take a moment to feel your body around your shoulders and lower neck. Feel the tension there? Did you also notice tension in your stomach, just behind your navel? Relax the muscles in your shoulders and upper arms by literally dropping the arms and shoulders so your shoulders sink downward. Take a slow in- and out-breath through your nose. Drop those arms, shake your hands around, and feel the weight of your arms pulling down on your shoulders. Breathe even slower, deeply through your nose. Realize that you were taking short, restricted breaths and were half oxygen starved. Lift your chin and move your head side to side in an exaggerated no, pulling your neck muscles. Now throw your head back, close your eyes, and count to at least ten—long, slow, wholehearted breaths through your nose. You'll notice that you feel higher than you were before, and of course more relaxed and centered.

Did you trip out and forget to open your eyes at number ten? Or did you keep losing your concentration on the numbers and space out around number four? Ha ha, that's cool, no worries. ... With meditation practice you will notice your concentration improving.

Meditation can change your physical, mental, and Stoner outlook.

Part 2: Go back into the original position, arms at sides, head back, deep breaths, eyes closed. Feel your stomach rise and fall. Stop and groove a moment, as if you were in water floating on your back—rising a little on the in-breath and sinking a little on the out-breath. With each out-breath, feel your shoulders relaxing more and more. If you get really stoned, just lie back as long as you like and dig it—if you are tired, just fall asleep for five minutes, or get horizontal and take a nap.

Zen Master Thich Nhat Hanh said: "Sometimes your joy is the source of your smile, but sometimes your smile can be the source of your joy."

Part 3: All Stoners must develop a good, honest, trusting smile that arises from inside their heart of hearts. A great Stoner smile can easily be learned, and once your smile becomes sincere, it opens the way like a magic wand.

Stand up, but stay relaxed, mellow, stoned. We suggest you stand in front of a mirror, reach into your heart, and practice a righteous smile. Force it, fake it if you have to at first; eventually it will become natural again. You can give smiles to people every day of your life—you might even start to laugh once in a while. If you are going to dance down the street, please do it gracefully. We might as well enjoy our ride, it's the only one we have – we can choose to be happy. We highly recommend dancing.

Yeah, I know. Nobody smiles anymore. But you're not like them anyway. We can start a new trend—Stoners smiling at people. Smile at your lover, at your parents, the cop, the grouchy teacher, your enemy.

The smile should be used each time you have an interaction with another human, especially if the other human is having a bad day. Kind, sincere words help too. If someone gives you a hard time, take his or her aggression without knee-jerk reactions. Instead, stop your emotions, and then smile. You should at the minimum give a head nod to beggars and other suffering people, worldwide—a smile is good also.

Extra Credit: Direct your attention to the middle of your chest (sternum area again) and feel love emanating from your heart chakra and spread that love outward with your smile. Imagine you are giving your energy to the world just by smiling, and it will keep you from being self-absorbed. Try flowing energy at children and see what happens—they can really feel vibes. Expand to older people, dogs, strangers, demons, gorgeous sunsets and rising moons, and smile at your own foibles, laugh at yourself stumbling through life.

Lao Two says: "Marijuana can induce telepathic awareness."

More Extra Credit: This wizard telepathic, sensory experience is optional. You must be stoned. Next time you are in a crowd, like a subway where people are standing around, pick any random person – the opposite sex seems to work best. Stare at them for a few short moments, making sure they don't catch you looking at them. Now look at some inanimate spot and become unfocused for a short time in non-ordinary reality. Then look back at the subject, and there is a good chance they will immediately turn their head to look your way—even if they are reading or listening to music on headphones. Some part of their mind picks up on your energy. If they do turn toward you, smile. Your smiling will cause them to focus on your smile, and sometimes they will return it. But don't be creepy; it's customary to look away after a moment. This empathic telepathy seems to be hardwired into our genetic makeup. I've used this effectively to meet women, but that's another story...

Described above is only the visible nature of what's going on. There are many levels of telepathic experience. There are subtle vibrations happening also between two strangers, and energy ripples in groups of people. You might experience this telepathic, connected feeling as a rolling wave, or a type of good-feeling chill on your body. See if you can notice this subtle vibration when it happens.

End of Exercise 6.

No matter how funky, miserable, fucked up, or gutter splashed you are feeling—keep going back to that mirror and try to smile. Physical exercise is also good for bummers. Have some fun, get stoned, put on your favorite music, loud, louder. Or go to concerts and support the music scene of your choice. Play air guitar and dance the dance of life!

Take a moment and think about the smile exercise. In Western nations we have unrivaled prosperity and great opportunities, but we also have a lot of very sad, disenfranchised, and angry people. Now that Asian nations are becoming more Westernized, it's probably true worldwide that Earth people need to mellow out and get rid of anger, so find ways to love each other, and creatively solve our problems. Think about how fortunate Stoners are to have access to great weed in this country even though it's currently illegal. Sure, we struggle with habits, relationships, the workday world—but having marijuana, psychedelics, and meditation as tools gives us the ability to utilize more of our potential.

Zen Master Dogen said: "Those who regard worldly affairs as an obstacle to their training do not realize that there is nothing such as worldly affairs to be distinguished from the Way."

We need to appreciate life, including the day-to-day struggle. All our chaotic life, bummers, confusion, and anger are gifts, and teachers. Ask yourself what you have to be grateful for; it's not an idle question. Our smile is the affirmation and appreciation of the life experiences that come our way. Remember, if you aren't living, you're dead—so live. Often life won't be smooth and easy, it will be tumultuous, and bad stuff will happen. But no matter what's happening, each of us has that spark inside, and that spark can light a candle. Once our heartfelt candle is lit, it can light other candles. Smile.

Your Man, Your Woman, Your Partner

Sex is the celebration of our most magnificent gift, our human body. To be able to let passion overtake thinking mind and completely let go of attachments during orgasm is similar to what we've been trying to teach. The power to let go during orgasm releases thinking mind and transcends into bliss—we let go of ego. When we consider the intense powers of desire, libido, and climax, we have to show some appreciation and respect—what a miracle! Then, to top that, we can have sex stoned!

Before we jump right into bed and start having sex, we need to meet someone. There are too many people who are alone, lonely, shy, and depressed. On a planet with 7 billion humans, there is no excuse for not being able to meet someone and start a relationship. If you really don't want to have friends, a partner, and be part of the community—you don't have to. As we've said before, make your own choices.

We'll give a few tips here for creating relationships in hopes that people can crawl out of their shells and partner up. Remember, we are vibrations, and vibrations can be shared, focused, and become orchestrated. For this part we'll be using some illogical references, generalizations, and personal observations—so if anything doesn't work for you, skip it.

Women usually give men subtle clues by flirting and eye contact, but most men are clueless and don't pick up on women's subtlety. Men are often awkward—either too shy or too brazen. How do we get through our differences and lack of skills to bridge the gap to socialize?

Note: Women, please give guys a chance to meet you, and don't laugh at them or be brutal if they approach you respectfully. If you are not interested, then show some kindness, so the guy won't be overly discouraged for his next attempt. Thanks.

Note: Men, be respectful. Don't make women into abstract unreachable angels or meaningless conquests. Manipulation and aggressive power trips over women are wrong. Using physical power because you are stronger is just anger – physical abuse is always wrong. Let go of negative emotions and see women as equals. NO means no. Thanks.

Love is universal; it's extraordinary, potent, and a primary force in our lives. Everybody deserves emotional, romantic, heartfelt love and a relationship. Who really cares what shape love takes as long as it respects human rights?

The fear that discourages people from developing relationships is based on the unpredictably of people, and the desire to have things work out in their favor. If we already know that there is a likelihood of failure, we are reluctant to give something a try. To put this in perspective, we need to realize that life itself is not predictable—tomorrow a comet or meteorite might slam into Earth and destroy all life. Because life is so tenuous, we need to be able to put aside our fears and risk some unpredictable outcomes now, today, right away. We can instantly change our mindset and develop courage without being attached to the result. "Would you like to get some coffee?" "No." "Okay, take care."

On a very realistic level, we are fine risking our hard-earned money through investing, gambling, or expensive material goods. Our culture has taught us that it's cool to be reckless, powerful, and shrewd if it concerns money, and even though we take those risks, we feel comfortable. We took chances, we're cool, and even if we lose money we're still cool. We're okay because investments don't talk back—money is emotionless in this instance. The same can be said for being risky on our computers, using drugs, too much TV, most contact sports, and risking our life and limb in other ways.

But not relationships, we're afraid to risk there. Or we go too far the other way, with carelessly risky behavior. A good balance of courage, respect, common sense, and mutual enjoyment is probably best.

Stoner Meditation is useful for self-understanding and seeing ourselves clearly. Instead of being weak, afraid, and ineffective, we can be brave and powerful.

Story: After Lao Two drove across country he lived with roommates near the prestigious University of California at Berkeley campus. Unlike his studious, shy, insecure, and brilliant roommates, Lao Two was meeting women right and left, bringing home a different woman two or three times a week. Lao Two drove a motorcycle; he was dealing marijuana, taking LSD, perpetually horny, and going to a junior college where he rarely did assignments or attended class. This was during the beginning of the sexual revolution (women's contraception), so Lao Two was getting laid by a variety of women—even a few virgins. Being so close to the college, Lao Two quickly discovered women to be energetic, intelligent, experimental, and easily sexually aroused. Lao Two was obviously hip in his motorcycle jacket and engineer boots—edgy, a little above-average looking—and gave the impression of impulsive danger.

One day all three of his shy roommates cornered him in the kitchen and demanded to know how the hell he was always getting so many women. He told them that he knew the magic word that women found irresistible. He then paused for effect: he told them the magic word is "hello."

Continuing, he told them that contrary to appearances, women are also shy, lonely, and awkward in their own way. It's up to men to say the magic word. His roommates had to realize that their own shyness was keeping them from meeting women—physical attractiveness is helpful, but being average looking has never been a deal breaker. They had to get over their poor self-images, gather their courage, take a risk, and let the chips fall where they might.

Lao Two told them that not only did they need to quit looking inward, but they were probably missing the clues that women were already sending them. He told his roommates to keep their eyes open for women glancing at them, and try to make eye contact instead of averting their eyes as they usually did. Then smile and go over and say hello.

Being incredibly smart geniuses, they changed their ways, and all three roommates started meeting women. It never occurred to them that women were shy too, and it was their role to say hello and smile. And most importantly, it's not the end of the world to be rejected.

End of story.

We live during a time where people are reluctant to meet new people for many reasons. Many people have had bad past experiences, sad love affairs, or not been treated right—splitting up is hard. We live with the scourge of AIDS and other sexual diseases, sexual predators, and even the question of which form of contraception to use weighs in. At least we now have contraception; having kids is a serious business. The materialistic nature of our modern world keeps us working long hours, so even finding time to get together can be difficult. The idea of supporting a family is so expensive that having children is often put off until careers are secure. Some responsible people are limiting families to one or two children, considering overpopulation in this mix. There are as many options as there are people. We sometimes choose career over family, have friends with benefits, feel the biological clock ticking, or have long-distance relationships. It's no wonder we are sexually stressed out.

Yet we yearn for someone to spend our years with.

Story: Lao Two met his current (third) wife at the airport—she sat down next to him in the crowded waiting area before the flight and immediately turned on her computer and started working away. Lao

Two could see she was a data wonk, so he asked her about all the data on her computer. She briefly described her job. ... The point is, she didn't mind being interrupted. The conversation turned this way and that, but Lao Two got the critical piece of information he was looking for—she lived near his town, not halfway across the country.

They boarded together and sat next to each other (Southwest, no assigned seats), talked briefly, and exchanged e-mail addresses before Lao Two fell asleep while she worked on her computer the entire flight. They e-mailed back and forth while she was traveling. When she returned it happened she was in a nearby town at a meeting, it was agreed that she would stop by Lao Two's house. They went into town for a snack and coffee, then they walked around a park briefly. Lao Two stopped walking and told her that he smoked marijuana, lots of marijuana—and if that was a deal breaker, then she should back out of the potential relationship right away because he said he wasn't going to change his ways. She thought for a minute, then accepted his precondition—she used to do drugs but quit when she got pregnant. To this day his wife will only very rarely get high, not stoned, but she doesn't mind that Lao Two smokes. So being a Stoner with a straight wife is not a problem. He and his wife have been together for nine years as of the writing of this book.

Note: His wife remembers it somewhat differently—she was reading the *New York Times* and says she remarked out loud about some issue and this led to their initial conversation. Interesting how memories differ, isn't it?

End of story.

Note: People on the phone, or who have earphones, or are in groups are more difficult to meet. Quite often if someone won't meet your smile, it could mean they are already in a relationship, are not heterosexual (or conversely, homosexual), or are just not into you. There's no need to stress if you don't have success. It's like finding a parking space, you only need one.

Most bars are stupid locations for Stoners to meet partners—immoderate drinkers will demand lots of attention, are potentially high maintenance, and will probably play sophisticated games that you will not understand. We know personally some chronic drinkers of alcohol who have tapered off by using marijuana. Don't underestimate the powers of marijuana. Alcohol is a strong drug; marijuana is a strong medicine.

During our primitive times we humans had to continually scan our surroundings for potential attack or ambush—we were tasty food back then. Cannibals call humans "long pig" and say we taste like Spam. ... I read somewhere that when the first Westerners met the American Indians in Northern California, they found that most people in the tribe had deep scars from bear attacks. It's genetically important to survive, and one of our tools is constantly discerning friends from foes—we can pick up on very subtle clues. We modern-day folks inherited this acute ability that makes us on the one hand alert to the world around us, and on the other hand potentially paranoid.

When walking down the street, we still do this scanning. But some of us are semi-defeated and look down at the ground in front of us instead. Most Stoners have had the experience of instinctively feeling something strange behind them—just suddenly picking up on a strong vibration—then turning and looking behind them to find a cop car, having just "telepathically" picked up on the cop's vibrations.

The good news is that we can use this genetically etched skill to our advantage. Remember, magic is only magic until we figure out how the trick works. Stoners can meet a woman or man who isn't gazing at the ground when they walk, or burying their head in the sand with modern technology. In other words, we want people who are looking around, at least enough for there to be eye contact, even for the briefest second. This instant is when your smile should start. Not some stupid, moronic grin, but a heartfelt smile that you learned from standing in front of your mirror doing the smile exercise. You want your approach to be human-to-human equals. Overcome all fear by saying the magic word: "hello." Sometimes that means smiling, crossing a large room, and deliberately making contact.

Lao Two says: "Your partner is not just one person—your lover is every fantasy and desire that you carry, they are every man and woman who lived, or will ever live. Your partner is a key to reveal enlightened eternity."

Wizards use magic, and Stoners learn from wizards, until they become wizards themselves. In this instance we take advantage of a natural, primitive human survival skill. Knowing that people are naturally scanning their surroundings is this magic ability. The more aware they are, and especially if they are a Stoner like you, the more they will be looking around them. They will inadvertently notice you for a brief instant, and that is your opening.

For example: Let's say you are attending college. People are always walking from building to building, or milling around—so imagine a guy or a woman sitting on a bench looking over some notes but glancing up at the people passing by every now and then. The painfully shy Stoner's usual response would be to pretend not to be really looking at that person sitting there. Instead of connecting to his or her glance, the shy person will quickly glance away, avoiding all eye contact. This is the pitiful no-results method.

Instead, give a slight nod of your head and your heartfelt smile—and hold it even after the person's glance has passed by. If, in that split second, they are curious or interested, they will look back. If they smile back, keep smiling and walk toward them, saying "Hi." Ask where they're from, or what they're studying, or where they work, or if they know of a good coffee shop, ethnic restaurant. ... Watch body language carefully—things like folded arms across their chest mean slow down. On the other hand signals like touching hair supposedly mean go for it, they're interested.

We suspect members of the opposite sex use a mysterious subtle language to get each other's interest. It's beyond question huge amounts of money are spent on cosmetics, clothing, and hair. Unfortunately, we all tend to think that we're being obvious, but often we're not. Even more unfortunate is that others rarely pick up on our smaller, subtle signals.

You will fail to connect with someone, miserably and often unless you take direct action. It has little to do with beauty and looks and everything to do with trust, communication skills (like humor), maybe pheromones (secreted chemicals), and definitely vibrations. Everyone wants a person to date who has some confidence—but I've noticed that people will be very forgiving if they see someone making a real effort. Everyone likes to have attention paid to them; however, it's all in the methods used—don't be weird, scary, or a know-it-all. Give them a chance to talk about themselves, find out their interests, dreams, and hopes. Hold back those sex vibes and remain human. Be real, considerate, and show your best ideals, principles, and honesty.

Lao Two says: "Our brain is also a sexual organ."

Absolute beginner: When you are dating for the first time, relax. Get any sexual ideas out of your head, and just enjoy the interactions in the moment. Don't fantasize about past and future; be alert in the now. If the vibes are right, touch their arm while talking, or reach over for some hand-holding; it's okay to be corny. Touching is an important communication and a very strong body sense—the slightest touch can be electric and telepathic. Sometimes sex happens on the first date, and that's fine—but if it does, let it happen naturally, and always consensually. We absolutely believe in love at first sight.

When you move on to a second date (or fifth date, depending) put your arm around his or her waist and draw them in to you. Full body contact is very loving and sexy. Tell them that the vibes are great and you are really enjoying their company. Give a little neck rub if they seem open to it. Go in for a kiss, pulling him or her over to you gently, slowly—then be passionate. Bodies should mesh. Now that you both know what's going to happen—bring up the subject of contraception. It's important and very responsible to be able to discuss anything and everything; it can also be amorous. Discussing sex openly and in good faith, without fear, is not only the adult thing to do, it's also caring, and sexy.

Lao Two says: "Lust, desire, libido, passion—there is so much sexual energy inside of humans. We need to understand and harness powerful energy, channel it, and use it for realization."

The secret is out—sex is better with marijuana. Smoking before, during (take a break), and after sex is magical. The human body is an excellent conduit of electrical, vibrational, sexual, and other, more subtle types of energy.

I was going to describe some sexual techniques, but Lao Two pointed out that there are much better skilled teachers (not porn) on the Internet for that. All I'll say is dig the person you are. Be loving, enthusiastic, and skilled, and play fair.

The joining of two people is a sacred act. Do not take sex lightly or superficially, or play someone for a fool. These days there's really no reason for anyone to be alone. Meet people on the Internet dating sites, in special interest groups (sports, hiking, volunteer), college classes, supermarkets, yoga classes, and everywhere else. Be the first to smile.

Lao Two says: "If you are a Stoner and are depressed and anxious, then change your ways. Smoking marijuana should make you happy, aware, and give you the ability to understand the cosmic joke."

If you have the courage to smoke marijuana—you already know you can get busted, but you smoke anyway—then you should also be courageous in relationships. Use your rebellious energies to meet people. No matter what your sexual preferences, refuse to be shy or unhappy. Liberate your ideas regarding sexuality and find what makes you, and your partner sexually happy.

Lao Two says: "Humanity needs to turn on the love-light."

In the hippie days it was possible to meet people just by asking if they wanted to get high. People were always sharing smokes, and strangers always felt they could join a circle of unfamiliar people passing a joint around. But I don't see that happening these days—people bring their private stash and smoke alone, or with their close circle of friends. I always have some high-quality smokes in my pocket in case a smoking session materializes. But I can't remember the last time that happened, so I've been giving the spare joints in my pocket to people begging on the streets instead. Times have changed. ...

When you interact with an unknown person, don't go into the situation expecting to be rejected. Expect that at the least, you will communicate with someone new—don't make it into a big deal. If you are rejected, be polite and graceful and realize that you had the courage to take the risk, so give yourself some credit. Remember, other people are just like you—painfully shy, or having a bad day, or just too busy—but generally it's harmless to casually talk to someone. Many people are into the good-looks syndrome, but they can't help it, and are looking for some ideal that doesn't exist. They will have to flounder around until they understand superficiality.

We suggest you keep every relationship fluid: don't solidify your friends, give them permission to change by seeing them as new each time you see them. Please don't forget humor in relationships; sex can be funny, and even words have sexual power. If a person harms you, it's up to you if you want to give them another chance to make it right—there is no rule saying you have to hang around abusive people.

Lao Two says: "Fair must be fair for everyone, or it's not fair. Even very young children know what it means to play fair."

Love can be understood as two types of lights: one is vast and expansive and lights up everything. The other can focus like a spotlight. Both of these lights, by nature, are completely free to illuminate, not limited in any way. No one can grasp a handful of light, hold on to it, or keep it indefinitely. We have love-lights inside all of us, it's part of our presence; we are connected to love whether we know it or not.

Expansive light has no innate boundaries, and once opened or turned on, it does not fade away, nor can it be covered or obscured. But it can be turned off, or even turned down—and that's the situation most of us find ourselves in: our love-light is turned down. Open up the emotional dam and the light bursts through, illuminating everything and everyone around us. The expansive light is love without obsession, attachment, judgment, or emotional dependency—it is love for everything and everybody.

But we also have a spotlight of love that can focus toward a particular person. When that person returns our focused spotlight with his or her own spotlight, it increases the light exponentially. Focused love-light is vastly powerful, and that's what we feel when we are "in love." Concentrated love-light is not just a one-to-one ratio, because love exceeds physical explanations, as we understand them.

For further study on the expansive and focused ability to emanate love—see the essential teachings in the Vajrayana system of Tibetan Buddhism.

Lao Two says: "Be grateful you have a person to share your love-light with."

Accept whatever physical features you have. Your status is not low, your clothing is adequate, your car goes from here to there, or you know how the bus schedule works. Everyone has something that makes him or her interesting, funny, loving, or desirable.

Realize that modern advertising has programmed us since we were old enough to hear and see. Beautiful, desirable, sexy, passionate, rich, latest, greatest, famous—words trigger our emotional desires. Most people are influenced; some are exploited and taken advantage of. We all yearn for acceptance, being part of the tribe. Advertising tells us god is money, and worship of money will keep providing us with toys to distract us. ... We live in an age of technological miracles, but it's a dark age too. These are dark and lonely times for too many people.

We have to reconsider what we want out of desire and see sexual attraction in a positive way. Desire is a human attribute, an emotion, neither good nor bad in itself. We can open our heart to another person, and use our desires as a focus, a bridge, and a beacon for others. Then together we create love, peace, awareness, and compassion.

Stoner Meditation wants you to desire love. Experience all the levels of love, from masturbation, sexual fantasy, and sex, to meditative bliss and cosmic consciousness. Again, love is the most powerful vibration in the universe. Start on the journey to meet someone. Try to be open to everyone, even people who don't fit your preconceived perfect-partner ideal. Go on dates, experiment, don't be serious or obsessive, and have fun in the present moment.

Be aware of the world around you, flirt, use your courage, make eye contact, smile, and be aware of body language. Touch, shake hands, joke around, be on your best behavior, have fun. Someone wants to love the person you are, and you want to love the person they are. Simple.

Contemplate Fear

Fear is our wizard friend, a friend that challenges us, competes with us, and keeps us alert. Without it we would walk in front of moving cars. Yet we overcame fear when we learned to swim and ride a bike for the first time, and it liberated us. Fear is the best teacher of all. When we conquer fear, we gain wizard power and confidence. The primal fear of being alone makes us cross the gulf from loneliness to companionship.

Lao Two says: "Risk is our ticket to engage with life."

Fear is a cornerstone of our relationships. It can make us see the world as unfriendly out-there, instead of feeling accepted. Because of overpopulation stress we have lost community, and we're taught at an early age to fit in, play it safe, and do as we're told. This is a story we culturally make up; it's not reality. As usual, we want to see things exactly as they are, not some storyline version that we use to distort reality. If we can remove all the preconditioned thinking, worrying, and anxiety, we are left with the actual situation itself—which in this case is just humans standing on the Earth at this moment of space-time. In that way, all our interactions become magical, eternal, and without care for our fear, because our socializing is natural. When we can BE and open our heart, it's enchanting, spiritual, and joyous.

We are not only made out of Earth, but we are also the same material as every star in the universe. I don't know where this saying comes from, but it goes something like this: "what is not here is nowhere, what is here is everywhere." If, for some reason or other, you grew up with a poor self-image or body image, or with negative attitudes about sex, then this is your chance to free your mind. Do you want to look back on your life and wish you had done things differently? Live like you want to live, realize your fantasies, be bigger than your fears.

Lao Two says: "You will know you are doing life right if you are noticing compassion, love, and wisdom growing."

Our physical body is constantly changing and growing older, but many people are stuck not being able to change negative habits. Habits are powerful and arise out of fear. Challenging entrenched habits is profoundly difficult. However, life is a process and a path. Not every path will be level; sometimes we have to walk steeply uphill, struggle, and run out of breath. Meditation can help, but for those with obsessive behavior, or fear - therapy might be the answer. I always suggest Internet searches, reading self-help books, and trying to solve obsessive habitual problems on your own—but different methods work for different people.

Don't suppress your fears; try your best to bring them into the light. When you're tripping or meditating and you can't tell what's real or not, you've learned that there's no place you can go that you can't get back from, and thoughts and emotions sometimes lie.

Endings

Lao Two says: "In the infinite cave of darkness the smallest light illuminates instantly."

Somewhere along the line all relationships end. Death, divorce, separation, not calling anymore, or the mixed-up people who are "just going out to get something at the grocery" and never come back. ... Ouch. It hurts, and it's been shown by scientific research that breakups and endings actually wound our body/mind. Stoner Meditation maintains that partners also share vibrations, empathic feelings, and sensory telepathy.

We hear of people who stayed in a relationship way too long. No matter what they tried, it didn't work: therapy, reading self-help books, advice from friends. Why do we stay too long? Because the feeling of love that we experience is so strong, so important to us, that we don't want to let that feeling go. Of course our ego is hurt and on a level we are embarrassed—but more importantly, our together-body is actually ripped apart. Stoner Meditation says we naturally grow tuned to the other person on a whole bunch of levels. We must reiterate - we share our vibes, empathic feelings, and sensory telepathy.

Lao Two says: "Just because you love somebody doesn't mean you can live with them".

When love is suddenly removed, it's a down elevator. In time we work through the pain, eventually scraping the mud and dust off, and we heal. Still shaken, we continue, realizing at some point that life is not waiting for us. Our next love will not knock on our door and announce that they are our new partner. Endings take a toll of time, patience, and hope. But sometimes people have to move on.

In our Stoner Meditation practice we focus on the breath. There are a lot of reasons we do this, and one is to notice how things end. No matter how abrupt something like a relationship breakup feels, it's part of a large cycle that we will experience over and over in our lives. We meet someone, spend time in love with them, and then it's over, and we pull ourselves together. Consider: we breathe in, the breath persists, it starts to end as the out breath, and coasts to the next breath, maybe.

Sometimes it's effective to develop a ritual to let someone go. Using Exercise 5, you can develop your own ceremony. Lao Two has an ending protocol ritual that goes like this:

"Face in the general direction where the person or situation is. Close your eyes. Start with a Namaste mudra (hands at chest, palms together) and project peace and love. Then raise your arms above your head with fingers pointing up, palms facing forward, stretching your arms up to infinity. Feel the pushing upward, then let gravity bring the hands down to your sides, then outward horizontally so your body is a 't', palms forward. In an exaggerated motion bring your hands together in front, clapping loudly, then back into the 't', and then another clap. Do this three times ending up as a 't'.. Hands back to Namaste. Open your eyes. Pause to give a head bow, then lift your head back to normal position. Turn 180 degrees around—and walk away. Each step puts the person or situation in the past, and your walking pushes forward into the future."

At the end of each daily meditation, Lao Two does this ritual:

"When the timer goes off or the incense burns down, pause for a moment. Close your eyes. Make the Namaste mudra, and think thoughts about compassion, and try to feel love. Then bring the hands up to your throat chakra—thumbs at throat, index fingers at lips—and remind yourself of right speech. And then move your hands up to the forehead, bowing the head a little, and spread your wisdom to the universe. It's important to try to feel these subtle energies in the body; it's not just a mental experience. Next put each hand on a thigh, palm up, thumb and forefinger touching. Chant three AOMs, feeling the vibrations down to your toes into the ground below you. Finally, one last Namaste mudra with hands together."

Yes, in each life there is suffering, pain, arguments, worry, and end-ings where we separate. Everything we experience is temporary. In the scheme of things there is also friendship, contact, and joy—and living in the moment. If you could have a life that had no pain, passion, or bliss—would you really want it? I have a friend who has anxiety. His wife said he should see his doctor, and of course the doctor prescribed Xanax—a pretty serious drug. If he had been smoking marijuana, his anxiety would have been manageable, but he never smoked before. I sent over two joints for him to try, and I hope he switches to medical marijuana instead of the Xanax. Learn to live with moments of angst, enjoy temporary suffering—after all, it's part of life, nothing to fear. (Of course, if anxiety can't be cured by natural methods, then absolutely see a doctor.)

Allow happiness; enjoy your life, laugh a lot. When you wake up in the morning, go to the mirror and see if the person in the reflection is smiling at you. If you have to give yourself a fake smile, then stand look-ing at your image for a moment. Smile at your life-partner first thing in the morning.

Be cautious, notice negativity creeping in and counter with giving yourself permission to live a complete life. Smoking marijuana gives us a higher perspective; use that view to focus on yourself and pay atten-tion to what you find. We are a work in progress, constantly changing and growing, infinitely curious and filled with every single emotion that a human can express. Stoner Meditation is not only done with analytical thinking mind, it is moving on to doing mind. Feel your body and sensory system, and notice whatever is happening in the moment. Be as connected and engaged as possible. Also—give yourself permission to not be aware, to be clumsy, unpredictable, and human. Give your partner that same permission.

Lao Two says: "Accept family and friends the way they are. Try to encourage their good qualities, knowing that they will also fail sometimes. It's very powerful to let people love us, and love them back unconditionally."

Review

A generalized summary: Thoughts lie. We like to think our mind is perfect, but the fact is that thinking mind is habitual and learning meditative concentration keeps it from running amok.

When you sit in meditation, it's your time. Thinking mind will tell you that you have to listen to its negativity and thought loops, but say, "This is my time, I'll think about that later." You don't have to analyze during meditation, just sit and allow the future to play out inside you.

If you are extremely active, depressed, or just can't sit in meditation, try yoga or tai chi (DVD, or take a class), then sit in meditation for a short while after the exercises.

If you can meditate, try single-point meditation. We recommend focusing eye attention on the burning ember of a stick of incense. While doing that, also focus at the nostrils, feeling the breath come in and go out. When single-point meditation becomes more advanced, it's called calm abiding meditation.

Enlightenment is the mind outside of us watching inside mind—and both watching minds absorbed as One Mind.

All thinking is illusion (especially during meditation). Turn down the volume on thoughts, then turn up the volume on breath.

Keep meditation mellow, don't stress—and although Stoner Meditation is big on results, realize that there are ultimately no results from meditation. Remember meditation is all about attention, so just watch whatever happens when you sit. Let thoughts, emotions, and physical body just send you signals, without reacting to those signals—more importantly, just seeing them for exactly what they are, temporary and passing through. Don't space out during meditation; it's important to develop concentration. The time for spacing out is when we get stoned. Make meditation a priority in your life, and make it an everyday practice. Spend a little time at the end of your daily meditation practice to contemplate and feel compassion—then take that into your daily life. Be compassionate toward yourself too.

Stoner Meditation is not aimed at people who become monks, it's for people living in the world. Stoner Meditation does not require us to give up our dreams. What we give up is our attachment, clinging, and negative habits.

However, we are required to understand what attachment is. When we meditate we see that each breath is in the here and now (beginning, persisting, ending). We are not entitled to another next breath. This present breath is ALL we have.

It's attachment to grasp at the next breath. It's attachment to grasp at relationships or events in the world, they ALL end.

We can only love someone in the here and now.

Enlightenment is awareness. Awareness of what? Higher mind. Stoner Meditation teaches us to clearly discover the path to higher mind. Meditation combined with marijuana and psychedelics are shamanic tools that use higher mind to change our world. Meditation is powerful, it can dissolve the boundary between self and other (inside of us and outside of us). This is commonly known as ego death, when emptiness is discovered. Once emptiness is made "visible," compassion develops as we realize we are connected to each other.

We are our choices. Balance lets us walk the path effortlessly. Being too serious, or too frivolous is not the Stoner Meditation path. Extremes are not our way.

Smoking marijuana should be fun and enjoyable, but at the same time it should be a spiritual, meditative tool that gives us clarity and elevates our psychic adventures. Abusing it carelessly is a superficial misuse of good weed, a waste of our precious time, and our life-force energies. Respect your grower and dealer, and try to understand how much work, time, risk, and expended energy is involved to bring marijuana to the public. What we smoke is mother Earth.

Realize higher mind. The Stoners who are sitting on their couch smoking all the time need to get off their asses and start a daily sitting meditation. As a group, Stoners must start becoming active and loving, and start expressing their gift of creativity. Get involved with the world, read, inquire, and speak out. Now that marijuana is legal in some states, Stoners there do not need to hide underground anymore.

Distractions—Itch

This day will not come again. If you knew for certain that you wouldn't see tomorrow, wouldn't the rest of this day have a special focus? Even a life of 100 years is incredibly brief. Each breath, every sight, taste, and smell, is worth more than gold. The sadness we carry around is just part of the lie and illusion that keeps us from joy, and an effective life. Stoner Meditation is teaching that there is untapped power in each moment, and the deeper we go into that moment, the more power we find. But the real problem is that we're missing what's going on right in front of us—simply because of our habitual distracted nature.

We have thousands of different types of bacteria happily living on our skin. We scratch an itch no matter what else we are involved with, and we never stop to think about what we're doing. We got these great fingernails, perfect for relieving the irritation—seems natural enough. ... But for Stoner Meditation a simple itch becomes an excellent meditation tool.

As we said before, when breath meditation advances to become calm abiding, breath is actually transcended. To do this we need to be able to sit still, unmoving, quietly relaxed, without jumping around in body or mind. Calm abiding is both relaxed and alert; it's not a sleepy haze. When we're acting from the calm abiding mind, distractions are gone and our life is effective.

How hard is it to do this? Damn near impossible for people who are not full-time monks. But we laypeople can use Stoner Meditation to experience brief moments of calm abiding as a result of our daily meditation practice, along with insights from marijuana and psychedelics, and learning how the world works by honest observation.

Our basic meditation instruction taught that the breath has a beginning in breath, a short pause, then the exhale coasting to the end—each breath fulfills this cycle. Breath meditation retrains our attention to focus on something other than obsessive thinking mind, giving thinking mind permission to take a break. Concentrations on natural rhythms such as breath or heartbeat are perfect nonemotional meditation objects.

We find the same cycle in our thinking mind. Exactly like breath, thoughts arise, persist, and fade away. Other life cycles are less obvious—like birth, letting the child grow into an adult, then death. For our training here we use the cycle of an itch.

Our favorite distraction is a good solid mosquito bite, although any lesser itch will also do. The bite occurs, it itches like crazy, and then eventually the itching goes away. Our job is to experience the itch, sit quietly and undisturbed, and not scratch it.

Since itching has arising, persisting, and ending, we realize an itch is a temporary phenomenon. It teaches us patience, mind and body connection, and creates an iron determination to sit without moving. Lastly, itching is incredibly irritating, so it's excellent practice in patience under unfavorable conditions.

When you are in your daily sitting meditation and notice an itch, stay perfectly still, and do not scratch it—no, no, NO. Ask yourself, "When did the itching begin? What exactly are the itch sensations? How long will the itching last?" I'll bet you are noticing itching all over the place right now. ...

The strange thing is that our body is sending us thousands upon thousands of signals all the time, and we can pick up the phone and respond to the signal from the body, or let it keep ringing until it eventually stops. Sitting in daily meditation necessitates that you *stay still* and experience everything that comes and goes. We want to notice distractions that arise while we are sitting. An itch is temporary, and usually it's harmless if we don't scratch it, so it's a perfect item to zero in, and use that itch for witnessing the incredible power of body/mind at work.

I would bet you are asking, why go to all this trouble? First, because it's the distractions that keep us from being aware—being pulled this way and that, from this pleasure to that. And next, being able to ignore itching trains us how to ignore pain. Body pain is no different from the other cycles. We feel pain, it persists, and then it lessens.

From this ability to notice the signals our body/mind is sending, we can expand into other cycles. Annoying life incidents like an argument allow us to notice the arising anger and emotions in our body. Anger and emotions also have a beginning, middle, and end. Distractions are not good or bad, just like an itch is neither good nor bad. These are just physical, mental, and emotional events. We're learning when to detach from our hidden habits, but because they are habits, they will return again and again. Tip: Go to the bathroom before you sit down and meditate.

Here are a few examples of distractions you might feel while meditating: a wave of pleasure sweeping over your body—this is love. A feeling of tightness in the stomach—this is fear. Shortness in your breath—is usually anxiety. Headache—often tension; relax your shoulders, renew your concentration on a deeper breath, bring in more oxygen, relax the entire body. Noticing the top of your skull lifting off—a very concentrated high—whoa. Feeling the weight of your human body on the ground—awareness. Feeling the ground sending you energy back—you have just connected with the Earth. Feeling your body becoming one with the universe—ego loss. Hallucinations—letting thinking mind fall away. Whatever you experience with any physical/emotional sense is not real or important (during meditation); it is a form of communication.

Sometimes when concentration on the breath is going really well, we can feel subtle pressure at the third eye—sometimes it arrives as a mild itching feeling, other times as light pressure, and often leads to insight, as if a light were shining out of your forehead—and always when you notice the top of your skull lifting off. The name for these subtle energies is Kundalini, and there is nothing to fear in noticing them. However, for advanced Kundalini practitioners it's said that there is a rise of energy from just behind the sexual organs. It travels upward through the spine and explodes out through the crown of the head, and is extremely powerful. It's recommended you find a teacher if you are experiencing waves of body energy like this. Some people on marijuana and LSD have described these experiences.

Just like not reacting to an itch, when you feel anxiety in your breath, make peace with it. Allow the breath to be anxious, then welcome and include anxiety in your life—don't try to make the anxiety go away or let it distract you from your breath, just let it be there as another part of the dialogue of your breath movie. The first occasion we don't react to the stimulus, we see the wizard power of letting events happen without trying to control the situation. Then distractions occur around us, but we stay centered in our awareness, unaffected by the itch or the anxiety, or even body pain. For many people, ignoring itching might be the first time not mindlessly reacting to distractions.

Tip: If you have a serious itch like poison oak or ivy, this might help - Instead of scratching with your nails with force, just rub your fingers lightly over the itching area. Of course this works best stoned. Lightly touching will keep the itch from bleeding and getting infected. And it gives the same satisfaction if you zero in on the feeling, instead of mindlessly scratching.

Do you remember the itch you had on your ear last week? Do you remember the thought you had at 3:23 p.m. last Wednesday afternoon?

When the demanding distraction can be endured and transcended, we gain control of our body senses.

Trouble Sleeping at Night

The first thing we notice when we start to meditate is the relentless inner voice of thinking mind. Once noticed, this fidgety chatterbox monkey mind shows up everywhere and becomes a struggle. We want to control the content, make it be quiet, and even have the inner voice go away. Even after Stoner Meditation tells us not to struggle with thinking mind, we can't help it—the incessant nature of "should, would, could" of thinking mind can draw us inward, and the inner voice can become obsessive indecision. Not only is thinking mind noisy, the content can turn into a malicious, angry, and belittling voice, and weariness from the constant putdowns draws a few people into depression. To counter this we use meditation to first notice the frequency and content of inner voice for a while; then through analysis we start seeing that thoughts have no inherent existence. Many of our thoughts are just confused lies that have become habitual. Most of the exercises previously presented are designed to help us realize that there are creative ways to deal with and understand thinking mind.

I've said it before, but it's worth repeating: meditation is not a quick fix. Marijuana and psychedelics can give us insights into our problems, but the high is often too intense, so the great ideas float away by the time we've come down. If you suffer from depression, anxiety, and poor self-image, start reading some different therapy techniques on the Internet. I've found cognitive behavioral therapy very helpful. If you are considering an anxiety drug like Xanax, please try smoking different strains of marijuana first, because you will probably find one that can fix your anxiety or depression. It's the same with using sleeping pills—there are some techniques, and types of marijuana, that can replace pills effectively. For our sleep-mix we mix several types of Indicia together; right now it's Dream Queen and Bubba Kush mixed 50-50, smoked about an hour before we want to be asleep. Indica buds are also incredibly effective for people who wake up in the middle of the night and can't go back to sleep. Lao Two says that one puff of Indica in the middle of the night puts him back to sleep gently, effectively—sometimes right away, other times within a half hour. If you smoke a few hours before you are scheduled to wake up, expect to be a little hazy for a while. Regrettably, not everyone can grow (or purchase) several different strains of marijuana like Lao Two. And not everyone has a medical marijuana card, and we don't always have just the right kind of smokes on hand. Stoner Meditation has a technique that should help many people suffering from insomnia.

We go to work, come home, and get stoned. Then after a few short hours we have to lie down on the bed, close our eyes, and go to sleep. For most people the process from awake to falling asleep isn't immediate. Our worries, anxieties, and insecurities continue along happily even though our eyelids have closed. Now we start some thought loops, analyzing our situation, trying to find an acceptable solution to our problems.

At night we lie down and abruptly expect thinking-mind to quiet. But our recurring thoughts and emotions, the aches of our physical body, and thinking-mind bringing up past and future events are overwhelming. We suddenly expect our body tension, short breath, and raging mind to turn off like a light switch. But, thinking-mind is not finished analyzing and replaying some screw-up, argument, or financial dilemma.

On top of that, many longtime Stoners are becoming shamans without realizing it. They are finding that being awake and being asleep feels the same in some ways. Perhaps you've been experiencing some lucid dreaming—where the dreamer becomes aware during dreams and chooses to participate. For example, finding a gun in our hand in a dream, and an attacker in front of us, instead of shooting the gun, we deliberately choose to use it to knock out the attacker instead. For that matter, our dreams change in content too.

When Lao Two was younger he was always a worrier—he had plenty of reasons to worry, but that's another story. He would sometimes lie in bed stressed, sad, or angry, his brain running thought loops—tossing and turning, eventually becoming frustrated that he couldn't fall asleep. His life was probably similar to that of many readers: almost every morning he was doing a ten-minute yoga and twenty-minute meditation, working a day job, coming home, dealing marijuana, then hitting the bed early so he could get up refreshed for work the next day. Only, it rarely worked that way when it came to falling asleep. One night he serendipitously discovered (rediscovered?) a simple way to get to sleep.

Here is his meditation for falling asleep, or going back to sleep in the middle of the night. It might not work the first few times you try it, it might even take months to work—sometimes it won't work at all. If it doesn't, then get out of bed and do something constructive for a while. Give this exercise a few months and some perseverance. As usual, feel free to modify the instructions if you discover improvements that work better for you.

Exercise 7—Sleep Meditation: Position yourself lying on your back, no pillow. Close your eyes. Roll your head back and forth a couple of times to feel and release the tension there; let your shoulders slump. Put your arms by your sides, palms up, touching your thumb to your first finger. Or, put your arms on your chest at the breastbone, palms down. If right-handed, put your right hand under the left hand, and the opposite for left-handed people. Thumbs touching, so there's a thumb triangle above your hands. There's no spiritual reasons for these positions, we just find them comfortable.

No moving is allowed—at all. So get comfortable, but no crossing one leg over the other. No scratching itches, but anything automatic like passing gas or sneezing is fine. This exercise is based on the premise that, hey, if you are going to be lying there doing nothing anyway, trying to fall asleep, you might as well meditate.

Notice that your rhythmic breathing is probably short-winded; in about five minutes it will be deeper and more relaxed. For sleep meditation your attention will be directed primarily at the nostrils, but also feel the chest and stomach rising and falling. So far this is like your daily meditation—focused, aware concentration, and feeling the breath at your nose. For sleep meditation concentration at the nostrils is especially important—pay close attention to the breath no matter what distractions arise, even if you have to use rigid effort.

The huge difference here, compared to our original meditation instruction, is that in sleep meditation you must consciously stop each arising thought, right at the beginning. Each time a thought emerges from the noise factory of thinking mind, stop it right away, or ignore it, keeping your concentration on the present breath. No matter how important a thought tells you it is, keep attentiveness on the breath. There is NO thought that is important enough to interrupt this exercise—tell your mind you will think about it later if you have to, but this is YOUR time.

What we want in sleep meditation is entirely different: we don't want thoughts to keep arising and floating across our movie like floating clouds, as we described for beginning meditation. Now we want to silence every arising thought. Please understand that this intense concentration on silence is unnatural for the mind, so we are swimming upstream.

Pretend your concentration on each breath is a huge, muscle-bound bouncer who stands outside of the nightclub. This dude tells each arising thought it's not allowed to come in because the club is closed for the night. The thought will start to argue, but our muscle-bound bouncer dude kicks ass and the thought goes away. Every once in a while a thought will sneak in, but inside the nightclub is another bouncer who catches the thought and throws it outside.

When a sound or flickering light comes along, don't react in any way. If we were on a bed in the sleeper of a moving train, there would be countless lights, sounds, movements, and unusual noises—yet most of us can sleep on a train.

We promise that this is the most fatiguing meditation exercise you will ever do, and that you will shortly roll over and fall asleep from mental exhaustion. You'll know when you've had enough of this meditation, so go with your instincts—when I started it took about twenty minutes, now about five minutes and I'm asleep. Sleeping meditation gets easier after years of practice—and after some months at it, you will notice your pre-bedtime thinking automatically relaxing, with stress and anxiety falling away even before you hit the sheets. After you get advanced at this you will have taught yourself to easily fall asleep by silencing your thoughts.

End of Exercise 7.

Much of insomnia comes because we are listening to the thinking mind tape run over and over in our mind, or being acutely aware of sounds like barking dogs or other stimuli nearby. By forcing thoughts to stop, or not letting ourselves react, we short-circuit the arising thoughts by not allowing the resulting thought loops. And since stopping every arising thought takes such intense concentration, it's exhausting—sleep soon follows because the self-absorbed ego mind wanted us to believe those thoughts are really, really important. They're not urgently important, at least not at bedtime.

The reason for staying absolutely still is, according to the people who practice lucid dreaming, our body often enters a benign sleep paralysis before we drift into sleep. By staying perfectly still during the exercise, we trick the body to mimic sleep paralysis as a technique of sleep meditation.

Techniques—Habitual Thinking

Lao Two says: "Our habitually analytical thinking mind cannot figure out enlightenment because there is nothing to grasp on to. Call it what you will—enlightenment, wisdom mind, buddha nature, Natural Mind, awareness—it's our birthright."

It still amazes us how so many people took LSD and now, down the road, act like it didn't really affect them long-term. It seems there are only a few hard-core psychedelic takers—and the rest come along to feel the spiritual vibes a little. Somehow they missed the deeper levels of LSD insight and only saw interesting hallucinations. It seems to us that this demonstrates just how strong the ego and thinking mind is, and how they can come back even after being mind blown by psychedelics.

But some guys like Lao Two and me, and some of the older hippies, totally immersed ourselves in the psychedelic soup, and then for a long time we feasted at the Tibetan Buddhist table of ancient teachings. Right after the hippies started to disband, previously unreleased spiritual information was made available. The Dalai Lama and his people, in exodus after China's brutal invasion of Tibet, started teaching the dharma. We were lucky by the timing - of first taking LSD, and then having Tibetan teachers to help us to stay on that path, although it's unlucky for the suffering Tibetan diaspora who lost their homeland. Hippies were also doomed for so many reasons, and that's all right because as we keep saying everything has endings. But the clear-sighted hippie dream of an environmentally productive planet Earth, instead of the destructive planetary mindset we had, is still alive.

What a lot of people who took LSD missed was taking a good hard look at their propensity for habitual thinking. Simple tricks like when we settle into our stonedest self, feeling entirely mellow and relaxed, remembering to notice our breathing and vibes—instead of letting habitual thinking take us where it will. I'm not discussing the times we are successfully tripping out, where we let marijuana or LSD take us higher and higher, but rather, the times we get high and get stuck in thought loops.

The advantage of noticing breathing and vibes when we are stoned is that we can do the same when we are our straightest self out in the world. Running into anxious and stressful situations, remembering that they are temporary and have no inherent existence (on the highest levels), and emotions are unreliable sensory information. Instead of feeling tense, take a deep, slow breath. Take another, get out of your inside thinking mind, and feel your body. Realize that even in the stormy roller-coaster of life, you are connected to the flowing creative force.

Ojibwe (Chippewa) Indian saying: "Sometimes I go about in pity for myself, and all the while a great wind is bearing me across the sky."

Love is the primary, strongest vibration, and the farther away from love people get, the more their vibration is disconnected and negative. What is this process? Maybe we feel entitled to be loved without doing the work on our part by giving love back. Love is active, not passive. Anger is not only the absence of love—it is completely ignoring our true feelings. Good vibrations can be learned, and once proficient, we can summon our best positive energy toward suffering people. Wizards make the people around them feel better, without the people understanding what they are feeling. We do this by being connected to such a strong love vibe inside of us that people can't help but feel it.

Joy, bliss, wisdom, love, awareness—these are our natural state of being. That's how we all came out of our mother's body. Our negative habitual thinking is just that—habit. But our habits are tied closely to our emotions, so learn to feel what's going on when negative thoughts and feelings arrive. Feel the negativity coming into the body, get to know it, embrace and contact the feelings instead of automatically cutting off attention to painful experiences. At first we notice that thinking mind has been stopping that negative input, or at least suppressing it. Instead of being relaxed, the body tenses up, but we've been doing it for so long that we don't notice the tension anymore. The solution is letting the negative tension flow into us, feeling it, changing it into a loving vibe, returning the vibe as love—and it can be learned.

At least Stoners get a chance to get high and unconsciously let all the stress, tension, and anxiety go away—unless instead, we are in habitual thought loops where we process the negative energy in our mind and body over and over again—even while high.

Our habitual way of emotionally reacting doesn't have to bring us down; we can process the information once and let it go. If the thought loop comes up a second or third time, change the dynamic by putting your attention on breath and body. That way even strong emotions like grief can be experienced in the moment, processed as experience, and let go as we're moving through the experience. We lived it; we don't have to ruminate on it over and over again. This is how we let ourselves move on.

Another aspect of habitual thinking mind is judgmental thinking. This is the inner voice that speaks up immediately after seeing something, or someone, we don't like. Aversion is just a voice inside of us pointing out things we've learned to fear, another survival tactic from primitive mind that can give us wrong information. Our group is familiar = good. Their group is unfamiliar = bad.

Consider the people who give you a bad first impression. Is it the way they dress, their foreign accent, their skin color, or that you consider them ugly? Such overcritical judgments keep us apart from others and increase suffering. Governments have always promoted aversion by creating an "enemy" that we get emotional about ... next thing we know, we have to kill that "enemy" to satisfy some insane governmental purpose. The strangest thing is, we find ourselves angry towards complete strangers.

Judgmental thinking is also a learned way of avoiding our personal problems—we don't want anything that's ugly, smelly, distressful, or painful. This is good in some situations, like being sprayed by a skunk, when it's important to use aversion to get away quickly. But being judgmental can block the natural flow of our energy, and unfortunately, it can build up over time, creating stronger emotions like anger, and then inappropriately we explode.

Think of it as being swept along by the current of a river. We arrive at a narrow gorge where the swollen water is building pressure, and we are swept underwater. In our body it's felt as pain, anguish, burning, gasping for air, inability to lift our worn-out limbs or think straight anymore—we're angry that our judgments got us in this situation. Then finally, we're in an underwater whirlpool where we are stuck, gasping for air. To burst through, we explode by acting out in anger. Bummer.

It's obvious that we need to start noticing our habitual thinking, emotions, and what is happening in our bodies. All these habitual techniques we learned as we grew up, we now have to unlearn. On the meditation cushion, and off the cushion, we have to put our attention on the quality, repetition, and types of thoughts that come up. Take some time to really listen to the messages thinking mind is dwelling on for a while. Once we see how our habits are creating a negative world, we can discredit those thoughts by saying, "That's just not true."

It's endemic on this planet to think we are better than someone else, to elevate our own view of ourselves. We all know the results of this type of habitual thinking—wars, greed, injustice, and suffering – even starvation. Don't allow your thinking mind to take you on these types of rides. Bring the awareness of doing mind that sees everything exactly as it is.

The hostile, angry, frustrated inner voice chatters away like churning waves on the ocean. Underneath the waves, the ocean is calm. *You don't have to believe everything you think.*

On the one hand we have aversion, which is pushing away the stuff we don't want. On the other hand we have attachment, grasping, clinging for the stuff we really want. As I've said, aversion and attachment are not always good and bad; they can also be survival techniques. Thinking mind is like a magnet that always wants something, and it's used to striving to get what it wants: material happiness, to be successful, and not to suffer. You can see where this is going—we find pleasure in this or that, but all pleasure is doomed to end sooner or later. Or, even if we get what we want, we find it's less than satisfactory—the shiny polish of the new car starts to fade as soon as we drive it away from the dealer.

Habitual thinking could also be called the distracted mind, which keeps churning over and over at inappropriate times, like when we want to fall asleep. Habitual thinking can't seem to forget our past screw-ups, or stop worrying about what might happen in the future. Even our cherished beliefs in philosophical and religious systems are created brick by brick into a fantasy story that "makes sense"—we forget to keep our skepticism. Beliefs become solidified, and even if they are ridiculous, they persist. It is no different than the "I" clinging to the solidified, erroneous storyline that it has created instead of seeing directly, honestly, and authentically using doing mind.

The solution to habitual thinking is to be in the here and now, directly involved in noticing when thoughts arise, seeing clearly what is happening at this very moment. Then the cloudlike natures of thoughts float by, not as judgmental directives that we have to listen to, but as information. We take that information and if it's accurate, use it, and if inaccurate, discard it.

Do you think your brain is storing each thought you think, or that your thoughts are really important? Probably 99 percent of thoughts are not saved—they disappear. I like to think of my thought stream as a river. The thought I had five minutes ago is downstream now, gone.

Lao Two says: "We are being carried along by the unfathomable river. No matter what our mood, emotional state, intelligence, or level of awareness—we are swept along."

Tripping—Meditative Concentration

Lao Two says: "The future arrives by itself, but we have to understand that there are two valid approaches to meeting it. First, we are oneness with the inexorable movement forward in space-time that has no past or future. And second, paradoxically we are a conglomeration of the past, and have to make plans for our future."

Time does not move forward, since when we step off Earth into outer space, there is no time. In our case, time represents our transit around the sun and the spin of the Earth—time is always relative to something. In outer space (and here on Earth), what's always inexorably moving forward is expanding space. Our oneness with space is what's moving.

We take the karma we are born with and mold it as we go through life. We are born fat or thin, smart or dumb, strong or weak—or somewhere in between. We are what we are. Our judgments about our self-image are irrelevant. What most of us miss is that every precious moment has eternity within it. The true gift of our birth is the brief, splendid, aware moments we have in space-time. Wisdom is using our time wisely before the future swallows us up.

We need to use the best techniques we can find to make peace with silence. Because at the end when death comes, we have to deal with silence, and it's not what we normally think it is. Within stillness is a mysterious power, and we can use Stoner Meditation to become one with silence and "hold" on to presence. This is another way of describing calm abiding. Of course, as Stoners we are going to use marijuana and psychedelics to help us understand silence, along with our daily sitting meditation.

Tripping should feel like coasting, so let the marijuana or psychedelic draw you along, relaxed without any struggle, just grooving on whatever hallucination or insight comes. Tripping is tripping—it's not sitting meditation. And tripping only comes when we can shut down our worries, suspend thinking mind, and float downstream—techniques that are learned in sitting meditation. Or, if the psychedelic is strong enough, it will suspend thinking mind chemically, replacing it with the psychedelic gestalt—its characteristics, or types of experiences. Marijuana is quite benign compared to the intensity of magic mushrooms. And mushrooms have a somewhat different feeling than peyote, or LSD etc.

Lao Two says: "The key to successful tripping on psychedelics is to suspend the judgmental mind and just allow whatever comes along—blissful visions or horrifying nightmares—and honestly look into the mirror of the life movie we've created. Take comfort in knowing that the psychedelic you just put into your body is an extraordinary shamanic teacher."

Tripping is admittedly the chemical changes happening in the body/mind on marijuana or psychedelics, but it's also tied closely to where our head is at. So, by smoking some marijuana or eating some mushrooms, we're sending depth charges into the abyss of thinking mind, temporarily shutting it down. Eventually inner voice quiets, releasing us to enter doing mind—tripping unrestrained.

Lao Two says: "When the conditions are right, tripping is like riding a surfboard on an endless wave. It's knowing that all of this stuff, ideas, and all our beliefs are just puffs of smoke, dispersing into space-time."

If your thinking mind is keeping you from tripping, ask yourself exactly what you are holding on to. Try imagining that you are a comfortable void of atomic pebbles that stick together. And amazingly, this mess of atomic pebbles is aware soup. This might help you flow with the river, becoming a relaxed eye digging whatever passes by.

Meditative concentration suggestions: never worry about being judged—no one can really understand why you do anything you do. Give yourself permission to be as different as you want. However, it's important to remember that often people talk glowingly about freedom but are afraid and suspicious of people who truly act free. We can live in our cultural generation successfully if we can control our mood, personality, and emotions while stoned. This means being open-minded, aware, compassionate, and loving—and not being anybody's fool. If life is a stage, then become an actor.

All humans have to make decisions without sufficient information; this is part of risk, and sometimes we just have to go for it. Don't be overly earnest; we don't have to volunteer to help other people every instant of our lives. Help yourself too. Living a peaceful, wise, and compassionate life is sometimes enough. You are allowed your yes and no. Keep from being too somber—lighten up (or lighter up). Every day take the opportunity to laugh, smile, chuckle, and/or guffaw heartily without any specific reason. Do things you love. Tap into and express your creative power—everyone has a gift, find yours. Take some time to trip, and give yourself time to come down, reintegrate, and readjust to the new things you learned on the trip. Get together with Stoner friends and purposely encourage them to get higher, and become better humans—support their dreams. It's better to not have friends if they belittle each other and are negative. You don't have to end friendships, but you can use your time wisely and limit interactions with people that aren't worthwhile.

Let tripping pierce through your endless struggles and try to see them clearly as storyline illusions, brought on by habitual negativity. Artists and other creative people know that tripping is where ideas and creativity can come from. Change the way you think, and make suffering become opportunities to learn.

If a person doesn't like you and maligns you, turn it into lessons of patience, understanding, and compassion. Hypothetically analyzing why, what, etc. about a negative situation or person is a waste of time—maybe the person has issues of their own, it's not even your fault … probably you are, at least in their eyes, a harmless person, someone they feel it's safe to dump on. Often, just by being a silent mirror, you'll help the person learn an important life lesson. However, do not let anyone physically or verbally harm you; you have the right to defend yourself.

Invent the future. Life is a cosmic joke; it's also damn near impossible to be perfect in an imperfect world. Living each day as consciously aware as we can, trying to be real, trying to see things exactly as they are is Stoner Meditation. But don't ever forget it's all a mystery—not something to be solved but something we accept. It's okay to not know. Don't believe negative existentialism. We do have purpose, even if you can't understand what it is in the beginning; it becomes clear in enlightenment.

Create some new daily habits, something like this simple routine: get out of bed, do your bath stuff, have something to drink, do a ten-minute yoga practice, then go right to the meditation cushion for twenty minutes.

Meditation will be your wake-up event, saving you from the struggle of finding available time later on in the day. Stoners are usually too stoned in the afternoon to meditate effectively anyway. Also, a morning meditation is the dividing line between darkness and light. Each morning we wake from the dream of "unconsciousness" to the dream of consciousness. Lao Two and I like to get stoned immediately after our morning meditations.

Be patient in beginning meditation, don't expect much at first except a lot of struggle. Learn to relax a little and step back, letting mind do the work. Keep after it year after year, and like a dimmer switch being turned up, your inner light will increase steadily.

During the last few minutes of your meditation turn your thoughts toward compassion, and include everyone in the universe—especially your "enemies." Most importantly, include compassion toward yourself.

That moment's reflection on compassion will enter your everyday life, so you can allow problems to flow by without being caught up in them. Over time you'll start to realize how daily meditation is paying off for you.

Imagine your daily meditation is a small lake. When you sit down, the lake is muddy from storm runoff. After you sit for a while, the water calms and particles of mud sift down to the bottom. Hopefully when you finish meditating the lake is clear and calm. We will always have storms that deposit new mud, but we learn not to mind the mud clouding up the water again. From meditative experience we know it will settle to the bottom and clear.

Our life is a shooting star that burns out seemingly in seconds when viewed from the larger perspective of the end. Stoners, we implore you—start now to live your dreams as best you can.

Stoner Meditation increases the length in years and the quality of life. Quite a claim that we absolutely believe is true. If nothing else, just learning how to breathe slower, deeper, and more relaxed from Stoner Meditation will lead to a more healthy body. A life of short, stressed breathing repeated over and over clenches the whole body.

If you decide to become a mountain climber or trekker, you'll be happy to know there is also anecdotal evidence that being stoned reduces altitude sickness. Again, it could also be because marijuana smokers expand their chest by inhaling and exhaling deeply when smoking, and this greater chest capacity brings in more oxygen at altitude.

Sanskrit proverb: "For breath is life, and if you breathe well you will live long on earth."

One day Lao Two looked back at his magical life and saw how Stoner Meditation enabled him to let go of dualism. It wasn't a mental event exactly; it was more that Lao Two realized, or noticed, that he was living without dualism. He also noticed was in higher mind all the time.

When we look at our day-to-day meditation, the subtle changes are not so obvious. Meditation can sometimes seem like an added struggle to an already complicated life. If we told you that after twenty years of meditating you would be able to trip better, or be healthier and full of wisdom, would you start now? Stoner Meditation is not just sitting on a cushion; it is living life in meditative awareness—living a completely awakened life.

Lao Two says: "This is your time, your moments. There is nothing you do that is apart from sacred."

Totality

Lao Two says: "Attention is everything in meditation. Above all, pay attention."

I've said before that emptiness is not empty. It's easier to say what emptiness is not (Heart Sutra), but I describe emptiness as the creatively active appearance of the universe. The coolest thing about emptiness is that it must be experienced.

The concept of emptiness can be very confusing and difficult to understand—until it's experienced. The important thing to know is that emptiness is not empty. The only thing left of us when in emptiness is pure attention, or awareness.

In the 'Heart Sutra' version we used the Buddha version. He was able to abide in sustained pure attention when he was in highest nirvana. If you read the Heart Sutra, you'll remember that the Buddha is absorbed in highest nirvana meditation—he's not talking, moving because he's in a transcendental state. His best student, Sariputra, is asking the god Avalokitesvara what the Buddha is experiencing. Avalokitesvara tells us what nirvana is and at the end, Buddha comes out of highest nirvana and says that Avalokitesvara's description was right on. Even though

Buddha was in highest consciousness he was aware of Sariputra's question, and Avalokitesvara's answer.

I always think that I'm not being understood when I discuss emptiness. I have to rely on previous descriptions by masters, and my own limited experience of being absorbed in momentary emptiness. However, like the Buddha in his highest nirvana awareness, emptiness is indescribable. But just because it's difficult to describe is no reason not to try, so I'm saying that if we have non-ego attention (awareness) in emptiness, it's not completely nothing, void, or nihilistic.

Psychedelics can get us to low-level enlightenment, but the truth is the enlightenment gained by tripping is temporary, ineffable, and overwhelming. Does this mean we should avoid eating mushrooms or not smoke marijuana? Obviously Stoner Meditation believes that there is magic in psychedelics—and if the opportunity presents itself for you to get high, then the universe is offering you a rare gift.

Your first few trips will be spontaneous and new, with your feet being swept off the ground. But after you get used to smoking or taking a psychedelic, it's time to take up the wizard path—cash in your ticket and start hiking through the forest. Unfortunately, too many people take a psychedelic once or twice, fly around in the mystic sky, then give it up, so they never really leave the valley. They get high in the valley, but they don't get stoned—it's not authentic Stoner Meditation. But even people who take psychedelics over a period of time come upon a place where they don't get higher—they're stuck on that path and it's time to move on. That's the famous quote by Alan Watts: "When you get the message, hang up the phone." That's where sitting meditation takes over and reveals the rest of the path. Slowly but surely, you cut through all obstacles and arrive at tree line.

There's a point where we question if we're smoking too much marijuana, spending too much time getting high. We have to look in the mirror of our lives and ask if we have a psychological addiction. If you do, you should research about being attached, compulsive behavior, and even addiction dependency. Obsessive behavior will hold you back just like habitual thinking does. To be immersed in enlightenment means we have to become invisible—leaving everything we are, everything we do, and all our cravings behind—in other words, let go. We don't let go forever, just for a few moments, learn what there is to learn, and return enlightened.

Old joke: "I've been smoking marijuana every day for forty years, and I'm not addicted yet."

Lao Two says: "If truth be told, I find the most addicting drug of all is drinking water."

The purpose of enlightenment is not to become a better person or to have some big self-improvement goal—although these are often the positive side effects from seeing reality. The goal of enlightenment is to become one with the raw, unadorned, pure, spiritual nature of the reality that surrounds us. Stoner Meditation calls this reality Natural Mind. We can't look somewhere else to find it, because Natural Mind is what we're immersed in—it is exactly where we are every moment.

Smoke with your friends. Experiment with psychedelics with your friends. Talk about serious stuff; get into the heavy of tripping. But during those trips, take some moments alone to close your eyes and delve into what's inside. Don't spend all your Stoner time watching TV in the valley. Take a look at exactly where you physically are, feel your presence—when you are examining reality, you are walking through the forest.

Many people don't realize that there's an important coming-down period after we trip. It can last for several days and can be as important as the psychedelic trip itself. If some incredible insight manifested itself when you were stoned, spend some time thinking about it. Again, discuss your insights with your tripping friends—learn from each other. Be good to yourself while coming down, eat healthy, keep your thoughts mellow, and discredit any negative thoughts that arise. The habitually arising "lower" thoughts of thinking mind become amplified during coming-down.

When we come down, thinking mind reenters but we see it differently, precisely, vividly. We're not used to looking at it directly—usually thinking mind is in the far background. Most people have no awareness of what thinking mind is doing to them, and think they are living their own life. Unless people trip, meditate, or somehow suddenly become aware, they are at the mercy of thinking mind. Over the years on the path through the trees, Stoners will confront all three minds—thinking mind, doing mind, and Natural Mind. When the three become one, you have passed through tree line.

Lao Two says: "All varieties of meditation produce the same result; there is only one place to go. Everybody climbs the same mountain."

For beginning meditators, there's so much happening inside thinking mind—with the noise, chatter, and distractions, we feel our head might explode. We're not sure what we're supposed to filter, what to accept, what's effective and what's not. ... Go easy on yourself and give meditation a while to show results—it's not a quick fix. You don't have to figure out the whole meditation package during the first few sessions. Take a few moments during the exertion of wild thoughts, body pain, and impatience to remember to smile, relax, experiment, and listen to your body. The cycle of meditation goes something like this—you love it for several months and get a natural high. Then you really start to notice thinking mind and it drives you crazy. You quit, but you keep remembering the natural high you got, and the world seems to be closing in on you again ... so you start meditating again. Your concentration improves, you start to feel a little expansive, then your body gets used to the insane position required to sit and meditate. Then you start to relax, and your concentration lasts for more breaths, and down the road you really can pay attention. Thinking mind stops seeing meditation as a threat to its existence and even starts to cooperate with doing mind, giving up control now and then. At some point you notice that your meditation is carrying over to the rest of your life, making it better. Negativity starts to fade, and you smile more. Finally there comes a time when you really look forward to your meditation practice because the day just doesn't seem to go as well without it.

Lao Two says: "Trying to describe what it's like to be stoned is like trying to describe tasting an apple. It's inexpressible, and the only way to experience an apple is smoking one."

Unknown (found on the Internet, anonymous): "Before you judge others or claim any absolute truth, consider that you can see less than 1% of the electromagnetic spectrum and hear less than 1% of the acoustic spectrum. As you read this, you are traveling at 220 kilometers per second across the galaxy. 90% of the cells in your body carry their own microbial DNA and are not 'you.' The atoms in your body are 99.999999999999999% empty space and none of them are the ones you were born with, but they all originated in the belly of a star. Human beings have 46 chromosomes, 2 less than the common potato. The existence of the rainbow depends on the conical photoreceptors in your eyes; to animals without cones, the rainbow does not exist. So you don't just look at a rainbow, you create it."

It's not necessary to treat enlightenment as some big deal. It's much more simple and elemental than imagined, and more obvious than I've been able to describe. If we told you that it's simply standing in the world without adding anything, just existing, it would seem too simple. So naturally we overthink enlightenment—it must be fireworks, a complete transformation—it is, but it's not. Enlightenment has many levels, some as simple as seeing the beauty and miracle in each blade of grass, or looking at the moon and falling into rapturous love with existence. Stoner Meditation is seeing every facet of existence as spiritual—even our insecure suffering, our screw-ups, successes and failures, courage and fear, joy and wonder. It's also when in here and out there, and both together, are empty. No independent, ego-based me, no solid world outside either, but together they are awareness (view) ever creating, ever destroying in each moment.

Stoner Meditation is being gentle with the world around us. We have to deal compassionately with those who don't understand where we're coming from. This consideration for others is the beginning of the higher path. Stoners are mellow, so being holier than thou, being prideful, or trying to prove something is right is not Stoner Meditation. Only if someone asks why you've changed, why you seem more happy and content—then explain your philosophy, ethics, and belief system. In discussions, express your views from your heart, and if they ring true, they're only true because they're rational and universal.

Be skeptical, even of Stoner Meditation.

Realize that the people around us are often stuck, suffering, lonely, disappointed, and feeling negative emotions. We need to always strive to see people as real and new, every time we meet with them. Don't get stuck in a previous image of a friend; allow them to change, see them as they are at this moment in time. We could die tomorrow, so we can't treat people badly today—we might never get the chance to make things right. Never criticize so it hurts, only if requested. Encourage instead. Give your best good wishes to anyone in love. It's important for humans to be in love. Love is powerful, elemental, sexy.

A thousand years from now, will anyone remember what we worried about? Maybe you had something terrible happen to you, or you've done something terrible—but every day dawns with promise, and a year from now life will be different in so many, many ways. Forgive and forget. ... Sometimes it's good to look into the distant future and realize that our entire culture is an insignificant speck of time/space. Imagine the world a thousand years from now. Maybe you are the only person obsessing about your "crummy" situation.

Lao Two says: "Drugs are a shortcut to enlightenment, only if we treat them as entheogens, and are willing to do the hard investigative work inside."

Sometimes during my meditation I like to think of breath as energy instead of air, imagining that it re-creates my entire body on the in-breath. On the out-breath my entire body disappears; during out-breath cruising (silence) I become a shining, luminous being.

For some people chanting (mantras) works better than breath meditation. They chant constantly, mostly in silence, and like breath attention, chanting overtakes thinking mind, allowing doing mind to take over. If you do any chanting out loud, pay very close attention to what is happening in your body, like vibrations, emotions, or especially powerful connections, and of course your thoughts. Here's a mantra we use during the day: on the in-breath think a slow "thank," on the out-breath think "you." We like to inwardly chant this mantra when inhaling and exhaling marijuana. It makes us feel grateful for each breath, and for the unfathomable universe that provides it.

Do we expect Stoners to meditate every day? Enjoying it every minute, and sitting for the target time? Hahahahahahahahaha! No, not at first, but we promise meditation will grow on you over the years. At first you will feel body aches and pains, struggle with monkey mind, and find your patience wearing thin. Then, after many clumsy stumbles, you will learn to relax a little, and over the long run Stoner Meditation will start to make sense.

Wizard Journey

Lao Tzu—Lao Two

Lao Two didn't set out on his Stoner path some fifty years ago to write a book. It turns out the original impetus for his life search was hearing a quote by Lao Tzu—his homage dude.

Lao Tzu said: "The great Tao is like a flood, it flows as it will to the left or the right. Myriad things depend on Tao for life, but like water the Tao continues to emerge and provide. Tao achieves its work, but demands no acclaim. All beings are clothed and fed, but Tao wants nothing in return. Beings come and go, but Tao continues in greatness, not regarding itself as great. This is Tao's greatness."

At age sixteen, Lao Two went deep because of a horrific tragedy with a close friend's loss of life. It was like he too had died. He and everyone he knew suddenly became ghosts. Nothing felt right in his body; he could barely walk; food tasted wrong; all his previous adventures felt selfish and superficial. The contradictions of death burned a hole in his mind, and he dragged through each day. He was in crisis mode.

Months later at a friend's house Lao Two was introduced to Lao Tzu's book *Tao Te Ching*, which was sitting on a table next to the couch. While he was waiting for his friend, he read a few pages. The next day he went looking to buy a copy, but no store had it in stock. People didn't read books like that in 1961 in Miami. He ordered a copy, read it, and found a reference to Lao Tzu's student Chuang Tzu. So Lao Two ordered Chuang Tzu's book. He was hooked. The next book he read was *Zen Flesh, Zen Bones*, which really blew his mind. He got a part-time job at a library and searched the philosophy section, and started reading Western philosophers—but the books were scholarly and dry compared to Taoism and Zen's mysterious inscrutability. But the little he read had changed his perspective, and he was on his Way. He decided at age seventeen that he was going to become enlightened, even though he didn't know what that really meant or how to do it. But he liked the idea that you could get enlightened and then come back to help people. For the first time in a long time, he felt hopeful he could atone for the part he played in the tragic event.

At the time he was just discovering his good looks, as young women were noticing him, seeking him out—even though he had withdrawn into a shell. For awhile I was his shoulder to cry on, and then I saw him less and less. Before the accident, he was outgoing and always had a lighthearted smile; now he turned shy and irritable. His schoolwork, already just average, became worse. It looked like he would fail his last year of high school, but he got lucky and was in the right place at the right time. The Cuban exodus to Miami was doubling, and then tripling school class size—Lao Two was pushed out and graduated, to make room for the huge influx of Cubans. Or perhaps, the teachers knew his situation and gave him the pass.

Not being on very good terms with his father, Lao Two was desperate to get out of town. Not having many options, he joined the navy—a horrible mistake. He got through it without too much effort or trouble because he signed up for only two years of active service. Once again he was at the right place, at the right time—he got out of the navy just as his unit was being sent to Vietnam. When he returned to Florida he discovered marijuana, and read voraciously every book he could find in Eastern and Western philosophy. He started going to a local junior college and got involved in anti-Vietnam and black rights protests, though he was pulled aside at one event by several black guys who said that because he was white, his presence wasn't appreciated. At the junior college, being allowed to take whatever courses he wanted, he started to excel at his studies, and feel better about himself.

He started speaking against the Vietnam War at public events and on radio talk shows. He was idealistic but naïve—and Miami was generally racist and pro-war (any war would do). The antiwar contingency in Miami at that time consisted of maybe ten or twenty people. He went to a candlelight event on Memorial Day in Coconut Grove. I saw on TV that night an interviewer asking Lao Two why he was protesting war on Memorial Day; didn't he think it was disrespectful? Lao Two answered that he was protesting so other soldiers wouldn't die in the future, and it's possible to have world peace.

Lao Two was going on dates, and for the first time was having sex. He liked it. He would take dates into bars on Miami Beach where live jazz was played. Even though he and his date were underage, they weren't chased out. Lao Two made a point of never trying to order liquor.

The folk-music scene was also coming to Miami, at the coffeehouses, small venues that had a tiny stage. It was possible to hear national and international recording stars like Ian and Sylvia, or Fred Neil. There was something going on in the rebellious consciousness of some of the young people. Not everyone was opening up his or her mind, though. But for the disenchanted like Lao Two, their idealism was exploding on the American scene.

At one antiwar event at the junior college he and one other male and three females were going to stage a protest. Some two hundred students came, many with baseball bats. Lao Two was in way over his head, but luckily the school officials had heard about the protest beforehand and broke it up. A lot of threats were made.

Two weeks later, Lao Two left Miami for San Francisco. Three months later, Lao Two took his first LSD.

I've known Lao Two since before the first grade, but we parted amicably in our late teens when he joined the navy to get away from home and the tyranny of his father. We hooked up again about twenty years ago on the West Coast, but I didn't realize how much he had changed. I had changed hardly at all; I still carried my preppy desire for money, women, and being liked, and the more I struggled, the farther away my goals seemed. Lao Two was dealing soft drugs, taking a lot of acid, and would disappear for weeks at a time without telling anyone where he was going or when he would return. I would complain that I would run out of marijuana while he was gone (this was before cell phones), so he said to buy more quantity next time. He would come back from backpacking, staying at someone's house in the country, making a score up in the mountains, or just meeting a woman and living at her house for a few weeks until the love affair turned sour because of his moodiness.

Lao Two kept his insights and awareness hidden from me initially, knowing that I wasn't really interested in mysticism—I just thought he was overcompensating for the accidental death in his teens still affecting him. Several times when we took psychedelics together he would cry for long periods. Over the years we started getting closer again and I realized that there was wisdom and a calm, self-assured spiritual quality to Lao Two. I started asking him questions, learning, progressing, and pondering the meanings of his "teachings." He always said he wasn't a teacher; he was a friend helping a friend. Here we are now, both of us in our late sixties, writing a book together. I had to twist Lao Two's arm to produce this book, as he would be quite happy to fade into obscurity, taking what he's learned with him to his death.

At first our resumed relationship was awkward and superficial—I would buy his marijuana and we would casually talk while he carefully weighed it out on his triple-beam scale. I started asking about his life search for enlightenment, and he told me shyly, in a subdued voice, that he'd had many enlightenments, each one different in some way. Back then I had no idea what he meant. He also spoke of amazingly high levels of realization, and mentioned his encounters with wizards and shamans he met. I laughed, but I could see by the expression on his face that he was not joking.

I always considered Lao Two a flake and would gossip that he never took anything seriously except pleasure—I really didn't want to hang around him when he was younger. He was too reckless and angry, and was a completely free spirit. I didn't know that during our time apart, he was quietly studying science, philosophy, and Buddhism—leaving a trail of books, teachers, and like-minded friends on his path behind him. My unshakable image of Lao Two stemmed from an experience we'd had together as kids—maybe nine years old. He inadvertently started a fire in an empty weed-filled lot near houses. We tried to put it out, but then we ran away when we heard the fire engines. He was always having an accident and getting stitches, or being punished and sent to the principal, and getting just-passing grades in school. I always won our academic and sports competitions and there was jealousy between us, but we both always respected the value of the underlying friendship. We only physically fought one time, when in frustration Lao Two gave me a surprise punch in my jaw, but I didn't retaliate because he was right, I was being a jerk. Each time I would see Lao Two he would be with a new woman, even more beautiful than the one he'd just thrown away.

Lao Two says: "If you are on a very high level of realization, you will 'meet by chance' other people at that same, or higher levels."

Buddhist saying: "When the student is ready, the teacher will appear."

From our first conversation after our many years of absence, I went home and wrote down some of the things he said, which for some reason stayed with me for days afterward. I had a small cardboard box under my desk labeled "Lao Two," and I would throw in pieces of paper with notes on them after every meeting. Eventually I brought a notebook and wrote down stuff as we were talking. This took some doing, as Lao Two grumbled that it interfered with the flow of our discussions and was a distraction. He said over and over that in a thousand years, none of his words would matter. Over time we got into a teacher-student relationship, but I don't remember that ever being said out loud. He taught me to meditate and made me stick to it. We often meditated together at his house. More recently he gave me a mind-to-mind, heart-to-heart transmission of shared awakening. We sat across from each other, looking into each other's eyes, unmoving, invisible, with no ego, in the same enthusiastically telepathic infinite space that I call loud silence. My mind was blown forever. I realized that my intuition had been correct—he really did have something unique to share with Stoners—a new (rediscovered?) way to realize awareness, in this case by using the combination of marijuana and meditation. But he wasn't finished; he gave me a few secret instructions that he said should never be shared. I disagree, and I've divulged many herein.

It took several years of pestering him to let me write this book. I showed him my notes and he finally said he would collaborate, as long as I did all the typing, editing, and publishing. Not being a professional writer myself, I hope you readers will forgive my clumsy attempts. I originally wanted to do his life story, but he refused, saying that although he'd had many interesting adventures, what was important was what he learned. But since many of his adventures teach us too, I've patched together as best I can some of his exploits.

Lao Two says: "Although separated by vast distances and the length of many years, good friends pick up the conversation right where it left off the last time they were together."

Lao Two is an old recalcitrant hippie, ex-dope dealer, a free spirit, longtime daily meditation practitioner, a blissed-out longhair love child from the 1960s, and now an astute sage. During the early 1960s he was in Berkeley, then San Francisco, and finally Marin County in the late 1970s; currently his whereabouts are unknown. Honestly, even I don't know where he is, and he said he'd get in touch in a few years after he read the Stoner Meditation book.

His younger years were filled with psychedelic music, getting laid, backpacking, Steven Gaskin's Monday Night Class, selling LSD and marijuana, and taking every psychedelic available. He took LSD somewhere between 300 and 500 times. He was busted a few times, and spent a little time in jail for "drugs."

He's a prime example of "if you can remember the 1960s, you weren't there." He lived in a hippie van alone, then with his girlfriend and their child, traveling around California. He's never had ambition to make money, but money always magically comes his way, and even in retirement he's financially comfortable. Hell, he's hardly ever spent any money, living frugally, simply and without extravagance. He only travels to low-income countries, so his dollar goes farther. His current car is fourteen years old and runs perfectly.

He's had lots of women in his life and two sons and two divorces, but is now married again and happily settled down. As he says about why he's mellowed even though women are still interested: "It's a case of been there, done all that. Every place is here now, now." He and his current wife make a great couple and are happy together.

Lao Two was a neglected child and always said he couldn't wait to escape from his strict and overbearing father, and too busy mother. Looking back, he said he was lucky to have time to spend alone when growing up. After the accident he wasn't very social and is still almost shy, but he was so good looking that women would approach him; he never had to make much of an effort. I was with him one day in a supermarket, and in the vegetable aisle a woman came over and started talking to him. They got together that night, and she made him dinner. They had a hot relationship for several months.

He's trekked in Nepal, Southeast Asia, Peru, and the California Sierras, and loves solo backpacking. One of his favorite pursuits these days is getting totally stoned and staring at the moon. Lao Two has faced death many times, but somehow survived to take even more risks. To his credit, he stayed away from hard drugs and avoided straight jobs. Lao Two told me this story:

When Lao Two was a hippie he was invited to join some friends for a few days at a cabin in the mountain redwood forests of Big Sur. He sat in the back seat with two friends, with three more in the front seat. Joints were being passed around the whole drive. During one of the stops a woman in the front asked him to change seats with her, as the woman sitting next to her had not bathed. Lao Two said sure, it wouldn't bother him, as he was rolling and smoking joints constantly.

They parked the car in mid-afternoon and hiked uphill, about an hour or two later arriving at the small cabin under the huge redwood trees just as it started to rain, hard. It was beautiful, dreamy, and Lao Two felt at one with nature, surrounded by his friends. Two men were already living there, and unknown to Lao Two, they weren't too pleased that so many people were crashing on the floors, with sleeping bags everywhere. Lao Two thinks one of the women was secretly bringing hard drugs to those two men. There was a nice fire going, a dinner was made, lots more joints were passed around, and Lao Two fell quickly asleep.

In the middle of the night a friend shook him awake. The two men were pissed off about all the people and to avoid any weird situations they had to leave, now. But, even stranger, not everyone had to leave, just the three of them were being thrown out immediately. Fortunately, one was the driver of the car that was left down below. Lao Two was too groggy to figure it all out and complied with a few protests, countered by angry threatening words from the two men.

The rain had stopped, but the clouds still covered the brightly moonlit night. It was easy enough to find the trail in the dark, but then the rain started again even harder than before. Lao Two found a huge redwood tree to stand under, but it didn't do much good and they were quickly soaked. The driver said they should keep walking, but as they were heading downhill he suddenly took a different trail uphill. At a motor home, he broke open the door and went inside. Lao Two stood out in the rain, refusing to go in, but was talked into getting out of the weather eventually. Exhausted, Lao Two fell asleep in his sleeping bag while the other two, raided the refrigerator, drink the owners liquor and had sex on the bed.

Again he was hurriedly awakened in the early morning. They did a quick cleanup and tried to fix the broken door, but it was ruined. The rain had stopped and the morning was gorgeous. Lao Two was happy to be on his way, as the trip wasn't turning out well so far. Out of nowhere two unknown men jumped onto the trail, knives drawn, yelling about our breaking into the motor home. We all denied it and tried to escape, but since the men had knives, we had to comply. The men said they had called the cops and walked Lao Two and his friends downhill to the highway.

A police car was waiting, and the officer wouldn't listen to any of the hippies but instead started talking to the knife guys. The guys with the knives told the policeman their story, and he started to take out his handcuffs for us hippies. Lao Two said: "I want you to arrest these two men too, for pulling knives on us and threatening our lives. And I want to talk to my lawyer in Berkeley before I say anything else." The cop was incredulous; he looked at the knife guys and asked if they'd pulled knives. After their conversation, Lao Two could see the frustration of the officer, who then turned to us and said: "Just get out of here. If I ever see any of you again, you will go directly to jail."

They got into the car and split.

Lao Two heard a few days later that on the day they drove away, a group of local people along with the police forced the two men in the cabin, and our remaining group of friends, to leave. Thankfully no one was hurt, as everyone vacated the cabin right away.

Lao Two says: "Smoke this: intellectual knowledge is not wisdom. Wisdom is found in silence. Act according to the demands of this very moment."

Believe in Yourself

Please do not try to become Buddha, Christ, Mohammed, Lao Tzu, or Lao Two—become you. You were created in this mysterious world to exist, live your dream, and realize love.

Our advice is to take a few months or years out of your life to get really, totally stoned—take the psychedelic wizard journey. There is plenty of time for job and family afterward, but being young is your chance to explore and have adventures—it's much more difficult when you are older and have a job or other responsibilities, and you'll lose the stamina of youth when you're retired. Another good time is after a divorce or some similar life-shattering event. In our opinion, both men and women should take a few years tripping on various psychedelics. Plenty of people will tell you to go the safe path, remain in the valley with your materialistic-acquiring, TV-watching, pharmaceutically chemically numbed half-death. Others might tell you to acquire some fundamentalist belief system, or fight a war. Well, it's up to you—it's your choice ultimately. Stoner Meditation recommends the path through the trees into the unknown, walking the high wire without a net, seeking the spiritual path. Just remember, we all will die, and the only thing we can take with us is the wisdom and awareness we possess.

Lao Two says: "When smoking marijuana, listen. The plants are speaking."

Close your eyes and trip out. Plants don't use words to speak; they use images, insights, perceptive life force, subtle energies, dreams and/ or hallucinations, and third eye emptiness. The wizard journey, is the psychonaut entheogen shamanic path, and our enthusiastically choosing to get stoned.

Lao Two says: "Always remember, getting stoned is food for the mind. Do not experiment with uppers or downers, opiates, or prescription medicines—those are not the Stoner Meditation path."

In primitive cultures there's always some forbidden cave or mountaintop that nobody is allowed to visit. The story goes that anyone entering will die at the hand of the gods. Only a few of you Stoners will join Lao Two entering that rarefied cave and climbing through it to the other side. Here's some stuff I wrote in my notebook when Lao Two was talking:

Lao Two says: "I took LSD for the first time in 1964 or '65; it was two small, clear capsules of pharmaceutical Sandoz acid. I don't think LSD was even illegal yet. The reason I took two capsules is my girlfriend decided not to take her share when we arrived at the house of her friend. It was a huge house in north Berkeley, and her friend's parents were gone for the weekend. I was disappointed that my girlfriend wasn't going to trip, as she had taken LSD several times before. I took one of the capsules, and sat on the couch alone listening to music for an hour while my girlfriend was in the kitchen with her friends. But nothing was happening. I said to myself that I would wait another half hour, and started smoking some marijuana. Still nothing happening a half-hour later, so I took the second hit of Sandoz. But as soon as I swallowed the second capsule, the first capsule hit me like a sledgehammer—I was beyond stoned, completely enthralled and loving every moment. This was what I had been looking for my whole life, and I felt completely liberated in the world of hallucinations. I had an amazing, wondrous trip and look back on it fondly. I remember standing on a street corner in the suburbs watching a stoplight for what felt like hours in the middle of the night. No cars would come, but the light would keep going through the cycles—I found it hilarious.

"About three hours into my trip, my girlfriend came over asking for the second hit of Sandoz acid I had, but it was already in my stomach. I told her that I ate it and she got all huffy. I tried to explain, but my words got tangled up in the music playing. I think she found some acid from someone else at the party, but we didn't hang out together. There were probably twenty young people there, almost all of them on acid. I was in an upstairs bedroom looking at some books when a boy and girl came in, took off their clothing, and started having sex. I watched for a while, but found it too freaky—it was hostile or self-serving or something— they didn't seem to be enjoying the experience much. I tried sex on LSD a few times, and it turns out it's a pretty interesting experience with lots of highs and lows, confusion, and ecstasy, especially the orgasm, where I seem to turn into a hallucinating god.

"I've been dosed several times over the years; each time was at a rock and roll concert. Once I made the mistake of taking a drink of apple juice from a friend's bottle, and another time an ex-girlfriend put several hits of LSD in some crunchy chocolate—which I thought was uncool. But it was a Rolling Stones concert, so I just went for it and had a great time. The worst time being dosed was when I was at a benefit concert. There were Hell's Angels going around with squirt guns that they would use to shoot the liquid into people's reluctantly open mouths. A particularly surly Hell's Angel squirted me again and again, as I protested that I'd just taken a hit of LSD. Apparently this was the Hell's Angels way of introducing PCP to the population of San Francisco. In about an hour my feet would no longer support my body, and in slow motion I sank to the floor, listened to the music a while, then suddenly went into darkness. This was of serious concern to the friends I'd come with, who found me crumpled up on the edge of the dance floor. I woke up in a bathtub of warm water naked, with my worried friends looking on. But I was feeling great, ate a big breakfast, and was soon on my way. Apparently I almost died.

"The first time I smoked marijuana was with the son of the mayor. He also sold me my first marijuana. It was packaged in a small matchbox—yes, it's true, before plastic Baggies existed we used things like matchboxes. I immediately took the marijuana over to my girlfriend's and we smoked some together, it being her first time too. We went for a walk, and at one point the oncoming people's faces were melting, changing; it was like their inner personality was displayed on the outside of their faces. I looked at my girlfriend to see if she saw the same thing; she looked back at me and we broke out laughing as we both had a telepathic confirmation. We became telepathic for several moments in a way I can't describe. We went back to her place and had a big make-out session."

"Another time, a friend of the mayor's son came down from New York city. He was a young, tall Mafia guy wearing a tailored suit. He had a rented Cadillac and we drove all around Miami Beach smoking marijuana and drinking alcohol. At one point the Mafia guy drove right through a red light. A motorcycle cop pulled us over and wrote a ticket. The Mafia guy tore the ticket up in front of the cop and threw the pieces at him, defying the cop to do something. The cop did nothing and drove off. I had never met anyone like this Mafia guy up to that point in my life. When we arrived at his Hotel the Mafia guy lit a hundred dollar bill on fire and threw it in the pool. A hundred dollars in the early 1960's was like a thousand dollars today."

Lao Two is legendary among our mutual friends for his risky behavior, willingness to be the first one in the water, and iconoclastic ideas. He often remarks that he never expected to live this long. But Lao Two is not you nor me. No doubt you are reading this book in a completely different world from the one Lao Two lived in during the 1960s and '70s. That was then, this is now. Stoner Meditation respects risky behavior, but remember dangerous and irresponsible choices are often caused by depression or other maladies. Our choices define us, and risk without reward is foolhardy. Choices like drinking and driving are considered foolhardy, not risky. It's the same with marijuana and psychedelics, and comes down to responsibility for our actions.

Lao Two says: "Do you think only the Buddha can experience nirvana? Don't get lost in words, concepts, or moralistic rules. It's the experience we seek—the same experience that every master has achieved. Call it whatever you want, Buddha did not discover it. He rediscovered it—we can too."

Note to high school students, and young people living at home with your parents: Believe in yourself. Believe in your dreams. High school is temporary, and you need your high school years to prepare for being on your own. Don't make the same mistake Lao Two did in thinking that school sucked, his parents sucked, and he sucked. So he did nothing. He wandered off on aimless hikes and bike rides, busied himself drawing, and daydreamed. He wanted to be a chef, but was so embarrassed by the peer pressure in his small circle of friends and completely alienated from his parents—never told anyone or did anything to make it happen. It was tough watching my childhood friend drift so aimlessly and be so unhappy.

Don't bring marijuana to school or break your parents' rules. No matter how misguided your parents are, or seem to you, you are spending time in their environment. It's debatable if smoking marijuana at a young age is bad for you or not; Stoner Meditation thinks you should give yourself a chance to develop your senses and mature. Remember, the brain is just another body sense. Think about standing in front of giant speakers at a rock concert and blowing out your ears—not too smart. It might be the same with smoking marijuana at a young age. Again, make up your own mind—don't be coerced by peer pressure, and don't automatically obey rules without thinking about what they mean.

Lao Two says: "You are not lost. You are directly above the center of Earth."

Your eyes should have wonderful things to see; fill your ears with awesome music, give your brain knowledge, and develop educational maturity. Learn how to learn. Materialism is not god, your spiritual quest is god, and so you must take care of your body and senses. We live in an economic world, and your school years are your chance to develop the tools to survive in that world. It's entirely possible that being stoned every minute of your teenage years will discourage developmental skills needed for life. Save your tripping for weekends and summer vacations.

Believe us when we say you won't like being busted—it's a life lesson you just don't need. The obscene expense, spending time in courtrooms, in jail with no privacy, on probation and constant drug testing. ...

Do everything you can to be blazing smart and successful. Do well in school using your curiosity, because you are needed to fix the mess Earth is in—you are extremely important for the future. Learn meditation to increase your concentration and calmness and become self-assured, creating a multifaceted set of abilities. Hard physical work and exercise are how a Stoner expresses love for the gift of our body. Letting time pass you by and wasting time in confusion is not the path.

Lao Two says: "Time is the gift we give in a relationship. When someone joins with us with love, they are sharing the most valuable offering of their life – their time."

Stoners in a relationship: Think about the percentage of effort you put into your relationship. We suggest each partner meet the other halfway, and give one hundred percent enthusiasm. The trick is to remember the very beginning of the relationship, when you saw that person as faultless, beautiful, sexy, and loving. Back then you gave your heartfelt effort, anticipating your partner's needs. Being stoned and becoming mildly telepathic is not enough—don't expect your partner to be a mind reader, tell them what's going on. Don't be subtle, be direct – but don't use words to hurt. As in everything else we do, balance is the goal. Remember the instructions on ego-death and keeping your sense-of-self? In a relationship it's the same, for example have some outside friends and interests, don't be too clinging. When stoned be especially loving giving up any rigidity, and try to find a comfortable flow to the high. If your partner doesn't get high on marijuana, tell them when you are really stoned so they can let you trip. Do not surprise your partner with "Guess what, I just took magic mushrooms..."—plan your psyche-delic tripping carefully (set and setting).

Lao Two says: "Words have power. In all discussions, we must make a strenuous effort to slow down and be aware of the words we are using. Speak with wisdom and compassion."

Now that a few years have gone by in your relationship, it takes compassion when your partner is suffering, confused, or in physical pain—and maybe most importantly, loving them even when you don't like them. Due to the limitations of the human language, tensions and frustrations can build until an argument begins; you want to win and convince your partner that your view is right. Fight fair. Listen to your partner, keep your heart open, look to the future, and be grateful that your partner cares enough to become as exasperated as you are. Don't say words you will regret, because you can't take them back. Focus on the issue at hand; don't bring in any other issues. If you get too aggra-vated, take a break—don't let emotions escalate into threats, demands, or ultimatums. Give space to let the person talk as much as they want, and then talk as long as you want—use a low voice, keep emotions relaxed. Instead of telling your partner that you love them like 'crazy', tell them you love them like 'sane'.

Lao Two says: "Sometimes I want to say something important, but I think it might be stupid, or even hurtful, or I'm just seeing things wrong. So I say, 'I don't know how to say this, so I'm just going to say it as best I can because it's been rolling around in my head for a few days...' and with that setup, my wife understands my difficulty—and I'm able to say anything."

Fight for your relationship, not for your point of view. When you and your partner are nearing agreement, use the sense of touch. Human touch is electrically powerful and has many forms and characteristics. You should be using the sincere tool of touch every day to connect. Hug, kiss, hold hands, be physical, playful, and remember your partner is a gift that you slowly unwrap, exposing the imperfect vulnerable person inside. Be compassionate, encouraging, sensitive, sensual, and have sex now and then even if you're not initially into it.

Lao Two says: "The test I use in my relationships is to ask if I want to be with this person a year from now, five years from now, ten years from now. If the answer is no, then it's time to take a close look at my life."

Story: One New Year's Eve, Lao Two decided he wanted some edibles around the house so he wouldn't smoke so much and give his lungs a rest—a kind of New Year's resolution. He planned to put them in the freezer, carefully identified as pot brownies because his wife doesn't get high. So the morning before the New Year he made pot brownies with a packaged mix. Marijuana must be cooked to effectively release the chemicals we want for getting stoned—it can be eaten raw, but takes a lot more buds to have the desired effect. Being new to making marijuana brownies, he first followed the recipe on the box, using melted butter instead of oil, as the fats are necessary. As you know, Lao Two grows marijuana, so his weed is very strong, and he mixed four different strains of *sativa* together. He used a coffee grinder, and finely ground about an eighth, or quarter ounce of buds. He added all the finely ground marijuana to the gooey brownie mix. He added nuts also, as he says nuts are not optional. Put it in the oven and cooked away. ...

While the brownies were cooling, he ran some errands. When he returned he noticed his wife had come home and eaten a big chunk, not knowing it had marijuana in the mix. His wife hasn't smoked in over thirty years. As soon as he saw that she had already eaten some, Lao Two figured the best thing for him to do to help her trip was to eat some brownies too. Actually he ate lots more than she did—hey, it was New Year's! He found her in bed, already very high and somewhat pissed off that he didn't put a note on the brownies reminding her that they had pot added. As it turned out, he had used a lot of pot, way too much pot.

Within the hour she had butterfly stomach, was aggravated and unable to comfortably move. She's had heart problems in her past and was starting to get worried, as her heart was racing, her breathing was labored, and her thinking became a mass of restless LSD-type images. She started to panic because of the strength of his brownies. On a scale from 1 to 10, she was an 11.

Lao Two had overdosed on edibles several times before, so he had no fears. As he was coming on to his own brownies, Lao Two started to realize he'd made them way too strong. Since he was on the same intense trip, he knew what was happening to her, so he kept reassuring her that in two or three hours she would feel better. He kept talking softly and giving her physical comfort priority. He rubbed her neck and back, but she said it was annoying and she was feeling chilled. He put on all the covers over her, then got the heating pad and plugged it in.

Lao Two put on music he knew she enjoyed and made her feel as secure as possible. He gave her fruit juice, lit incense and candles, and put on the TV so she could watch a lighthearted, funny movie. For the next several hours he continued to comfort her, reminding that it would pass. He told her to make sure she got lots of oxygen by breathing slowly and deeply, and apologized, probably too many times. The day after her "overdose," she said that she would never, ever use marijuana again.

Obviously the dose was way too strong, not an uncommon mistake in making and eating edibles. Lao Two sadly threw away the rest of the brownies. They were ridiculously strong, even for him. He made a new batch using about a sixteenth of an ounce of his powerful buds. Without doubt, this was the New Year's Eve they both will always remember. Actually, she's reminded him of it on every New Year's Eve since then.

Lao Two says: "Unfounded belief is illusion, denial is destructive. It's as if we shut ourselves up in a dark room, tenaciously denying that there is such a thing as light."

Relationships are filled with unpredictability. From the awkward first date through the years together and letting go at the end, anything and everything can happen. But Stoners have tools to make a relationship sublime.

Lao Two says: "Life is in the living of it, don't squander your opportunity."

Which Way?

Don't be anybody's sucker. We advise against joining up with any philosophical or religious system that demands unthinking, unquestioning, blind acceptance on faith. Stoner Meditation again warns you to question, be skeptical, and not follow rules uncritically—think, analyze, know truth when you hear it. People who worship gurus are missing the point. The point is to listen to the message, and if it makes sense, then try it out for a while. All gurus give off heavy, wise, and loving vibes, and we can easily be sucked into an unhealthy alliance, or just a bad fit.

However, a truly honest relationship with a guru is adult to adult, friend to friend. A true teacher will do nothing except bring out higher-mind qualities in us, by pointing out the right direction.

If there is something to experience, you should be able to experience it directly or it's not valid and provable, and it's possibly nonsense. What you want is verifiable experience by empirical observation and insight. In our experience, if you sit in meditation or smoke marijuana, you will experientially understand Stoner Meditation. If it's not fun and enlightening for you, then move on to a different method to explore your inner universe. It is possible to be your own guru. You don't even have to smoke marijuana or take psychedelics, so don't feel pressured— go your own way.

Lao Two says: "Some psychedelics don't feel compatible; avoid them. LSD let me explore the depths of inner heart and mind, magic mushrooms for body bliss, and Peyote cactus for understanding community. However, PCP made me feel like I was wrapped in plastic, and speed made me feel like I was fading fast."

The essential point of meditating for years and years is to learn how to sit in calm abiding and give validity to personal ethics. The essential point of smoking marijuana is to gain insight, spiritual experience, and an understanding of the dreamlike nature of life.

Zen Master Dogen Zenji said: "To study the Way is to study the self. To study the self is to forget the self. To forget the self is to be enlightened by all things in the universe. To be enlightened by all things in the universe is to cast off the body and mind of the self as well as the demands of others. Even the traces of enlightenment are wiped out, and life with traceless enlightenment goes on forever and ever."

How do you wake up each morning? Are you depressed, angry, frustrated with your life? We're not saying to be a pretend-cheerful person, or not feel your moodiness—we are saying to fight your demons. If you feel emotionally bad, then realize that these emotions are habitual and not real (in the sense of permanence). Learn how to change and take charge of your body, emotions, and mental negativity at will—this is part of the secret teachings, changing shit into gold.

There is nothing wrong with seeking enlightenment. Or not seeking enlightenment. We all choose our path and live our own life. It doesn't matter what you think about the way other people practice their meditation. What matters is how you practice your meditation. Which way? Your way.

Money

Lao Two says: "The best way to keep people poor is tell them that it's possible for them to become rich, than make them feel bad by saying they are just not trying hard enough. Guess what, though? There's no more room at the top—the greedy few plutocrats have solidified their positions, and the needy many are expendable."

Not only that, but there will be fewer and fewer jobs. Overpopulation is a real issue, possibly the underlying problem of all problems - and it's not something that will be happening in the future, it's happening now. Jobs are shipped to countries where people can do the same work for 10 percent of what they'd be paid in the United States. Robots and computers are able to work 24/7, also for less money. We need a new economic model, and we need to redistribute wealth because the need for cheap labor is a thing of the past. I recently saw that a CEO's salary is 380 times that of the average worker. Why, when they can't even spend what they earn—do they just hoard the money? It's absurd.

Money is life force; it abstractly represents all the resources on the planet at this present moment. Resources like oil are finite, and as limited raw materials are depleted, they become more valuable—as we've all seen with the rise in gas prices. At this time, we have nothing to effectively replace oil. Seven billion people on Earth and as population rises, we'll start to see resources like fresh drinking water become scarce—a situation in many countries already.

So, what does this mean in the real world? We are in the midst of a huge planetary change that will reshape, and perhaps destroy humankind simply because the greedy leaders of corporations refuse to act responsibly. It's also the uneducated, Neanderthal, disenfranchised part of our planet still intent on fighting wars. But it's not just the bosses or terrorists—it's also ordinary irresponsible humans who have more than one or two children, who continue to buy cheap throw-away crap, and who have no respect for Mom Earth—those folks throwing a cigarette butt out a car window, burning down acres of forest. We watch news reports that tell us the glaciers are melting, species are disappearing, and poisonous chemicals infect our water, air, soil, and the very food we eat. Denial can be deadly.

Our nature is to survive, but what will be the cost when our continued destruction paves over the Earth with concrete and asphalt, cuts down every tree, nets every fish? Environmentalism is not a hobby or a politically liberal fascination—we are very close to massive die-offs. It will only take one rogue communicable virus plague, a nuclear war, or the ocean systems crashing. Wouldn't it be so much better to change the way we do things instead now, while we still can?

This doesn't have to be a depressing scenario; we can rethink our methods on a planetary scale. Scientists have answers, but corporations silence them. It's time to look at money in the bigger picture. No longer can we just see things from our smaller perspective. Just because you don't have the money you feel you need, or live in a prestigious house, or have the perfect life doesn't mean you can't find satisfaction and joy in simple responsible behavior. Become environmentally motivated. Meditate, smoke marijuana, and see the truth behind the lies.

Lao Two says: "Knowledge is important, but I would prefer to be remembered for having a good heart, rather than a quick mind full of facts."

If too much money is printed it becomes worthless—it no longer represents the real cost of goods or services. Our collective agreement as to the worth of money is what gives it power and value. Printing money does not give it power or value; it's just paper. How money is acquired carries the same responsibility as how money is spent. Greed, selfishness, and denial have imbalanced world resources to the point where a few highly developed countries have the largest share of material goods. I've been to countries where people have only popcorn for breakfast and a meal of rice and a few vegetables for dinner—and they are the lucky ones.

Compassion requires us to collectively share resources with every single person on the planet. The acquisitiveness of systems like capitalism must stop; it is no longer free enterprise, it is plutocracy and has become despicable and ignoble.

Why do we see people walking the city streets preoccupied with worries and concerns, their brows wrinkled, their heartbeat irregular, and their breath stifled—constantly worried about money in one way or another? People worldwide should be joyful, free from want, able to love and laugh, grateful for our magical bounty that sustains us all, equally.

World governments have only one obligation: to benefit each and every human alive on the planet—no exceptions. Regrettably, the system is turned on its head: the truth would appear to be that governments are organized for the protection of the rich. Because of this lopsided equation, the poor are often marginalized and lack basic needs. The deception of campaign promises pretends there was once a perfect world or promises an unlimited future of prosperity, but these are just lies. Although we have many technological wonders, it's the continued military conflict, poverty, and environmental destruction that tear at the fabric of civilization as we squander our resources.

Lao Two says: "Everyone should read Martin Luther King's 'Letter from a Birmingham Jail' in its entirety. It's a little long, but worth the effort."

With just a little organization, planning, and a drastic change of purpose, governments could provide for everyone. Stoners, please develop a social conscience and social awareness toward the disenfranchised. You Stoners are not like the establishment, but group pressure and propaganda is strong and they want you to conform. Take a Saturday or Sunday to join a protest, be a human body standing tall for what you believe in. And vote.

Each time we deal with money, we have a responsibility. Consider your money as concentrated power, or life force. Each time you earn it and spend it, ask yourself if you are creating or disrupting life force.

Earth has thrown species off the planet in great extinctions, and we have no reason to imagine that humans are an exception if we don't change our ways. If we change the oxygen-carbon dioxide balance to only carbon dioxide, then humans are gone. We need to use our inventive abilities to evolve into caretakers of Mom Earth.

Common saying: "Science flew us to the moon. Religion flew us into buildings."

We are absolutely *NOT* advocating any type of violent revolution. Any revolution in the future must be a peaceful change of group mind, in other words—change the way we think. This doesn't mean we sit on our ass passively—instead we can stand together as a group and demand positive changes. Whenever a few million people show up in

Washington, D.C., to protest, the corporations and government take notice. Fifty thousand people protesting is too small of a rally. Organize.

Inventions and discoveries by science might save us, but few scientists these days are working on peaceful or visionary projects. Even pharmaceuticals are based on the marketplace and they won't work on projects that don't have a big payoff. If you google top employers, you will find scientists mostly work for Big Pharma. Next is the defense industry, making bigger and better ways to kill and maim. However, it's almost impossible to investigate what the Department of Defense is up to ... but we've always thought that developing more, faster, and absurdly destructive bombs is insanity.

It's exactly like the gun debate in the United States. To us, it seems the argument is insanity versus sanity. At the time of this book there are 330 million guns available in the U.S., and approximately 80 people die each day from guns. Anybody can get a gun, and it's crazy.

We need new ways of thinking about it. How about we make only one type of gun available worldwide, that shoots one round at a time? No more fancy guns, or automatics, no magazine clips, and not even any automatic repeater shooting guns. Everyone will have the same gun and to use it they shoot one bullet, pull out the shell, reload, and shoot again. Or even better, outlaw all guns from planet Earth. You know, evolve instead? Guns have one purpose only – to kill. There must be a zillion alternatives to the insanity we have now. Think deeply about this issue, and others like it – don't accept the status quo if it's messed up, be controversial, different, a heretic. You don't like my ideas? Come up with your own – but make changes because what we're doing now isn't working.

We can't start to fix all these things some nebulous time in the future, because it's already too late. Destroying buildings with bombs, killing strangers, and putting poison in our own food are insanity. Nonviolent protest is the only viable option we have; let's use it—get involved.

Lao Two says: "Earth could be a paradise instead of a hell. With just some honesty, organization, and good-natured persistence, everyone could be free from want."

If your life is a hellish down elevator, then you have to realize that you can press the emergency-stop button, and we hope Stoner Meditation has provided some similar tools to help. Conversely, if you have a heavenly life, filled with riches way beyond your needs, and you are not working to help people less fortunate, then your heaven is an illusion and will only bring you suffering. Hoarding huge sums of money is pathetic and despicable—and worse. If you are not part of the solution then any drug you take will only numb you, so you will be missing the benefit of Stoner Meditation. Ignoring the world around you is completely the opposite of Stoner Meditation.

It seems Stoners will have to fix the Earth; we cannot leave it to the politicians to fix anything anymore—they are either drunk, megalomaniacs, in the pocket of corporations, or deluded by religion. Folks, prayer doesn't do any good—it's action that does good. Let's be outraged at ecocide and lack of planetary organization.

Lao Two says: "We have only a limited time on Earth. Make time to enjoy it—go for hikes in nature, find peace in profound silence and meditative calm abiding. Give yourself permission to realize your goals, wishes, and dreams. Give others the same permission. Do this and your anger will disappear, and you will become a calm, kind, selfless person—and helpful to the greater society."

LSD, Psychedelics, and Entheogens—Lotus Eaters vs. Psychonauts

Lao Two heard a story attributed to Timothy Leary: a young man called him on the phone saying he was freaking out on LSD. Tim asked if anybody was there with him. The caller said no, he was alone, but he was seriously lost, scared, disoriented, and confused. Tim asked who dialed the phone, and the caller said that he did. Tim asked the caller to give the phone to the guy who dialed the phone.

Bad trips have been given a bad rap. They are not all that bad, and at the back of our mind when we're freaking out we have a tiny voice saying, "You're on a drug, it's just scary pictures, feelings, and thoughts. It will be gone in a few hours." Bad trips can be excellent teachers if we can let the bone-chilling and nerve-wracking images just be whatever they show us, without fear. Then we can then watch the "movie" without being intimidated. Lots of people take psychedelics at night and forget that their body is physically tired or perhaps they didn't eat beforehand, or they let the pressures of the unpsychedelic world enter into the trip. You are not disappearing into nothingness; even if a bad trip seems to last a long time, it's really not.

Fears arise because of the nonstop horrible visual images, monster hallucinations, negative thoughts, and magnified emotions that feel overwhelming. The monster we are experiencing is not in the psychedelic; we didn't get a bad drug (you should know it's quality before you take it). The monster lives in our habitual thinking, primal fears, and our ignorance of reality. Take a deep, slow breath, realize you are zonked, and let go of fear. Then the images will become interesting; even if they are unresolved, you know them for what they are—illusions, hallucinations, and not a psychedelic crisis. This is precisely the cure for all psychedelic freakouts—transmuting fear into courage, and then the magic can arise again.

Prepare for your trip in advance. Be in a safe, comfortable, and secure place, and in a relaxed, positive, experimental state of mind. Being with good friends you know and can trust to speak the truth is also good planning. Use common sense—if you have serious mental issues, resolve them first through therapy and meditation. On the other hand, psychedelics can sometimes resolve intense inner conflict—but buyer beware, psychedelics are heavy medicine and shamanic magic.

Story: This happened in 1967, when Lao Two lived alone in his hippie van. Before that he relied entirely on hitchhiking and public transportation, but he had to give up his apartment because he wasn't making enough just dealing marijuana and LSD. He wasn't alone; there were lots of people living in old bread trucks or school buses. At first Lao Two drove aimlessly around the area surrounding San Francisco, pulling off each night in a different place to sleep. He had to be in San Francisco for the weekends and on Monday's to make his money buying and selling drugs. On Monday, it was the Monday Night Class, which had just changed its name when it went off campus. Lao Two was partial to the old class, North American White Witchcraft, because of the interesting people he was meeting, the discussions on philosophy, and the esoteric books that were shared. But the thing he liked most about the class was the opportunity to discuss the drugs that were going around. If there was a green-colored acid and a blue-colored tab of acid, he was able to find people who'd taken both. Then he would buy in wholesale quantity whatever seemed the best.

This schedule enabled him to drive all over California Tuesday through Thursday. This story takes place along the Eel or Navarro River in the second-growth redwood forests of Northern California. He was driving in the rain along the highway looking for a turnoff, as he was getting tired of driving, and the river parallel to the road looked beautiful. To his right was a cliff face and to the left redwood trees and river, so he would have to cross over the highway with a left turn. Each time a place to turn presented itself, either it was too late or there was oncoming traffic. He got to a fairly straight stretch of road and noticed a turn ahead, and quickly crossed the highway. Suddenly he found his van accelerating down a steep slope. For a moment he thought he might crash through the trees into the river, but was able to slow down and found a place to park so he wouldn't be visible from the highway. He realized his old underpowered truck would have a hell of a time getting back up that slope in the rain. Oh well, maybe it would stop raining in the morning. He got out to look around and noticed some other hippie vans were also camping nearby under the redwood trees. No one was around, so he swallowed a tab of LSD that he'd just bought, so he could tell his customers about it from personal experience. He took note of where his van was parked and started walking in the light rain parallel to the river.

In about a half hour the acid was starting to come on, so he stopped to watch the dance of the forest. A soft breeze would send the ferns on the forest floor into a sublime drifting flow, as if the wind were water. The raindrops started becoming rainbows on the leaves and would speed up or slow down, or come in bursts if a redwood tree branch got loaded with the weight of water and sprang back upward. Insects were making their way as best they could, birds were on branches, and time had stopped.

A few hours later he was completely stoned as he wandered among the giant trees taking in the sweeping play of nature. A break in the clouds brought the sunshine briefly, while above him, the branches of the redwood trees would shift in the breeze, allowing sunlight to change from shadows to bright light for a moment on the fern-carpeted forest floor. His face was locked in a perpetual grin as the vibrating hallucinations moved through him. Leaves would fall, birds sang, sunlit clouds could be seen drifting overhead through the canopy. A perfect day to be stoned on acid.

Suddenly, he had an acid rush and stopped walking. He focused his gaze on the scene right in front of him, allowing everything to shift— the whole scene becoming one integrated system dancing together. His individuality shifted from sentient to totality, then became both together. The visions of his eyes were only a small part of his ability to see. He was no longer Lao Two, he was an Indian from two hundred years ago walking through the forest in an initiation ceremony. He was an alien who had landed in this strange forest, trying to make sense of the exotic scene. He was an explorer that had no body, only awareness. He was only feet walking. He was the last person on Earth. ...

Lao Two felt so tiny compared to the huge redwood trees surrounding him. Another wave of LSD rush proceeded to turn him into an infinitesimal and insignificant bug; he became invisible, and the wind blew through what was once his body. He saw himself becoming smaller and smaller while the trees towering overhead became skyscrapers reaching into infinity.

Because of the LSD, he could see in a way that had no distinctions. He had faded into a spacious world that had no edges, where separate and together became the same thing, and the inside of Lao Two was no longer disconnected from the outside world—he was the trees, ferns, birds. The air took on a thickness, becoming for humans what water is for fish, and he felt like he was moving through it in the same way. He heard himself saying, "This is really good acid!"

All his worries and cares completely fell away, and he became an integral part of his surrounding environment. With his raincoat on he lay down on the soft wet moss, looking up at the patches of mixed clouds and blue sky through the redwood trees—he felt himself to be a part of the soil. Closing his eyes, he cascaded into a series of unobstructed patterned mental hallucinations, with no thinking mind interruptions or judgments—just a roller-coaster fantasy ride. He was free, with nowhere to go and no place to be, and no one knew where he was.

At some point he wandered along the fast-flowing river and came upon three men fishing. Lao Two was so high he was basically unable to speak, but having no defenses or artifice he kept that huge smile on his face. To the fishermen this was obviously one of those stoned hippies from San Francisco they had read about in the newspapers. Lao Two started wandering away when one of the men called him back and without a word inexplicably gave him two huge, freshly caught salmon linked together on a rope. Lao Two has no memory of speaking a word to the fishermen, but it would be unlike him to not say thanks. Still absolutely stoned, Lao Two went back to his hippie van and placed the fish in his cooler. Later that evening, the salmon would be shared with all the hippies who were parked nearby.

By evening he was starting to come down a little and became hungry. Everybody was back at their vans, so dinner was organized after Lao Two showed them the salmon. One truck would boil some brown rice, another would make some vegetables, and some other hippies cleaned, prepared, and cooked the salmon. Lao Two had to beg off, telling them he was still too stoned to cook. So an impromptu potluck dinner was created, everybody eating communally. The exact minute dinner was finished, everything washed and put away, the heavens opened. It poured nonstop heavy rain, with strong winds and thunder sounding not too far away. To Lao Two, sitting in his van smoking marijuana with the door open, it was heavenly.

He was just about asleep when he heard another hippie van pull up and park nearby. It was raining hard, but for some inexplicable reason, or instinct, he put his clothes, raincoat, and hat back on and went out to say hello. Hippies during those times weren't strangers for long; he found a couple just traveling around, rootless like himself. But they obviously had even less money than he did, as their truck was sorely neglected. Lao Two lit up a reefer as the woman started pulling out some rice to boil, and in conversation Lao Two realized that they had no other food. Even the candle they lit gave off very poor light—he was thinking, and feeling: "These people have so little; spirits-that-be, please be kind to them." Instantly the light on the candle got very bright and the couple remarked how strange to see so much light, because they bought these really cheap candles that lit up their truck so poorly. Lao Two didn't say anything but suspected something magical had just happened. They remarked that they had not eaten all day, so Lao Two told them about the salmon and said he could share some food. Lao Two went back to his van and brought over the remaining cooked fish and leftovers. He also gave them some of the groceries he had bought, and in a small bag some free marijuana, a couple hits of acid, and a little cash. Now he was ready for sleep, so he went back to his van.

This time he quickly fell asleep, but was startled in the middle of the night by a huge crash. It was so loud and violent the ground shook. He put on his raincoat over his naked body, slipped into his boots, and went outside. Fluttering down were thousands of needles from the redwood trees, along with heavy rain. Just when he got outside, a car on the highway above them slammed on its brakes. He hiked up to the two-lane highway to find a huge redwood tree had fallen, completely blocking access in either direction. Another car was coming fast but also hit the brakes, coming to a screeching halt. This was happening on the other side of the tree also, and quickly all the hippies were shining flashlights to warn new cars arriving. Soon the police and highway patrol arrived and there were a lot of blinking emergency lights. They soon had everything organized, and cars were making U-turns to return the way they came. Lao Two decided it was best to go back to his van so as not to raise the curiosity of the police.

Down below, one of the hippies had obviously decided to get the hell outta there, and made several attempts at getting their van up the steep, muddy incline between the camping area and the highway, without success. Each attempt resulted in the van rolling back into the parking lot. But finally, gunning the engine and popping the clutch, the van barely made the incline, reluctantly reaching the highway, and they went on their way. Lao Two knew that his truck was older and weaker and would never be able to duplicate their strategy. The thought of it being stuck in this remote location for months occurred to him as he walked back to his van, then watched the police lights in the trees and cars turning around and returning the way they'd come. He went back to bed, lit some incense, and slept peacefully amid all the noise and lights of cars above.

He woke before sunrise and ate a peanut butter sandwich as he watched the tractor backhoe loaders already in action. Men had been cutting the fallen tree, but it was very thick. A line of cars stretched beyond sight. But they were almost done and a few cars were already passing through one cleared side. Lao Two quickly packed up his equipment. By the time he was ready cars had been moving for a while, and it would be a good time to try to enter the highway. He drove to the incline, gunned his engine, and made his attempt, but his tires would not grip in the mud, just as he imagined, and he would coast back down on the clutch. He would get just past halfway up the incline, lose traction and power, and drift back down. Again and again he tried to get up the hill, with the same results.

One of the highway crew ran over to the incline, yelling at him from the road. He yelled down for Lao Two to wait. A tractor driver had noticed his predicament and drove down the incline, got behind his van, and pushed Lao Two up the hill, while the other worker stopped traffic. In a few fortuitous, magical, wondrous minutes, Lao Two was on his way to the next adventure. He lit a reefer, enjoying the rain and the rhythm of his windshield wipers, thinking how the universe was magically cooperating, almost protecting him and his precarious hippie lifestyle.

When he arrived at the ocean he thought again about what had happened ... the excellent LSD trip, the fishermen, the hippies he met and bonded with so easily, the seemingly magical candle getting brighter in the impoverished hippies' truck just because he wished it, and the tractor operator who helped him. Even the fallen tree seemed to be in on the events, bringing the tractor right there to help him ... all coincidence?

LSD is nothing more than ergot mold from rye, and when synthesized, exhibits predictable extrasensory-type hallucinations, insights, and mystical events. Sometimes these events come together in a fluid way and it seems we are in sync with the universal creation around us—if we know how to look for it. For Lao Two sitting on that beach, even the clouds spoke to him, not in words but in shapes, and the ocean sparked a rhythm that mixed with the beating of his heart. His realized that all hallucinations are Mom Nature's way of expressing herself—and our mind interprets everything on LSD as part of an organized whole that is more than the sum of its parts—the gestalt. Each single leaf, every grain of sand, has a story to tell us if we know how to see it with all of our senses.

End of story.

A discussion has gained momentum recently, concerning Lotus Eaters versus Psychonauts. The Lotus Eater is from the *Odyssey*, where Odysseus describes the lotus fruit and flowers as a sedative; people find so much pleasure under that spell, they want to continue forever, but it makes them apathetic to everything around them. In other words, a Lotus Eater is someone who takes psychedelics for pleasure, never digging into the shamanistic depths.

A Psychonaut, on the other hand, takes a psychedelic for the serious purpose of seeking wisdom, and considers all psychedelics entheogens. Each trip is a search for transcendence, as in our metaphor, pushing through the forest toward tree line, higher each trip.

However, we think this argument is somewhat silly. No one becomes a Psychonaut without first being a Lotus Eater. The psychedelics themselves turn us into Psychonauts. We don't necessarily choose to become a wizard or shaman, and unlike other cultures, no one chooses us. It just happens the way it happens, perhaps magically. Many people ignore the call and turn back to ordinary life, and perhaps those are the Lotus Eaters.

Lao Two says: "Don't even speak out there on LSD; keep that intrinsic, spacious enlightened balance. No words; be still, be silent."

You've certainly noticed that Stoner Meditation considers all psychedelics as entheogens. Anyone taking them will recognize the spiritual context, the cleansing of their problems, and the transcending and opening of body and mind.

Lao Two says: "Psychedelics are an advanced meditation practice."

Psychedelics are so profound that we now have a new tool in the search for enlightenment. LSD has entered the same arena as any other sophisticated meditation technique to leave ego behind. The only problem is our lack of ability to control the intensity and direct it. We are forced to accept the tumbling waterfall of hallucinations without intermission—not that that's a bad thing ... intense fun, but still overpowering. And too often the awesome insights, answers, and revelations slip away from us.

Many people have successfully taken their first trips at concerts, but as we've said, we recommend a comfortable, secluded, and safe environment, with good and honest friends you can trust. Don't even think about driving, and for some people on acid, it's even difficult to walk.

When you are tripping with friends, do not mess with their head; be on your best behavior respecting the spiritual nature of their trip, and the greater trip you are on together. Do not tell somebody on LSD that they are invisible and pretend you can't see them. Something like that can lead to a psychedelic crisis in an unstable person. Then you've got a freaked-out tripper on your hands.

Honestly, Stoner Meditation is not going to say for certain that the psychedelics we are putting into our bodies are a good path, or the best path. We are going by both our personal experience and what other people have told us about their trips. Psychedelics are a new path, recently rediscovered—so we, and you, are all pioneers of the inner voyage. It might or might not be one of the highest paths like meditation, but for those of us who are Psychonauts, it rings true. After we come down from a psychedelic, we're sure grateful we were fortunate enough to be able to take the trip. An aware bliss, a kaleidoscope of images and thoughts, but at the end the struggle was better than not knowing.

Lao Two says: "Just like spraining an ankle, we can sprain our brain."

Coming down: the period after taking psychedelics, although not as dramatic as the trip itself, is equally important. Take very good care of your body and mind, eat right, be positive, and have no fear. Enjoy any recurring visual, auditory, or mental imagery that arises. Your dreams during sleep can be your teachers.

Cherish your bad trips; they are the best teachers. Always remember that everything that's happening on your trip is illusory and although something seems real, solid, and factual—it is just passing through. Lastly, be sure to only take psychedelics. Do not drink alcohol or take downers, uppers, or any other strange combinations. Let the psychedelic be a spiritual influence by itself, bringing you the message you need to experience. Take a few days after a trip to learn from it, and let yourself come down easy.

Lao Two says: "It always strikes me as funny, or maybe ironic, that many people who took some LSD twenty or thirty years ago act like nothing ever happened. But I can only infer from my own point of view, maybe it did go away for them. I always assumed that even one LSD trip changed people profoundly."

Story: In 1966 Lao Two would hitchhike from San Francisco to Los Angeles with 500 to 5,000 hits of LSD to sell. He would buy them for twenty-five cents, and sell them for a dollar each. For a while he was doing this every month, staying in L.A. for a few days, then hitchhiking back to San Francisco. Every trip was eventful in its own way, considering it took two days. He would always go via Highway 1, the twisty-turning highway that in some places sat high on the cliffs overlooking the Pacific Ocean. He would camp in Big Sur, but one month they started charging money, a commodity he was always short on, and Lao Two really didn't like being around so many straight people. He would arrive in L.A. and then call his girlfriend as soon as he arrived—this was before cell phones, and long-distance calls were expensive. He also had a girlfriend in San Francisco with whom he stayed when he was there, but he had a key to her apartment.

He called his L.A. girlfriend at her office, but they told Lao Two that she suddenly had to go out of town and would return the next day. Lao Two was calling from Venice Beach, but he didn't know anybody there. He sat on the beach thinking about what to do next. He decided to just hang out there and sleep on the beach. He went swimming and talked to the locals. They told him not to sleep all night on the beach because it was cleaned with trucks that swept the sand, pulling out the small objects. He walked up to a very pretty girl who was swimming near him and talked for a while. She said she lived nearby, so Lao Two asked her if he could crash at her house for the night. She said he could, but she was a restaurant worker and wouldn't be home before midnight. She told Lao Two where to meet her if he didn't find anyplace else. She left to get ready for work, so Lao Two had hours to wait for her return. All kinds of sexual possibilities started to form in his head, and he thought she might be interested. Cool.

Lao Two decided to drop some LSD, and gave a few hits away to his new beach friends. He doesn't remember what "brand" it was—Purple Haze, Blue Cheer, or something, something Sunshine. ... Everyone he was hanging out with went home and the beach was mostly empty, so he walked down to a completely secluded part of the beach and sat on an elevated section where he could scan the ocean sunset clearly. He instinctively sat in a meditation position, letting the LSD move through him. He says he was completely unmoving for hours, and unlike previous attempts, his body accepted the meditation position without complaint. Sunset turned into night, and the crashing waves on the beach, the stars, and the heat of the night connected inside him. His hearing picked up the rhythm of the waves forming at the edge of the ocean, then cresting and falling, crashing loudly into the sand—his meditative breath joined the cadence of the waves crashing, synchronizing with the endless tides.

Spontaneously, he started chanting the AOM mantra, and each tone became synchronous with the waves and his breathing. He says he was chanting for hours and hours, when he lost himself and became the ocean. After awhile he quit chanting, but the AOM sound continued rhythmically, and the person that was Lao Two was completely gone, replaced by deconstructed emptiness mind. Something impossible to describe was happening to him as he experienced a unique type of mind that was more expansive, yet more aware than anything before. Here was concentrated creative energy, pure love, aware superconscious-ness, and intense wisdom coming from some unknown source.

He suspected this was enlightenment—he had never experienced anything as clear, so filled with wisdom and awareness on any of his other acid trips. He sat in calm abiding for what seemed a short while, he says he has no idea how long, but at some point he questioned if he had gone schizophrenic because what he was experiencing was a completely alter-nate reality. He didn't understand what he was experiencing, because this elevated state of awareness was different from every previous trip. When he came out of it, he was no longer who he'd once been: he intuitively realized he had seen a pure consciousness that was awareness in concert with creation. It must be emptiness. Even though Lao Two had read many Buddhism books about enlightenment, the experience was completely unlike any description he had read. Also, having no teacher, he didn't fully understand the magnitude of what had transpired. From that moment on he has searched for validation of his experience, and in rereading the books from his new viewpoint he realized that the authors and the Buddha were indeed describing the exact experience he'd had. Maybe.

He looked at his watch and it was 11:45; he had been sitting still in his meditation posture for over five hours. He noticed the trucks positioned far away on the beach, sweeping the sand clean, so he left to meet the woman who'd offered a place to crash. She let him sleep on the couch and went right into her bedroom and closed her door. In the morning Lao Two split, leaving her a thank-you note and a few hits of acid in appreciation. He never saw her again.

End of story.

Lao Two says: "Psychedelics can enable us to look back upon Earth as angels floating through space."

When we think about the potential of psychedelic inner exploration, it starts to seem plausible that humans might just be able to communicate with the weather gods, talk to animals, or heal the sick through our inner energies. I don't want to get all New Agey here, but maybe someday in the future people will unlock new parts of their brain. Stoner Meditation wants to keep an open mind on these subjects, because over the years we've heard lots of stories from people describing their entheogen experiences. And we've had a few elemental communications with the "spirits" ourselves. ... If you get enlightened and find you can heal people, we certainly don't want you to dismiss the ability—please go out and heal people.

When you've had a few inexplicable events interacting with Mom Nature, some magical experiences, and transcendental unexplainable and profound spiritual connections, you will think back on the person you once were. That person is still you, but was volume one, in a long series. We don't blame modern science for being suspicious of our anecdotal reports; we do blame modern science for not investigating, however. Trippers love to tell their most "out there" stories to other trippers. Does magic really exist? One of the instructions for advanced Buddhist monks is to vow not to perform magic.

Lao Two says: "If there is such a thing as black magic and white magic, realize it comes down to this—negative amplifies negativity, and positive amplifies positivity. What you put your energy into intensifies it."

Enlightenment can come in several ways. One is the flash of insight, lasting only a few moments as the third eye opens. Or to put it another way, it's a waking up, putting aside all dualism, and standing in view. Instant enlightenment is an "aha" moment of realization that completely transforms your viewpoint. When this occurs there is a new connection to reality, and our relationship to the world around us changes. It's similar when we take a hit of strong LSD. Please note that there are other types of enlightenment; sudden enlightenment is only one. The view is the same, but the attainment is different.

Eventually we hit the ceiling and LSD won't get us any higher. What's happened is that our aware consciousness has adapted to that higher LSD level. We reached the first spacious plateau of enlightenment, but ahead of us looms the top of the mountain. This is where meditation takes over. This is the practice of the wizard.

If you consider taking the LSD path, please understand that you will be an outcast, struggling to keep your feet on the ground. You will be investigating an unmapped path that explores the highest highs and the lowest lows—the shaman's path.

Zen koan: "What is the sound of one hand clapping?"

Earlier we told you not to look into a mirror while you are peaking on a psychedelic if it's your first time taking it. Now that you've tripped for a while and understand Stoner Meditation's demand that we confront our demons, it's time to stand at a mirror. This time we personally know what emptiness is, have overcome fear, and understand illusions. We see our reflection without fear or judgments of what we see arising—we can accept it all as hallucination. If you are peaking on a psychedelic, the mirror might possibly cause an out-of-body experience, exploding hallucinations, or archetypal visions, and you might lose your ego temporarily—wonderful. Lao Two told me that several times he saw his past lives while doing this. Or at least he saw his face change to different faces, male and female and young and old, in a long succession of metamorphosing faces, monsters, animals, and gods.

Lao Two says: "The only time I was ever able to sit in a full-lotus meditation position was when I was peaking on LSD. My legs easily folded over each other without the usual excruciating, distracting pain."

While tripping try to notice our planetary group mind, and feel the other humans on our planet, become them. Our individual minds are all connected, each a part of the whole. On LSD it's possible to be telepathic, but it requires a lot of trust. Beware of both erroneous superstition and erroneous science. On LSD, not much is certainty, and reality is bendable—learn to appreciate mystery and living without answers. We feel it's important to not know everything, to see everything as new and be present in each moment—that's where the magic is.

Buddha You

The 14th Dalai Lama said: "Buddhists say the self is not separate from the physical body, feelings, recognitions, etc., and consciousness. When we die, the body is left behind and feelings, recognitions, etc., cease; but a subtle consciousness remains." —Mussoorie, India, September 18, 2012

We create our confused, mistaken life story by expecting the outside universe to make us happy, but that damn universe sure is doing a crappy job of it. We do feel entitled, and we are impatiently waiting to get the outside of us fixed just right; then our life will be fine.

Unfortunately, too many people think that they can fix the outside vto meet their expectations. They think they have permission to blunder and bully through life—using people, buying a new car every year (because they have the money), discarding energy and even time wastefully, and not respecting the precious nature of all life. Too many of the very rich and powerful have this mistaken attitude, a tunnel vision where the universe exists for them alone. And, as Earth gets more overpopulated with humans, life itself becomes cheap, worthless of respect to them.

Ignorance, anger, greed, and bad manners have become the way of life of many on Earth in the twenty-first century. Even if the universe gives us the winning lottery numbers, we still want more. Is there a better way we Stoners can participate in determining how life is to be lived, and died?

The bigger picture we've tried to describe herein is that we are responsible for our behavior, goals, practices, actions, and emotional drama. We expect Stoners to be unafraid to grasp the secret teachings as they are revealed to us in marijuana, psychedelics, and meditation. Your Stoner Meditation path leads to understanding the nature of reality and your place in it.

Why is it so difficult to understand what nirvana is? Because all humans have a built-in survival mechanism that diverts our attention from what we actually focus on—in other words, we don't see the world outside our eyes as it is; we would rather create a sugarcoated storyline world. We see an apple with our eyes, and in our mind we have already decided how it tastes—before we've even taken a bite. Then, when we do take a bite, we are distracted by other events and don't even taste the apple while it's happening.

If you decide to study Buddhism, don't try to follow in the Buddha's steps to become like the historical Buddha; become Buddha you. The Buddha gave excellent teachings, but after he died other buddha-type masters expanded on his teachings, and now we have lots of excellent techniques. Be practical—use these shortcuts, read up on stuff, try to understand what those masters are pointing at. But don't quit meditating because, from our experience, meditation is the key to unlock Natural Mind.

Buddhism isn't the only method, and if it's not for you then find some material on secular reality, or various other philosophies. Every one of these teachers and systems is discussing the same reality—the ecstatic, spiritual, transcendental direct experience. Most importantly, remember that nothing is written in stone, except for the advice to remain skeptical. If you hear people saying that their religion, philosophy, or method is the only way, then we suggest you get the hell outta there.

It seems the psychedelic drugs we take know what to reveal to us. They will not push us off the cliff into emptiness in the beginning; we need to learn some stuff first. There are "advanced" teachings that are revealed naturally when we are secure enough to accept and understand them. As we've said before: magic only remains magical until we see how the illusion is performed; then it becomes science.

Our bodies live on average about 68½ years—that's approximately 25,000 days. The fact is that humans are not overly special on the cosmic scale. Our research tells us that human monkeys have existed for 5 million years, at the most, and our intellectual evolution started 400,000 years ago. Recorded history started only four or five thousand years ago in caves and then in places like Egypt. Five hundred years ago, even Columbus thought the Earth was flat. We hope it's sinking in how brief a period this is for us individually. Or to put it more bluntly, if you are thirty, you've used up perhaps almost half of your life.

Predictions are that the entire universe is filled with life. Recent observations suggest our Milky Way is fertile ground for intelligent life. Some kinds of life out there might be more backward than us, others more advanced. If aliens already have the ability to travel through space, they have certainly noticed Earth. The fact that aliens don't try to contact Earth anymore shows their intelligence and wisdom. I wouldn't be surprised if astronauts someday discover a type of billboard at the edge of our solar system flashing a quarantine warning, saying, "Stay away, the third planet is toxic and filled with insane life forms."

We on Earth like to think of humans as the miracle of the universe, a perfection of some sort—but it will probably turn out that we are far surpassed. Until we can understand that we're just a jumble of piled-up vibrations, we will continue to be deluded. We all know that life is more than we see with our senses—we are a mix of matter and emptiness, but there is stuff like dark matter, dark energy, and other invisible-to-us energies all around us.

We Stoners exist on disorienting higher levels while we continue to exist on ordinary levels—it's the paying attention that determines what level we are experiencing. There is no way to achieve enlightenment without our physically existing bodies. As a matter of fact, realizing enlightenment is dependent in some ways on the intense feelings that arise in the body. Enlightenment is not a singularly mental experience. All levels of awareness are contained in one vessel: Natural Mind.

We develop some pretty strange mental habits from our childhood that we carry throughout our lives. Some of us have aberrations like depression, anxiety, or just plain confusion. Others are deluded into thinking their belief structure and their unexamined life will satisfy all their needs. We are certainly told often enough that our success is measured by our delusions—wealth, beauty, power.

Meanwhile time slips away, and our karma leads the deluded blindly on. Lao Two discovered a simple method that helps keep your focus on what is real and valuable. This exercise takes repetition to be really effective.

Exercise 8: This can be done anywhere you can close your eyes. Bring your attention to your breath and do several very deep, slow-motion breaths using intense concentration. Notice all the smallest details—the in-breath, then a very short pause, the long out-breath coasting to the brief pause before the next in-breath.

Take a very deep in-breath, then stop breathing, and hold your breath gently for as long as you can. Then, during the long out-breath, imagine your next breath is your last ever. This next coming breath is the important one, because your death is imminent and it's the last breath you'll ever have.

Ask yourself what mindset you want to have for that last breath to take into your after-death experience. If done right, it will entirely change your attitude.

The gift of continued breathing is not to be taken lightly; and should be filled with purpose, gratitude, heart-filled hope, and attention.

End of Exercise 8.

Lao Two says: "Enlightenment is a shift of perspective."

We all have emotional, environmental, and mentally inspired moods—sometimes down, up, neutral, aware, not aware, angry, loving, and maybe emotional outbursts that come and go. Over the short time we have, just how important are these delusions? What if we let go of how important, or how angry, sad, self-absorbed we are? Stoner Meditation says to just let these delusions go, let them fly away, and become involved what is really happening in the here and now. It takes some time and energy to learn to let go and recognize what is really happening, but it's worth the effort.

Investigate meditative philosophies like Buddhism; Zen; Vipassana; the forms of Tibetan Buddhist, Hindu, and Sufi meditation; hatha yoga; kundalini yoga; kung fu, and any other technique that suits you. We've even heard of secular, Christian, Islamic, and Jewish meditation groups. No matter what your discipline or school, remember it's the daily repetition of meditation that will produce "results." Some people like to meditate in groups and others on their own—try out both.

Remember to judge a teacher or master by the students. Are they serious, respectful, thoughtful, and kind in their speech? Or are they frivolous, immature, distracted, and abusive, with complicated negative habits?

Lao Two says: "I don't think it's possible to become 'enlightened' unless there is an ego death experience. Superconscious awareness is, and is not in our brain."

Story: A few years ago Lao Two went to New Delhi, India, with his wife. He had been to Nepal four times and had always wanted to experience India. But India is quite different from Nepal—the tourist sites are farther apart from each other, and many are decrepit. If the traffic is bad in Nepal, it is horrible in India—especially the highways, where no rules are enforced, accidents are common, and there are just too many cars. His wife didn't want to stay in India for more than a few days, so they explored Delhi a little, went to the Taj Mahal, and then she caught a return flight to northern Thailand—her favorite destination. Lao Two planned to stay in India and take a train to the town of Dharamsala up in the mountains, where the Dalai Lama and the Tibetan refugees reside. Then he would return to Delhi and continue north to the holy city of Varanasi, and onward to Nepal again. It's common for them to split up for part of their vacation because of their differing interests, and sometimes it's just cool to experience things on your own as a tourist in a foreign country.

Lao Two had learned that marijuana is currently ambiguously illegal in India, but it's basically a marijuana-friendly country. The plan was to brazenly ask anybody who seemed to have a connection for some marijuana (ganja) or hashish. The first person he asked was his bicycle rickshaw driver dropping them off at their hotel, who coincidentally was named Ganges. Lao Two kept asking for "ganja," and the rickshaw guy thought this stupid foreigner was pronouncing his name wrong. After a while of this and some hand gestures, the rickshaw guy understood, but said no. A few blocks away from their hotel was a huge shopping area, constantly filled with thousands of shoppers seeking wedding gowns, jewelry, food, and just about anything else you can imagine. In some passageways it's so crowded with people walking, or making deliveries that there is almost no forward movement. The aromatic smells from the spice shops set their heads spinning, and the food in India is mostly vegetarian, so they were eating everything. At every hookah shop Lao Two asked about ganja but was rebuffed. Finally he was directed to a part of town that backpackers frequent. The taxi let them off and Lao Two was standing still on the street, waiting for his wife to window shop. A young man walked up to him and asked what he wanted. Lao Two said, "I'm looking for some ganja or hashish, preferably hashish." The guy said to follow him. As Lao Two was following him, he gestured to his wife that he was going to score. She tolerantly and good-naturedly understands "his hobby," as she calls it, and went into a jewelry store.

Lao Two was led down a narrow, dark alley to a locked shop door, then into the shop that was pretending to be a shop—it had a few cheap tourist items that might have been for sale, if any official inquiries were made. The young man dug into the loose wall sheetrock and pulled out several plastic-wrapped chunks of hashish. He weighed one and it was 15 grams, a huge amount of hash, and said it was US$200. Well, Lao Two had done his homework and read that hash costs around $15 for 10 grams, or if it's cream, up to $40. Lao Two got the feeling that he was being taken for a rich tourist, so he started bitching about the price, expecting some negotiation. But amazingly, the young guy wouldn't budge. He wouldn't let Lao Two smoke any either, but Lao Two ate a small morsel and it was definitely hash (in Nepal he'd bought hash on the street that turned out to be part road tar). Unexpectedly, the young guy pulled out a photo album of his visit to the north Indian mountains. The photos showed him harvesting the plants, and his hands covered in thick, sticky hashish tar. You can imagine how much Lao Two was enjoying the whole adventure of sitting across from an Indian dude, looking at his photographic trip to the mountains of north India to make hashish ... just sitting there buying hashish in India—what a cool experience!

The guy kept repeating that this hashish in the pictures was the exact stuff Lao Two was buying. No matter what Lao Two said, the guy wouldn't lower the price. The fact is that money is not a problem for Lao Two, but he hates being cheated, and he really didn't want to look elsewhere after that morning's episodes of asking at shop after shop. Lao Two explained he couldn't possibly smoke that much hashish and bought half the package, about 7 grams for US$100, still a huge amount of hashish. You know that old homily, "A bird in the hand is worth two in the bush." Lao Two was thinking, *this better be good hashish at this price,* and noted where he was in case he had to return to complain about the quality.

He pocketed the stash and rejoined his wife, who was still shopping. She picked up right away that Lao Two was bummed out, because the first thing he said was that he'd paid too much. She was tired of hearing about it all, and had put up with his searching all day long. After all, here they were vacationing in exotic New Delhi, and Lao Two was spending the whole damn day asking for hashish and then when he got it, he went cheap. She had a point... They stopped at a restaurant, and there was a dreadlocked guy standing out front. Lao Two showed the hash to the dreadlock, who smelled it and said Lao Two paid way too much. ... It's possible Lao Two was irritable from hunger, because after lunch he thought what the hell, he'd been ripped off before in foreign countries, it was no big deal, might just as well enjoy the journey, so he pulled himself into the here and now and brought on his smile.

As the sun set, the vibes changed from people working to people shopping, laughing, and interacting—it was a delicious, magical scene, and they were enraptured by the sudden change. He bought a small hash pipe, some incense, and a cool metal box to keep the hash in. As it got dark the lights went on inside the shops, incense was lit, and a population of a zillion people flooded the streets, making the city alive, vibrant, earthy, and they both fell in love with India right then and there. India can definitely be a love/hate experience.

They were pretty far from their hotel, so they took a motor rickshaw, watching the goings-on along the way. In the room, Lao Two brought out his new hash pipe, opened the window, and took about four deep hits. It was instantly Stoner heaven, and he realized that he'd stumbled on the infamous "Cream," the very best hashish of India. He was so stoned, in fact, that he could barely sleep that night. His wife, mildly sick with intestinal problems, was not in a mood to hear Lao Two praise the hashish over and over again. She complained about how he'd wasted the day searching for the hashish, and said something to the effect that Lao Two spent so many hours looking for drugs that his life was consumed by it. She said; "Life is what we put our energy into." Lao Two answered, "Rrrrrright," as he felt the hashish he just smoked was well worth all the effort he'd put his energy into—not her meaning at all, but he was much too mindblown to argue his perspective. After all, she was feeling a little sick and had probably been embarrassed, worried, and exasperated by his actions that day, so he cut her some slack.

One of the lessons learned here is that we Stoners can't always expect people to "get us" or understand the reasons we do some of the crazy, risky, and probably irresponsible things to get high. Straight people just can't always understand why we make Stoner Meditation our focus. Just love them anyway, and know they love you back.

End of story.

Do not engage in risky behavior like Lao Two did in India. It's much better to take a break from getting high. Lao Two likes to tempt the fates and confront life head on. As we said before, enlightenment does not solve all our problems, or change all our behavior or karma – it's a life-long process and there is no perfection. Lao Two is a perfect example of this, but on the other hand, his approach has always been to be fully human, not saintly and inflexible.

Buddha you is being who and what you want to be and living your aware, awake life on your own terms, as much as possible. We are alive right now, and we should be living as fully as possible right now. If instead we are constantly caught up in our neurotic problems, our *relationship* to our thoughts is the cause. Ascertain how sitting in meditation and living life without judgment can help you unlearn habitual inner criticism and free you to participate fully in living.

The point is not avoiding thinking, stopping the mind, or even reaching enlightenment. Develop a healthy relationship to your thinking and change the habits that hold you back. When you get high, remember to relax your breath, relax your mind, and open your heart. Be your body, mind, and presence.

Our wish is that every Stoner will have that enlightenment moment when duality stops and self merges with other. Being appropriately responsive to your body and mind, appreciating the gift of life, understanding the mysterious, and being compassionate to others and yourself is Buddha you.

Wisdom

Stoner Meditation points out that the only worldly goods we really own are our physical body, our time, and our current breath. Regrettably, so many of our early years are focused on superficial leisure as life slips by.

We are stardust that has become aware. We can't begin to understand what stardust considers important, but we can live peacefully with not knowing all the answers, accepting the incomprehensible mystery, and opening up to experience.

Mohandas Gandhi said: "Many people, especially ignorant people, want to punish you for speaking the truth. For being correct. For being you. Never apologize for being correct, or for being years ahead of your time. If you're right and you know it, speak your mind. Speak your mind. Even if you are a minority of one, the truth is still the truth."

Primitive humans had to know about all the plants in their vicinity, testing and tasting—so it wasn't long before the first Stoners appeared. Back then they didn't have nice pipes, bongs, or rolling papers, but they had fire, and it's pretty certain they threw some marijuana plants on it to burn. It became obvious that if you got caught in the smoke of certain burning plants, you got high. Shamans discovered that if you ate certain mushrooms, cacti, flowers, or vines, you would have transcendental visions.

Almost every location on Earth has hallucinogens of one kind or another growing wild. Because of the power of these psychoactive substances, shamans were eventually chosen by the community to safely interact with the spirits through visions, and hallucination. Many cultures restricted psychedelics to only the shaman and other cultures allowed all members to get high. These shaman wizards were allowed to have extreme personality changes, while other community members were expected to remain normal, unless they were cooperating with the shaman to make a specific personality change. The shaman would map the unfamiliar territory of the mind and emotions and exchange everyday consciousness for expanded transcendental non-ordinary consciousness.

The argument about who should get high continues unabated, but many of us don't really care. We're going to get stoned anyway. Stoner Meditation believes that some of the shamans in primitive cultures got just as enlightened as the Buddha.

Stoner Meditation opens the door for those willing to open their minds enough to leave the trees and make the farther journey to the mountaintop. We celebrate the yearning of those few Stoners who MUST know what's behind the door. Stoner Meditation claims there is an ever-flowing secret fountain, unknown only because we are too deluded to see it. All religions, philosophies, and scientific insights originate from the exact same fountain.

Zen koan: "The finger pointing at the moon just points the way. Once we see the moon, the finger is no longer necessary."

Once we understand enlightened reality, mentally descriptive words are no longer necessary, because we see the world as it is. Generally, people are caught up in the world's illusions and don't even notice the moon when looking directly at it. That's because they are separated from experience by thinking mind's distractions. Stoner Meditation can point to the moon forever, but thinking mind holds tightly to our delusions and keeps us distracted from truly seeing it. If we can silence fear, insecurity, anxiety, and negative self-image, we then stand naked with the moon.

Intuitively, everyone appreciates that there is a deeper layer of mental awareness. Stoners physically and mentally connect with this deeper layer from their first high experience. A few hits and the door opens a crack, and they have their first taste of Natural Mind. This initial connection lights an emerging flame inside them, as they take their initial steps away from darkness. They might misunderstand and try to smoke more and more, but ultimately the flame only flickers bright to dim ... but adding meditation stabilizes and enhances the light. Together, as

Stoner meditators, we turn up the flame of our natural wisdom, and the blazing fire of love develops.

The egotistical love we usually practice is survival, inner-directed love born out of loneliness and fear. Tension, sexual anxiety, and our own body image criticisms make us hold back on outer-directed love. We become constricted, with our muscles clenched tightly, and become crippled inside. Being uptight is endemic in the modern world.

When we can love everybody equally, and that includes loving ourselves, then body and mind can become one. If we condemn other people judgmentally because of the way they look, then we are condemning our own body image. They are our mirror, and if we're afraid to dress differently from the norm, then anyone who does dress differently will be criticized in our thoughts. It seems strange to think of it that way, but when we form an opinion of someone we see, it's coming from our judgmental thinking mind. Listen to the actual voice of the inward criticism—try to catch it word for word. Also notice your thoughts, emotions, and judgments, like *That bald guy dresses weird.*

To change our body image from negative to positive (or neutral), we have to start with our thinking. When you think, *that bald guy dresses weird*, add an echo of *I'm afraid to dress differently,* or perhaps it's the misplaced superiority of *I have all my hair* to the disapproving judgmental comment. What we are doing here instead is mentally changing the inner voice of habitual thinking. Ego is insecure about our body image, and that becomes part of our inner voice. We can defuse our volatile, hypercritical inner voice, and in doing so, accept our body image.

That bald person is your mirror replica as far as ego is concerned. After doing this mental rebuff a while and opening up your mind, you'll find you will have developed a new way of thinking. You'll notice your thoughts saying something like, *that bald guy dresses interestingly.*

Nobody can match some preposterous body ideal, so why are we overly concerned with desiring a perfect body? We are insecure because we are lonely, we want a partner, and we mistakenly think the only way to connect is to be beautiful, alluring, flawless. As a culture we spend millions on cosmetics, body-care lotions, and whatnot ... and the result of all the programming by advertising is social confusion. We find someone who meets our criteria as physically beautiful, not really seeing them as they are. From that we form a superficial relationship with hollow conversations. It usually ends in disappointment once we see through the façade we've built. Little by little we begin to see the unadorned faults of our partner, and more often than not, we break up, then unthinkingly find another physically beautiful partner, and repeat it all over again.

If we can break free of social convention, we can achieve our own freedom of expression. Then our clothing becomes art, and we become a confident artist dressing from our individual creativity. If you wear cosmetics out of habit, then please rethink your actions. Don't be overly hard on yourself, but dig a little deeper into superficiality, discover the real person you are—not the person that advertising says you should be. Create your own look, learn to be comfortable in your skin. Body image then celebrates this incredible gift of the body we get to live in.

Many authoritarian cultures strictly enforce the prevailing costume— like Muslim burkas, hijabs, niqabs, chadors, or khemars. But in the West we can wildly choose our costume—we can wear makeup, go without makeup, or maybe do both on the same day. If you need to wear a costume for a job, remember you are not defined by that costume—no one can judge you. We are all deserving of love regardless of our clothing.

Change the way you look at your body. On the most basic level, we are guts with a skin covering. It's amazing how much attention skin gets in our culture. Stoner Meditation has been saying all along that we need to look at the subtle-inside body, discovering the essence of what we are at our core, because within that essence is vibrational love. That loving essence has guts and a human skin surrounding it, protecting it. This is why we can be accepting of other people's bodies and the way they dress: once you connect with your inner essence, you will begin to see it in other people. We know intuitively if that person has connected with love, or is sad, defeated, or angry inside. The bald guy in the interesting clothing is seen as a totality.

Society and advertising give us unrealistic body perfection as a goal. Many people focus on a specific body area, believing if it were "fixed" they would fit the ideal. This is unrealistic self-loathing, or at least obsession and delusion. Change your focus, and find freedom—and remember, if you never make any changes in the way you are living your life (letting habits rule you), you are stuck on your path.

After learning how to deeply feel the body we live in, we can begin to amplify that love inside. Just as there are levels of realization, there are levels of love we can express. Being able to express love is not some hippie-trippy giggle; this is powerful magic. You must discover what your body can do; it's so much more than we've been led to believe. Projecting love, instead of anxiety and fear, is a secret esoteric technique—find out what you can feel when you go way, way deep.

Exercise 9: It's time to break out your best smokes and get super high again. If you usually get off on smoking one hit, then please take two, three, or four. Wait for the smokes to come on.

Then take a nice warm shower.

We always feel better after a shower, but don't really think much about the actual showering because it's become one of the many repetitious parts of our life in the West.

We understand that warm showers are not available in all parts of our planet, so maybe substitute a cup of tea, or a cool shower on a really hot day, or simply very slowly eating your lunch—this exercise involves using the senses, and potentially a sensual or sexual encounter. The goal here is to be super conscious during an ordinary, habitual physical activity—something you do with your body every day without thinking about it. This is an excellent exercise during psychedelic tripping as well.

Normally, when you take a shower you just get in, soap up, rinse off, and get out to towel dry in a matter of minutes. Unfortunately this exercise will take a little longer, and we apologize for using extra water resources. A valid option is to turn the water off and on as you feel is necessary.

This is not your usual shower; this is a Stoner Meditation shower. Consider this a sort of once-in-a-lifetime brand-new experience—as if showers are a new invention. You've been hearing all about showers, and now you get to try one for the first time, wow! Get naked, look into the bathroom mirror, smile, and relax all your muscles. Splash your arms around and wiggle your body, feel your feet pushing against the floor, arch your back and roll your skull, feeling you shoulder and neck muscles, bring your eyes level. Close your eyes and let the marijuana trip your head wherever it will go—we don't want any mental controlling, just observation of the body. No music, please; sorry.

Open your eyes and very slowly enter the shower.

Pretend your body is being filmed with a stop-motion camera, so move slowly like a robot. As you move, try to notice everything one photo at a time. Examine every detail—the pressure of the water, the temperature, your breathing, the smell of the soap; feel all your body senses, and take note of the incredible utilitarian nature that is our body. Moan or make some euphoric sound; feel the vibrations in your throat. Can you feel the vibrations within your entire body? The most important thing is to keep bringing attention back to feeling the skin as a sensual organ, exploring the sense of touch and feeling—loving your body.

Stand on one foot, lifting the other foot slightly off the floor—do not slip. As you stand on one foot, dig your balancing, think about the awesome mechanical ability involved in balancing on one foot—even if it includes putting your shoulder against the wall for stability. Notice the process of all these actions flowing through space-time.

Soap up, and feel your hands rubbing over your body, feel your body feeling your hands. If you get a marijuana rush, close your eyes and take a moment to stand still, bringing Stoner Meditation presence and awareness. Do not get dizzy and fall, but feel and experience the sensuality of the water. Breathe in the water vapor, feel it fill your body, leaving through every pore. If the water spray is on your chest, feel the difference of the cooler temperature of your back. Move normally now, not robotically.

Optional: If you've never masturbated in the shower, give it a try now. Let your fantasy mind open up, feel the sexuality in your body and mind. It's said our mind is our biggest sexual organ, so move your hands to your genitals, and explore any mental eroticism. If it turns into a sexual event, then go with it, but go slowly. Continue feeling the interaction in each moment, and the climax at the end, and then pay attention afterward to your breathing and heartbeat, and again try to bring every sense into awareness.

Eyes closed, bring all the senses into concert, especially feeling the nakedness of your exposed skin. Imagine you are in the shower and the walls have suddenly turned transparent around you. You have no privacy, and everyone is looking at you. Your parents, all your relatives and friends, and countless strangers are looking at you shower. Maybe you just masturbated without realizing that they could clearly see you, and everyone knows your secrets. Unknowingly exposing yourself in this manner should be liberating. You have nothing left to hide because everyone has seen you sexually naked. If you have any residual shame and embarrassment let it go, because you are created of Mom Earth.

Feel sensuality and physicality with full intensity, bring mind and body together, imagining the marijuana turning on your senses, higher and higher. When you towel off, feel the towel taking the water from your body, feel the weight of the towel increase. Are you cold or hot? What is your breathing like? And are you even more righteously stoned?

Isn't it amazing the skill of the stoned mind to manipulate and be aware of so many layers of events? This concentrated paying attention to every event of life as it is passes by is called mindfulness, awareness, enlightenment—and if you feel your body sensations bursting the boundaries, expressing love and passion, then it could be called bliss consciousness. That's excellent.

Take this pride of nakedness into your day by feeling it under your clothes, remembering that everyone has seen you naked. Try being figuratively naked each time you get stoned, each time you meditate, etc. See other people as naked; imagine them masturbating in their privacy.

Learn to feel your body as beautiful, purposeful, and unadorned when you are naked. Even as you age, suffer from pain and the fear of death—thank your body for carrying you. Spend some time being stoned and naked around the house—cook dinner naked, or vacuum, or just sleep naked.

Free you body image by laughing, really laugh deep down into your belly, and force it if you have to. Practice this deep laugh regularly. All these ridiculous thoughts about negative body image are absurd because thinking about some fat on your body keeps you from feeling grateful. Instead take action by exercising, eating less, etc. Taking action is Stoner Meditation, not inaction and fixation on deluded thinking.

Munchies: Marijuana does something to the body that makes it crave food—it's a drug side effect. I'm guessing marijuana uses up the sugars or fats, or something that makes us crave more. The solution is simple if we want a healthy body image: we have to be mindful and not let the munchies run our lives. Several suggestions: eat a vegetarian diet, cut back on sugars, don't smoke tobacco unless it's organic and for shamanic purposes, serve small portions if you tend to eat four or five meals a day with snacks. Chew food slowly, mindfully, feel it in the body, relax while eating. Forge an exercise routine, take the stairs instead of the elevator, get up from your desk now and then.

End of Exercise 9.

Stoner Meditation wants you to have mental health. There is an abundance of scientific information on body and mind correlation. If you need to, change the way you eat, because some diets will affect the mind adversely. Get enough sleep. Learn the nature of stress and anxiety through meditation, and relax by smoking marijuana and daily meditation practice. Stress lowers the immune system's ability to fight disease, and slowly kills the body and mind, resulting in early death.

Our body is a container, and we can be imprisoned in it or break through the obstructions and use it effectively. Our body is neither good nor bad—it is the tool that allows us to move through space and time. Discontinue negative thinking, just by changing your thoughts.

Daily Meditation—Next Level

We assume you've come to the point in your daily meditation where you can sit in aware silence comfortably for short periods of time. Your meditation should feel like a bubble in the flowing river of Natural Mind. Remember that Natural Mind is the mind that contains us without duality (self/other). We suspect it's what gives us the serendipitous insights and artistic creativity known as perception, imagination, and wisdom. You have tried to locate where the various minds (thinking, doing, Natural Mind) arise, where physical sense acuity comes from, and the origination of emotions—without finding the source. Your body is starting to feel both a little invisible, especially when stoned, and surrounded by a very nice feeling of energy—the beginning of bliss. At some point you realized that finding answers is not as important as it once was. You have accepted that much of life is a mystery, and are willing to receive and deal with whatever comes.

Even science is still mystified about where highest-level wisdom comes from. Does it arise in our brain, or do we absorb insights from a group mind that's outside of us? The next step is to transcend where, or why, or even what—because it doesn't really matter where highest wisdom (awareness) comes from, even if we can't put our finger on it—it's there. It is, what it is.

Stoner Meditation's goal is to tune in to the very primal essence of BEing—the inherent awareness that unfolds when thinking mind is silenced. When we can transcend thinking mind, we become that essence. Natural Mind flows into brain, brain flows into Natural Mind, and we are enlightened. That mind, everything we are, is awareness.

Lao Two says: "Paradox. Wrap your head around imagining the impossible—expand your creative reach beyond the normal. Open to paradox and anything's possible—we can exist and not exist at the same time, and space, as awareness."

Our salvation is found in profound silence, once thoughts are stilled. Remember, Stoner Meditation is not stopping thoughts; it's ignoring the content by turning down the volume – then thoughts calm. We learn to take away the power of the judgmental, habitually controlling inner voice, and then Natural Mind creativity enters unhindered. This is the 'voice' of Lao Two.

Now that your meditation has become more regular, you look forward to it, and miss sitting when you have to skip a session. But sometimes we feel like an alien visiting this strange planet called Earth. When you get that feeling, take time to renew your spirit and inner being by tuning into Mom Earth—climb hills, hike forests and mountains. It elevates the spirit and helps us see our inspired aspirations. Pay attention to your dreams, and become a participant—both asleep and awake. There are infinite worlds inside of us. If you get the chance, trip on a mild natural hallucinogen and sit in meditation during part of your trip.

Lao Two says: "Plants talk to me; the plants will gladly talk to you if you will learn to listen. Value and respect marijuana, the Stoner's sublime gift from Mom Earth."

For those who have not progressed as far: when we gave you the beginner instructions for meditation, your only goal was to follow the cycles of breath and try not to get distracted. If you gave it a try, you now realize it's very difficult to keep attention focused and concentrated for more than a few minutes. Don't give up; if you continue with single-point breath meditation, it can result in exceptional concentration abilities down the road.

Our natural instinct is to jump up during meditation. We find it difficult to sit still and fear silence. We want to be (and think about) someplace else, other than exactly where we are. Anyplace else seems better than sitting in silence, or being alone, or not having what we want.

During meditation we might see flashing lights or have weird experiences, tremendous insights, or horrific fears. These might indeed be rarefied enlightenment experiences. Or they might result from simply not breathing in enough oxygen. Be aware of the body; Stoner Meditation is not about being only in the head. Accept whatever comes.

Set your timer for twenty minutes (or whatever), and concentrate on keeping attention at the nostrils, looking at the spot on the wall, and not letting thoughts take you for a ride. At the end of meditation we can really be exhausted from the struggle—but there's another way.

The next level of our approach is to completely give up the struggle. Give up on trying to control and stop thoughts. Give up on being frustrated that you can't keep single-point concentration as long as you think you should. All this fades into the background as you turn down the volume even on your practice method. Feel your body physically sitting there by expanding your breathing to fill your whole body, not just at your nostrils. Pay attention to the natural rocking movement as breath moves in and out. Let your skeleton remain rigid, but your muscles relax; then let your mind relax.

When you can really relax while sitting up straight, your awareness will expand—and like the exercise where we were having difficulty juggling, maintaining different attentions becomes easy. So that's pretty much level two. There is only one more level, and this "highest level" is sort of a joke you will laugh at when you reach it. This is because it is the natural essence of what humans beings are—the view that was with us all the time.

Being stressed out is not our natural state; our essential nature is meditatively persisting in peace and calm. One of the things we're looking for is the flow of events from start to finish, because this flow is a type of emptiness. Change the shower exercise above to your meditation practice—be minutely aware of physically sitting down on your cushion, setting the timer, lighting incense, inwardly announcing your intention, starting breath concentration, feeling your body, noticing your thoughts, and the passing duration of time while you are unmoving in space.

Then put your attention outside of yourself on the spot on the wall or the ember of the lit incense. By expanding our attention wider we can cast a net of awareness all around us. We "see" ourselves sitting still, meditating in that room, but moving through space-time. We are always in a flow of time, and the space is where we physically are sitting. And sitting in the flow of experience is what is worth noticing.

We should start seeing this scene as a type of stability. For twenty minutes we sit seemingly still and upright, but actually we are also breathing, thinking, sensing, emotionally experiencing life. The individual thought, or itch, or emotion then becomes unimportant. What becomes important is the moment we are sitting down to meditate, the time we sit, and the end of sitting as a cycle, a flow through space-time. We're not distracted because we are passing through. We still sit and watch everything pass by. There is no need to control individual thoughts, they come and go. From this a new awareness emerges.

So, at the beginning we concentrate on breath, and it leads to an amazing panorama of calm abiding. But we can't build the roof of a house first; we have to build the foundation, and proceed to framing the walls that will support the roof. We can't expect to sit in meditation for a few months and say we've built the entire house.

When we can remain stable in calm abiding for a longer period of time we will notice how clear and bright our environment is, like a still lake, without thinking mind causing waves; we can see clearly to the bottom. Sitting in this clarity is also called deep insight and wisdom.

This is the progression of concentration training.

We're not going to make this discussion into an exercise because there are a lot of different techniques, such as analytical meditation, chanting, Vipassana, and single-point concentration meditation, known as calm abiding. Just sitting there, thinking about something specific, is similar to Zen koan meditation. Meditating on a specific god, learning about the qualities, and becoming those god qualities is a practice of one of the Tibetan schools. There are many, many more types of meditation.

For Stoner Meditation, it's calm abiding. We discussed body image because now we will let our body be absorbed into the world around us—and the only way to do that is to be calm and aware, and see our body as spiritual. Our body is the instrument that allows us to go beyond dualism and consider our brain to be just another sense organ. Can you see in your mind's eye your awareness as hovering eight inches above the top of your head?

Lao Two says: "Meditation is a skill, like playing a guitar. When we start learning the guitar, it sounds rough, but in ten years we have mastered it and play fluidly with emotion. In twenty years we play effortlessly without thinking, and the guitar strings become passionate visions, expressing love."

Some other suggestions: we recommend buying a professionally made cushion and pad, called a zafu and zabuton. If sitting in a chair, be sure to keep your spine straight, no slouching or leaning against the back of the chair. Before you start meditation, take a moment to access where you head is at—notice your mood, emotions, and thought stream. Some people can meditate after eating; we prefer an empty morning stomach—find what works for you.

When you sit, get as comfortable as possible, but if you ache, try to go into the pain and figure out what it's all about before you move. If you have excruciating pain, consider finding a way to stretch, like tai chi or hatha yoga poses before you sit—people who sat in meditation for long periods developed these exercises. We in the West are not used to sitting on the ground, so please don't injure your body. There are many acceptable ways to sit while keeping the spine straight.

Then someday, you'll realize you are sitting without pain—it just went away. That's because your body, and mind, have stretched to accommodate your awkward position. When you finally get fairly physically and mentally comfortable, you can focus on not moving. Our center is around the belly button, and you will know when your body feels balanced. As they say, "immovable like a mountain." So, no shifting your torso, scratching itches, or falling asleep.

The room should not be dark or too bright, and if possible should be quiet and undisturbed by noise or distractions. Close your eyes, then intensely concentrate on the rhythmic cycle of breath. Next, focus on the pressure of your eyeballs pressing on the lids (or, should we say the eyelids resting on the eyeballs?)—yeah, feel it. Do you feel a little pressure at the center of your forehead?

Do not get frustrated or annoyed by thinking mind—remember that it's thinking mind's job to be a motor mouth. Allow both good and bad experiences to emerge, and view them both dispassionately—neither appreciative of bliss, nor disgusted with distress. Some days meditation will be better than other days.

Lao Two says: "Give yourself a break, don't be hard on yourself. Sit daily in meditation learning about silence, and what it means to have presence in the here-now. There is a flow in meditation; once noticed, it changes everything."

Exercise 10: Close your eyes, and do not think.
End of Exercise 10.

As expected, not thinking is not easy. And yet, thinking can go away by itself. All of the urgency of our thoughts can be taught to relax and even be silent during our meditation. Maybe it would be clearest to say we experience our thoughts instead of think about them.

Lao Two says: "You can't step into the same river, even once. The river, your stepping, and you are in constant change."

No matter what profound level of attainment we reach, we are never removed from the real world. Although it's possible to remain in a nirvana heaven, what would be the point? We are not alone, we humans are all connected. We live in a physical world and an immaterial world—and some other worlds besides. That's the mysterious paradoxical nature of our existence. The higher we get, the more important it is to assiduously maintain a grounded, honest, compassionate, and humble attitude. Enlightenment can't be reached if we are mean or hurtful—that's not its nature.

Zen Master Shunryu Suzuki said: "There are, strictly speaking, no enlightened people, there is only enlightened activity."

Stoner Shiva

Shiva is a god to many Hindus, and he has many characteristics or personas. We hope Stoner Meditation is in no way disrespecting or diminishing the reverence a large population feels for Shiva, but rather enlarging the base of appreciation for him here in the Western world, where unfortunately, he is still largely unknown.

Shiva is the paradoxical god of the endless cycle of birth, entropy, and destruction, and the reproductive act—but Shiva is not subject to birth and death, always existing in the here-now. Shiva is transcendental, persisting as Natural Mind. Shiva is also an earthy god and exhibits lots of different aspects, personalities, and energies—he's a meditation expert, a family man, and an ascetic wanderer, and he exemplifies nirvana for humans, and for that matter all animals. Shiva has no possessions and is represented in each poor, unfortunate person; we can see Shiva in each of them and hear them crying. Whirling inside of him is the cosmic dance—our heartbeat and breath. In some personas Shiva is half male, half female. He is able to see everything and is pervasive everywhere; he has the power to give blessings and stop time (death). Lao Two likes to use Shiva to describe the destruction of ego and the re-creation of a new us without form—the embodiment of enlightenment. Shiva stands at the center of the entire universe, right at the balancing point of creation and destruction, and uses his third eye for transcendental observation—just like us. Shiva also loves marijuana and hashish—a Stoner.

Lao Two personally encountered Shiva in the high mountains during his first visit to Nepal. Some of the followers who worship Shiva are called sadhus. These wandering ascetics live on the edge of society, owning nothing but the clothes on their backs; they carry a begging container usually made out of tin or stainless steel and a walking stick, often with a trident on the top. To the sadhu's the marijuana plant is holy and divine. Around the Indian continent there are thousands of sadhus who still follow Shiva to this day. Their goal is to achieve liberation, and by their example, the liberation of others. Many, if not all of them smoke hashish, also known as *charas*, and this practice has been going on for centuries. When in Nepal, Lao Two met a few sadhus. He describes them as an ethereal group, extremely good-natured, almost childlike, and often stoned. Interestingly, some sadhus do not wear any clothing at all, spending every moment naked or covered with ashes; others are snake charmers; some have a monkey that performs for donations; others have no gimmick. Sadhus give a blessing and expect a donation in return. After the donation, the sadhu places a vertical dab of red paste on the giver's third eye.

Lao Two says: "I can't help it, when someone wants to sell me hashish in a foreign country I usually buy it—a few times it didn't feel right, so

I trusted my instincts and refused the offer. In my experience I've found Temple Ball hash in Kathmandu, and when trekking in the Himalaya Mountains Nepalese Finger Hash seems available—all hand-rubbed. Some hashish also contains opium and although you will have interesting visions and dreams, opium can wreck your mind after awhile. Also beware the unscrupulous touts on the streets of Kathmandu, selling road tar that looks like hash."

Story: Lao Two was buying some hashish at a rooftop restaurant in Kathmandu, Nepal, when he heard this story from his dealer: the government of Nepal has historically allowed the sadhus to legally smoke hashish, as they had done for centuries. But since Nepal is an economically poor country, they had to bow down to the United States, who tied financial aid to drug prohibition. To get money to feed starving people, the government of Nepal had to agree to make all drugs illegal.

Unprecedented in known history, police started harassing the sadhus and confiscated their stashes of hashish and marijuana. They also disrupted their supply lines from the mountains, which affected sadhus throughout Nepal. The word quickly spread among them, even down to India.

Since sadhus can ride for free on public transportation, many sadhus from India arrived by train and bus to join protests in Nepal. At first there were only a few hundred. They sat in a circle chanting various mantras over and over. They defied the ban by publicly smoking hashish, but at that point the police did not interfere. After all, it's a Hindu country and was led by a Hindu king. Eventually the circle of chanting sadhus swelled to thousands, all sitting cross-legged day and night. After a few days a storm gathered, and on that night lightning repeatedly struck some government buildings, burning them to the ground. The sadhus quit chanting the next morning. The next day the government repealed prohibition and allowed the sadhus to continue smoking hashish and marijuana.

End of story.

We've never been able to substantiate this story, and it might be what's known as an urban legend, but it's such an interesting anecdote, and we thoroughly enjoy the idea that it's possible to work magic in modern times. We encourage you to go to Nepal and take a mountain trek, and experience some culture shock. Lao Two recommends the twenty-one-day Annapurna circuit, or Everest base camp trek. If you go you will discover that marijuana grows wild all over the western mountainous regions of Nepal and India. Ask your guide or porter to score some ganja or hashish. You will see sadhus walking the mountainous roads without a care in the world; all their needs taken care of. They travel for free, stay for free overnight, get fed, and have only one set of clothes and a stash of hashish. In Lao Two's experience, sadhus do not sell hashish to Westerners.

Shiva danced the universe into existence. As he continues his dance, his vibrations create the worlds of variety, manifestation, and distinctions. Because Shiva is formless, his vibrations become evident as mind.

The Vishvasara Tantra says: "What is here is everywhere; what is not here is nowhere."

Street Smart

Lao Two says: "What the DEA is most afraid of is that when marijuana becomes legal—nothing happens."

BEWARE: We live in perilous times, and although we have First Amendment rights to write this book and Stoner Meditation may often seem cavalier, rebellious, and reckless—it's just not that way in the real world. Getting busted is not funny—it's horrible. You can be calmly smoking some marijuana and be one of the most gentle, intelligent, worthy individuals—but if you get busted, you will be seen as a sociopath and treated cruelly by government employees. You are an anonymous face, a number, and the means to their paycheck. They're not necessarily mean, but they don't care about you, they only care about themselves. That's the reality.

So hide your stash, keep your three eyes open, watch what you say, and understand that when smoking marijuana and ingesting psychedelics, you have a good reason to be paranoid—it's not necessarily imagination, it could be instinct. There are people out there who hate us and are paid to completely mess up our lives—Congress, narcs, cops, D.A.s, judges, jails, etc. ... are not our friends.

Lao Two says: "Stoner Meditation is not about endless happiness and perfection. I only teach about reality."

Since marijuana and psychedelics are illegal, and because of all the misinformation invented by the DEA, we know this book will piss them off. Therefore, we repeat that this book in no way pressures anyone in the use, buying, selling, or even possession of illegal drugs. The writers, publishers, our old grandmothers, and all the sky dwellers consider this entire book fantasy science fiction—Stoner Meditation is our description of an alien world, a cosmic joke, the story of Alchemy. Right...

Lao Two says: "Marijuana could be completely legal and it would still not be for everybody—let's face it, some people just won't enjoy pot smoking. Not everyone is, or should be, looking for enlightenment either."

Intention

I doubt that any Stoners reading this book have not completely stopped in their tracks, transfixed and stunned speechless by a sudden and overwhelming feeling of love, after smoking a reefer or two. All Stoners have that "Ah, I get it" moment. We have humanity in common, we all fit into the picture, everyone together—and bad vibes only bring us all down. Act appropriately in each situation.

Lao Two says: "Do you allow people to change and improve themselves? The person you knew yesterday is not the person you see in front of you today. Give people credit for their successes, no matter how minor."

We have to allow people to change and grow by giving them room to be different each time we meet. Too often our friends and enemies become stuck in our mind as an image or a concept, and too often it is mistaken—they are no longer the opinion you had of them. We forget to zero in on people's faces to see them as they really are, in that exact moment. This is an ability we would like Stoners to cultivate.

Exercise 11: Focus in on someone's face. You should really see all their imperfections, beauty, makeup, beard stubble—and if your eyes are really good you can zoom in on the pores. Usually we just glance at a person and then avoid eye contact. This time, zoom in instead. Look closely. Do you see their pain, and their happiness written on their face? Do you see their anxiety, awkwardness, and their attempt to reach out to you or shy away? Can you tell by the way they dress how they feel about themselves? Do you hear their struggle in their voice, truly listen to their communication, notice their gestures, body language, and new hairdo/haircut? Try not to bring the person's past actions into each interaction with them—try to see them as new. See them as noble.

Look closely at someone who has seriously wronged you. Do you allow them to make a positive change, or are they stuck in your mind's image? Everyone deserves a second chance; the enemy we knew yesterday could be our friend today. See them as human, not as a statue. However, there's no need to be anybody's fool or dupe; be wise and alert. We're saying, see people exactly as they are.

This simple exercise can be the beginning of understanding and compassion, just by looking at people in a different way. In this instance, several world-views were happening simultaneously – and it's the life choices we make that results in ignorance or wisdom.

End of Exercise 11.

Story: Sometime around 2004 or 2005 Lao Two was on a trek in the upper mountains of Nepal. In each town visited, he would look at the Buddhist monasteries. In one town he discovered that Westerners were welcome to come to the evening chanting. Since no one else in his group wanted to go, he went alone. He left the communal dining room, the drinking and laughter, and walked up the hill alone, then up the steep steps into a part of the monastery where the monks gather to chant. It was a large room filled with mats on the floor for the monks, musical instruments, and *thangkas* (painting of buddhas, mandalas, and gods) on the walls. Everything was painted in psychedelic colors, and the views outside the windows were panoramic. The sun had already set, so Lao Two took a seat on a raised cushion in the back. The monks filed in, and then the high lamas and the rinpoche took their seats. Lao Two was the only Westerner at the ceremony, although the town was full of Western tourists—most were down the hill getting drunk.

Lao Two listened to Tibetan Buddhist monks chanting for over three hours during their evening practice. Being a longtime meditator, he was able to notice and ride on his emotional responses while listening to the monks chanting the different memorized passages. Even though he didn't understand the language, the voices and the occasional blowing of horns, rhythmic drumming, crashing cymbals, and ringing bells coalesced into universal music. He started being so moved by the chanting he was swept into an after-death experience, and at another point he was crying for suffering humanity. Lao Two wasn't stoned, but he closed his eyes and started to hallucinate as the chanting swept him along. It was as if the gods represented on the walls were in the room, invisible but present. He felt lovingly welcomed and embraced by all the visiting psychedelic gods, and the monks in the room as the chanting continued.

Several times his porter and guide came in to try to make him leave. Lao Two sat firm, shaking his head no. Then, toward the last twenty minutes, the music along with the chanting became euphoric, with all the monks chanting in a collective (telepathic?) group mind. As he stood up to leave, he realized he was as stoned as his trips on acid. Were the monks also this stoned, naturally?

Outside, the night clouds moved under the stars. A senior monk introduced himself and asked if Lao Two had a place to stay for the night, offering him a bed. Lao Two absurdly said, "I'm staying in a hotel in town, the Paradise Hotel." He again had the steps to himself as he walked down them, then downhill through the town. At a shrine he turned each prayer wheel as he walked by, still feeling connected to the monastery and the selfless monks. He walked into his hotel to find everyone still drinking and singing, and in the center an especially rowdy group of high-spirited young men yelling while one played the guitar. He sat for a few minutes, comparing the multidimensional worlds he was in, the irony that in an instant he could have stayed at the monastery and passed all this by. Instead of joining in the drinking, he excused himself from the party and went to bed.

End of story.

Lao Two says: "When our sense of self is realized as part of the whole of everything, then Natural-Mind appears."

Stoner Meditation is not about anything else but how to live an ordinary, aware life without suffering afflictive emotions. We choose what to believe. By the time we are about fourteen, habits have been instilled in us over and over until we've solidified them as beliefs. We can choose to change them now by the choices we make.

Lao Two says: "Stoners must learn to hear the wisdom mind inside. This is not the same voice as our habitual thinking mind."

Continuum

Tibetan Master Nagarjuna said: "Neither from itself nor from another, nor from both, nor without cause, does anything whatever, anywhere arise."

We are existing in constant creation every moment: being reborn, persisting, and perishing again and again. Our body gets older, but our higher presence remains, neither being born nor dying. Whatever that awareness is, it's both eternal and nonexistent at the same time.

We meditate not to get someplace, but to be where we are. This is contrary to our usual way of thinking, which is always moving into the future with purpose and destination. We are meditating to see the journey without a goal. It's important to want to become a better person, to not be angry; that is part of ethics, and the intuitive knowing or wise action that guides us.

In enlightenment we see that mind is not coming from inside of us, and that mind is not coming from outside of us—and it's not in between the two. We are contained inside of mind, and everything, including thought, arises from that ever-creating presence within Natural Mind.

Lao Two says: "Breathing meditation is not tightly controlling the breath—Stoner Meditation is letting go; this is our practice."

There was a rock-and-roll group named the 'Grateful Dead'. The leader, Jerry Garcia, died and the band broke up. Then several band members created a spinoff band, 'Further', that plays Grateful Dead covers. A lot of people take psychedelics and smoke marijuana at the concerts. The music is designed to help people trip, and a kind of group head develops where the band and the audience are in a synchronous musical telepathy.

A mutual friend, Franz, says (re: the 'Grateful Dead' group head) after hearing the band Further on New Year's Eve: "The Dead are a singular experience that some people get and some don't—the ones who got it seem to have high dosed and given up their ego at some point so that they can join in to the group head and not be threatened—the Dead and now Further have the ability to raise the consciousness—mainly, I think, because they took so much acid back when and float on that level somehow just like some of us do—they are also lucky that so many get it and come to their concerts ready to take off and dance—it really is a synthesis of them and us—they also have this free-form jazz thing that no one in the history of music ever had where they weave themes through and through—it is the music of the bardos—all their music is supremely good vibes—it is very spiritual and vibrates on rare and ethereal levels." (January 4, 2012)

Few bands and music groups can reach transcendental levels that carry both the musicians and the audience to magical places. Recently I saw 'Bassnectar' a completely different style of music, one electronic musician coupled with a light show. The result was not only a group head, but also a recreation of the LSD experience. In the future there will be more emphasis on places specifically designed for people to comfortably trip on psychedelics.

Exercise 12: Set your clock to wake you up in the middle of the night, best after five hours of sleep. Go to the bathroom if you have to. Stand in the darkness. Feel gravity, feel your human body pushing against the ground beneath you. Notice any breezes, hot or cold, changes of light and shadows, sounds close or far away. Pay concentrated attention to your breath and notice what, precisely, is going on during each breath. Feel the rising and falling of your stomach and the air going in and out of your nose; create a circular rhythm between the two. Feel the clothing on your body, your eyeglasses, tension in your muscles, and your two lips together. Wiggle and feel your toes.

Fill your body/mind with your vibrational energy and feel your presence in space-time. Next, expand that energy to surround your current location, no matter how big or small the room—it is now filled with your energy field. Expand your personal presence larger and larger to include the city you are in, like a giant circle of awareness. Imagine the entire city is filled with your energy. Then enlarge again to include the state, the country, and finally the planet, all filled with your vibrational energy. Wish peace and happiness for all living beings on Earth.

Let your vibes roam farther and include both Earth and moon—seeing a few man-made satellites along the journey—take a moment to say hello to the people in the space station—let them feel your good wishes. Mentally imagine expanding your awareness to include the whole solar system and onward to the galaxy beyond. Finally, send your vibes out beyond your imagination itself, without end or boundaries—all filled with your vibes.

Hold that thought, while simultaneously still seeing "you" still in your room.

Go back to bed and do the falling asleep exercise. Keep your concentration as aware as possible as you drift off to sleep, and announce you intention to participate in dreams tonight. There might be body sleep paralysis, feeling like you're falling through the bed, or imagining you're still standing in the room or roaming the stars. Hopefully you'll easily fall asleep, and then be aware as you participate in your dream.

End of Exercise 12.

Some notes on lucid dreaming—it's not for everybody. First understand that body sleep paralysis is normal, safe, and needn't be feared. We have body sleep paralysis every time we fall asleep—only now we are noticing it happen. Learning how to participate in your dreams is important practice. I suspect the after-death experience is like lucid dreaming. Lao Two is able to smoke marijuana and lucid dream, but others say they can't. With practice many people are able to control their dreams. Flying in dreams is Lao Two's favorite. Like all the exercises, if it disturbs you, then don't do it.

Black Elk (Oglala Sioux) said: "Then I was standing on the highest mountain of them all, and round about beneath me was the whole hoop of the world. And while I stood there I saw more than I can tell and I understood more than I saw; for I was seeing in a sacred manner the shapes of all things in the spirit, and the shape of all shapes as they must live together like one being. And I say the sacred hoop of my people was one of the many hoops that made one circle, wide as daylight and starlight, and in the center grew one mighty flowering tree to shelter all the children of one mother and one father. And I saw it was holy. But anywhere is the center of the world."

Our concepts of space and time are influenced by what we are taught. Stoner Meditation recommends observing space and time directly. Forget what you've been taught, and believe what you see and know. This doesn't mean to believe in a flat-Earth just because that's what you really see with your eyes. Knowledge has its place in our lives, but at some point on the psychedelic journey we have to look at the world around us with new eyes.

Lao Two says: "If you keep meditating year after year, at some point you will relax into it. There will be no more sitting aches and pains, no distracting thinking mind, and suddenly you notice that you are sitting in higher mind. Over time stabilize higher mind without effort—that's the relaxed sigh, and all the doors open."

Relax, give yourself permission to taste the pleasures of life. Don't be caught up in cultural conditioning, historical examples, or the demands of some spiritual discipline. Give yourself credit for being on a valid path, moving forward, learning and being—set your own rules. Being adult means to take control of your life. We live in this world, so be of this world awake, instead of sleepwalking through it. Ultimately, everything we do is meditation.

We only have so much time, then our journey is over. Maybe we start over again after death in a new rebirth body, or maybe we don't—it's a mystery. What matters is that every time we wake up in the morning we have an opportunity to BE, and to live compassionately.

We want to adapt to the world as we find it, finding productive ways to live. But it's a struggle sometimes—everyone becomes lost now and then. Here's a good place to start to get back on our feet.

Exercise 13: Get stoned and stand naked in front of a mirror (full-length is best) and look at your reflected image. Look exceptionally closely, seeing all your imperfections, aging, zeroing in on body parts that don't fit your fantasy body image. Then, stop the microscopic zooming and see the whole picture of your body. Do your best to see yourself exactly as you are at that moment—without body image judgments.

You are seeing a human monkey reflected, or you are an alien who just acquired this unfamiliar body. Don't back away from anything you see or think, continue seeing your entire body, listening carefully to the inner dialogue. Relax your gaze and expand your vision beyond your body to include the entire mirror image, the reflection, and the room that surrounds you—include the shadows, the gradients of light, and any movement. Maybe your face and body will change into multiple images, flipping through a hallucinatory sequence—just let it happen, ugly or beautiful.

See everything in the room as having no firm edges, just colors merging, blending, being together. This might take some spacing out, because you do not want to let thinking mind label or name everything; it's just a conglomeration of different colors, even your body is just a color in the room. Don't zero in on your body at all; your vision should be mostly peripheral. Relax your shoulders and feel your weight on the floor. Let your body disappear into the surrounding vision—relax into that for a few moments.

Next, come back into your naked body. Focus and take a moment to smile. Force the smile if you have to. Look at the two vertical sides of your face—is one side happy and one side sad, or are both sides balanced? Do you speak out of one side of your face? Can you hold your smile equally, is it sincere? Is one eye smaller than the other?

Listen to thinking mind judging the imperfections, wrinkles, and insecurity of body image. Can you accept who you are and what you look like, and still smile? Can you take that karmic face you received when you were born, put on that smile, and take it out into the world?

This is what we call being "real"—being authentically the person you really are. Underneath your clothing, makeup, or shaved face and carefully combed hair, you are still naked in the world. Your tool for the world is your body, and how you wear your body is what's really communicated. Your smile is the start of being genuine.

Here's a magic trick, good for people suffering from physical and mental illness. You can change the way you look and think, heal injury to the body and mind, by using mind. In the mirror, see the part of you that is hurt, and imagine it as healed. Imagine the reflection looking balanced, fixed and happy, and your eyes reflecting your inner wisdom.

Let the stress go, relax your face muscles, let your eyes rest in their sockets as if they were floating, let your jaw be effortless instead of clenched. Breathe deeply. In the full mirror, watch as you relax your shoulders, flap your arms a little, and let the energy of your body surround you like a comfortable blanket. You might see a light surrounding the lines of your body. From that moment on, start to see yourself as beautiful, with a visible glow that fills the room, everywhere you go. Become centered. Now, make a wish.

End of Exercise 13.

Get over any life reluctance and learn to be straightforward and real, developing courage and ethics. Take a chance on saying the wrong thing, and speak from your heart. Now is the time to make your life have meaning; there is no reason for waiting. Don't stand back—give yourself permission to have some impulsiveness, take some risks, and live your dreams. Meditation will teach you the way to ignore your fears and join in the dance of life.

These methods help us find peace of mind and live a complete life. Everyone living right now is thrust into this strange, sometimes inhospitable world. Some people are so filled with fear and denial that they shut down their questioning. Stoners continue to want to know why we were born right now, during this period of history, and what we're capable of. We are all on the same journey, but not everyone is willing to stand face to face with his or her nakedness.

But guess what? The answer is that existence is mysterious, unknowable, hidden, too huge and too small, inconceivable. This acceptance of the riddle is where we end up, but it's also a new beginning because we are now released to dance through life uninhibited and smiling. Fear is gone, and we can accept that not knowing is knowing, and paradox is in everything. What is surrounding us here-now is just fine – it's the clay we can shape however we want.

Lao Two says: "After you have learned how to smile, learn how to laugh. Feel it in your belly, your chest, and your skull. Stretch your arms up over your head, look up at the sky, and laugh from your toes."

What We're After

We can only describe these techniques and hope the reader will see what we are pointing at. However, if you meditate (stoned or not) for just twenty minutes to a half hour each day, paying attention to your breathing and thinking mind, and during your daily activities, acting in a loving and conscious way—then we can promise you that you will experience enlightenment. Afterward, you will not be perfect, always joyful, and have everything constantly go your way. But you will see all events as temporary, passing by, and not causing either happiness or sadness—things happen.

What we can't promise is that after you have opened up to low-level enlightenment, you will also attain buddha nature (nirvana). That's much, much more difficult—but obviously attainable, as demonstrated by the many meditation masters over the centuries.

Even if we sometimes stumble along through life, not understanding our place in it, after meditating for several years we start to feel connected to the flow and ebb of life arising. The seasons come, persist, then vanish; we are born, persist, then perish; our breath arises, pauses, and fades. Then if we are buffeted about like an object in the ocean during a storm, we know we are still resting on the calm sea underneath us.

You might live with people who do not understand what you are attempting by getting high and trying to find ways to make your life better. They may criticize, diminish, and discourage you. Maybe nobody believes in your dreams, or tries to hold you back from realizing them. The people around you might be lost, controlling, or desperately suffering from their own problems. Please see them as mildly mentally ill;

there's no reason to give them a hard time. Do the best you can, be as kind and wise as you can, and don't step on someone else's dream in retaliation. Stoner Meditation says we must be fair to everyone, including being fair to our own dreams.

These are provocative paradoxes and dilemmas, but this is how we Stoners must walk through life. If you are in this situation where people give you a difficult time, you already realize that no matter how peaceful and aware you are, or how good your arguments are, not every person will see your good side. Some will still find fault or try to make you feel less than they are—perhaps it's a power trip, insecurity, bigotry, ignorance, or hate. No matter what you say, no matter how accommodating you are, their perception of you is that you are breaking the law, selfish, prideful, and corrupted by New Age superstition.

Compassion, standing back and seeing them clearly without your own emotions brought to the table, will help you remain centered, bearing almost anything. This does not mean you let people walk over you— have your yes, no, and know.

Lao Two says: "Your immediate environment is your life mirror."

Even uptight people can give us good information, and how you deal with situations is how karma is either released or increased. By defusing an argument and keeping the peace, we can release bad karma. Keep in mind that it's important to stay grounded and real. Beware of arrogance, pride, and wanting to get the whole world high—some people just aren't ready for it.

You are welcome to teach anything you've learned from this book. But only teach if someone requests it, never to elevate your own status. Be sure you know what you are talking about, from personal insight, realization, and experience. Realize that everyone teaches and everyone is a student. The Stoner Meditation path has no self-important teachers—we are all in this together. It's like someone not knowing how to fix a broken bicycle—if you know how to fix it, tell them, or show them. That's how teaching should be, helpful and heartfelt teaching in the moment it's needed. Watch out for intellectual pride and hubris.

The terms "spiritual pride" and "spiritual materialism" suggest that we can still fall into traps even after years of meditation. Always make your meditation practice your own path that suits your needs and aspirations. Take some time to discover methods other than what we've offered here, create a successful daily practice. Become the balanced center in the storm that rages all around you. There is nothing we can do to stop the storm; our job is to be unmoved, joyful, forging ahead no matter what turmoil comes.

Lao Two says: "Treat today as an adventure, a new experience, a once-in-a-lifetime day. To exist at all is inexplicable enough, and each breath is eternity, expressing love. We each write the story of our life, our karma, and our death."

Humans have a heart of gold; the trick is how to draw their sanity out from inside them. Wisdom, humbleness, a humorous attitude, nonviolence, good vibes, good intentions, an open heart, a smile, and compassion are the right tools for most every situation. This is how a wizard reveals the rationality of everyone he or she encounters.

We have to constantly challenge ourselves as Stoners. Life is a work in progress; it's not finished just because you realized enlightenment on an acid trip. It's the same with sitting on the meditation cushion— peace, silence, and intense concentration is a great achievement, but it's not the end of our path. Living in the world being active and engaged, living our truth, is the path.

Lao Two says: "Meditation is a skill. Adjust perceptions to realize mind is eternal change."

Hidden within silence is the intensity of the universe, an ever-creating river of mind. This silent mind is not empty; even death has something that goes beyond the previous limitations of human skin and bones. Love is not only the goal, it is the essence of everything.

Lao Two says: "We are born into the karmic river."

We are born into a world that is already in progress, where events have already happened, and humanity is busy as bees. Babies born at particular months of the year are treated differently. In the summer you might be dragged out to the beach dressed in only a diaper. In the winter you will be placed close to a hearth fire, or swaddled in tons of clothing. These are your imprints. In so many ways, we humans are no different from any other animal.

Lao Two says: "You'll know if you are doing life right by your sense of humor. A mature, sane, stoned adult will feel bliss consciousness inside them. We are nothing more than a borrowed body, made out of stars—and euphoria."

We've heard enlightenment described as a large mountain. No matter what is going on around it—lightning, loud thunder, rain, earthquakes—the mountain remains sitting still, accepting the distractions, whatever comes. During your meditation, be like that undisturbed mountain. Don't fret about body pain or afflictive emotions, desires, past or future, mental tripping, or anything else that comes along. Just BE the flow of that mountain until your twenty or thirty minutes are finished.

Learn to listen to silence, and be comfortable in your own skin. Consider meditation fun time, not struggle time. Notice any stiffness of your body, and then relax that tension whenever you can. Let the skeleton hold up your relaxed muscles.

At some point in your day (or your life), step back in awestruck wonder! Consider how lucky you are to be a Stoner. Wow...

Stoners with a bad, uptight attitude? Get over yourself; you're not the only person having a difficult time. Learn to laugh at everything; take nothing seriously, especially whatever happened to you in the past. Sure, the crap that happened in your life is painful, and you are damn tired of things not working out, or you might feel burned out trying constantly to meet some of your basic needs. The fact is that most people on the planet struggle. See the bigger picture. We live in a society of greed, inequity, entitlement, and political/social systems that are in denial. A plutocracy of the few and the suffering of the many have made life unnecessarily difficult around the world. Everyone in the rain is getting wet, except for a few rich who locked us outside.

Instead of being uptight, work for justice, peace, equality. Make some time for getting stoned outside, and reconnect to Mom Nature. Instinctively feel Mom Earth under your feet as you walk. Be grateful for all she gives us, and help her out if you can. We believe all humans who smoke marijuana become caretakers of Mom Earth—the love we give to Earth is the love we will receive back.

If you can remind yourself to relax a little, it will open doors. Humans can sense vibes in other humans. Life will never be perfect, and there will always be dissatisfaction and having to settle for less, but there is still the possibility for joy. At a minimum, wizards can put their attention on the breath, then calm, intensify, and slow the breath. This practice of being calm in public has a calming effect on people around us.

Acting out in anger or being mean doesn't help, and is the easiest and fastest downward spiral. All the more reason to listen to your body and try to come to grips with the signals your emotions are sending to thinking mind. If we react with anger, we get an appropriate and similar response from the world around us. Perhaps we get punched in the face because of our negative attitude. Or, if our attention is not focused and we are cutting vegetables for dinner, we might cut our fingers "by mistake." Stoner Meditation is very real-world stuff.

You might think that life never gives you the birthday present you want, or at the very least life should let you win the lottery. Life often gives us auditions even if we're unaware of them when they are happening. Only a fool would say no to getting what they really need. A wizard prepares for getting what he or she needs, and expects to find creative ways to make it happen.

Everyone has some kind of a natural gift, and if you find yours, you are one of the luckiest people on the planet. Once you've learned your craft, think of each time you practice and perform as an audition. Maybe there is a producer looking for new talent in the audience of your high school talent show.

Question, debate, investigate, be skeptical, and discard what doesn't work. You are you; decide for yourself what shape you want your own life to take. Allow yourself to be incredible, brilliant, loving, profound, worthy, and capable. Don't wait another minute, life is passing by—become famous, legendary, shamanic, magical—a Stoner Meditation wizard.

Consider going vegetarian and perhaps vegan. At the least, eat less and less meat, milk, poultry, fish, and BBQ (Lao Two's downfall). Give yourself credit each time you pass up food that is unhealthy. Animals deserve a quiet and fulfilling life.

Work for peace, the eradication of endless war and gun violence.

If you are feeling awkward in a crowd, imagine that everyone is a child. Then open up to their potential as human-to-human. Know that they are beings filled with luminous energy, they just don't recognize their true nature—or maybe a few do ... try to feel their vibes. At social gatherings, always try to open your heart chakra and practice compassion and wisdom. The best technique in conversation is to let the other person talk about himself or herself, and listen – really listen.

Avoid crushing debts—loans and bank credit cards are playing us for suckers. Be ingenious, and learn how to make it financially in the world.

Negative thinking is endemic in the West. Don't overly stress about not having peaceful thoughts all the time, or believe your negative thinking all the time. The thoughts you had last Wednesday, where are they now? Also remember, much of advertising is designed to make you feel bad about yourself. Guilt is a mistaken concept that our human emotions are somehow bad. Not deciding to act on your harmful emotions is called wisdom.

The path, the Way, the method—has already been discovered. Learn from the teachers of the past.

In the End

Lao Two says: "In the end there is no achievement—there is only awareness. Everything, every action, every belief, will eventually be washed away by eternal change."

It's probable that we have mentioned things in this book twice, or even three or four times. Even in our editing we miss stuff because editing sessions are often separated by days or even months. Some of this book was edited in my home study, some at Lao Two's kitchen table; other times work was done in hotels, on the beach in Thailand, and in a cold November room in the mountains of India where my fingers almost froze. Hopefully the professional editor can make some sense out of all of this. Most often we wrote stoned, and other times we wrote even more stoned. It was great fun and we had lots of laughs.

We hope you forgive our excesses and lack of writing ability. Most things we teach are from close observations of how life actually works. We are fallible and sometimes a memory is mistaken, a lesson misunderstood, a past discussion misremembered—but the sparks of our lifetime of insights are aimed at starting a huge fire in your heart.

A book like this is a summary of something unfathomable and esoteric, so no words can directly point at those visionary experiences. We hope that each reader will reach the highest highs, and find a safe life harbor with love and laughs. We hope some of you will be inspired to make a better world and environment, and hopefully somebody will figure out a valid planetary economic system so everyone, without exception, is cared for.

We hope this new voice will inspire Stoners to start meditating. We also hope that people who've never smoked marijuana become interested in trying it. We welcome you new smokers to an extraordinary path. Marijuana is not for everybody, but for those it speaks to, it speaks profoundly, to the marrow of our bones.

We hope the narcs find it in their heart not to bust us and put us in jail for what we wrote. Instigators like us should be the vehicles for change, in our humble opinions. Lao Two is an iconoclast, but his heart is in the right place.

It comes down to this: a Stoner should be growing, learning, loving, and living. The people closest to you are your mirror—and if they are thriving, happy, compassionate, and open hearted, then you know that you are living right. Psychedelics should not separate you from the people who love you. They might not understand what you are up to, but it's up to Stoners to set an example—get your life together, work, raise a family, smile. Be who you are, follow your own footsteps.

Lao Two says: "Are you in this moment?"

Well, dear reader, it seems we have come to the end of our instruction manual. We hope your smokes, mushrooms, cacti, and chemicals will be insightful, your relationships meaningful, and your life filled with wonder after wonder, joy and wisdom.

Lao Two knows there are people who will search for him. He has moved on, and is donating all profits, money, and fame from this book. I'm also donating all profits, after expenses, from this book—but I'm not hiding out like Lao Two. Lao Two is ordinary, extraordinary, solitary, blending into the world as just another invisible man. Look around your city and you might see him, but it's more likely you will feel his loving vibes supporting your quest. Listen deeply and you will hear his voice.

Lao Two discussed the end of his life with me one evening. His plan is to put enough supplies in a daypack for a few days. You might see him on a trail on his old bones, heading out into the wilderness alone. When the location feels right, he will find his last breath, leaving his body behind, entering bliss, joy, and merging with universal love. He said he wants to make love to Mom Earth as he's dying.

This is by Chuang Tzu, a follower of Lao Tzu: "The man in whom Tao acts without impediment harms no other being by his actions, yet he does not know himself to be "kind," to be "gentle." He does not bother with his own interests and does not despise others who do. He does not struggle to make money and does not make a virtue of poverty. He goes his way without relying on others and does not pride himself on walking alone. While he does not follow the crowd, he won't complain of those who do. Rank and reward make no appeal to him; disgrace and shame do not deter him. He is not always looking for right and wrong, always deciding "Yes" or "No." The ancients said therefore: the man of Tao remains unknown. Perfect virtue produces nothing. "No Self" is "True Self." And the greatest man is nobody."

We know that some who picked up this book are beginning Stoners, and others reading have never smoked marijuana at all. Even though we have good intentions, we know they are not enough. We promise everything is true, including every wild story—well, maybe a few small exaggerations and lapses of memory. ... We also promise you can achieve the attainments we describe.

Lao Two says: "My view is that someone who has followed all the rules, never took a risk, never asked direct tactless questions, has wasted their life."

Meditation is your time, your short moment to be alone and relax with the breath and silence. Tell the people you live with that thirty minutes of quiet would be appreciated. They might give you a difficult time at first, but when they notice the positive effects Stoner Meditation has on you, they will accept your sitting meditation as quiet time and even close doors gently and walk and speak quietly so you can have that time.

Lao Two says: "You might read something in this book that sounds like a clear, ringing bell of solid gold. Often truth can be imparted this way, and if what we say works, then adopt it. However, my constant reminder is, don't take our theories, postulations, or instructions on trust or faith—be skeptical. Test what we say in the psychedelic fire."

A reminder that the plants we're using are given to us by Mother Earth, so always remember your connection to the planet each time you smoke, or take psychedelics.

Read books, attend lectures, and if you are fortunate, find a realized teacher to guide you. At some point you will know when to not read books, attend lectures, or listen to teachings. Effort is a two-edged sword, necessary for discipline and understanding, but it can also lead us away from enlightenment by becoming rigid. Learn to relax and let things come and go without attachment, clinging, or repulsion. Meditation takes effort in the beginning; it's like any skill where we see incremental improvement. What you want to notice is your heart opening over time.

The strangest thing is that just sitting on a meditation cushion, concentrating on the breath, gives the mind a chance to fix itself. Like when a rock thrown into a lake creates ripples, eventually the waves settle and return to calm.

Lao Two says: "All we have is a brief moment of time. We live in the space of here and now, carried along within universal mind. Make prudent choices—use your time wisely."

Old hippie saying: "Head in the sky, feet on the ground."

Lao Two says: "Do not take meditation lightly; in the long run, it's more powerful than the strongest hits of LSD."

Holy smokes!

Made in the USA
Lexington, KY
06 June 2019